Also by JESSICA MITFORD

Daughters and Rebels
The American Way of Death
The Trial of Dr. Spock
Kind and Usual Punishment

A Fine Old Conflict

A
Fine Old
Conflict

JESSICA MITFORD

ALFRED A. KNOPF   NEW YORK   1977

HX
84
M55
A-34
1977.

THIS IS A BORZOI BOOK
PUBLISHED BY ALFRED A. KNOPF, INC.

Library of Congress Cataloging in Publication Data

Mitford, Jessica, Hon., [date]   A fine old conflict.

Includes bibliographical references.
1. Mitford, Jessica, Hon., [date]   2. Communists—
United States—Biography.   I. Title.
HX84.M55A34   1977   335.43'092'4   [B]   77–2324
ISBN 0–394–49995–6

Manufactured in the United States of America

FIRST EDITION

To

Constancia Romilly

Benjamin Treuhaft

James Robert Lumumba Forman   Chaka Esmond Forman

Contents

Illustrations

(following page 112)

Acknowledgments and Sources

I AM INDEBTED to so many people, over such a long period of time, for help in putting this book together that it is hard to know where to begin. Many of those who read and criticized the manuscript—notably the Book Committee, which still functions, and splendid Bob Gottlieb, my editor at Knopf—have been described in Chapter 12. To these must be added some newcomers, who never failed to respond to my cries of anguish when things were going badly: Maya Angelou, Paul du Feu, William Abrahams, Bettina Aptheker, Miriam Miller, Clare Douglas, my children, Constancia and Benjamin. (After reading my account of their childhood, these two threatened to write their own version, insisting that it be included in the book; fortunately they failed to meet the deadline.)

Three people in particular stuck with me and gave prodigiously of their time and talent: Marge Frantz, who has been after me for at least seventeen years to get on with this book, and who helped me reconstruct our shared experience in the Communist Party. While she bore down relentlessly on the many shortcomings of the manuscript, she never failed to encourage (and to laugh at the jokes). David Nawi, of the New Left generation, to whom it was a slice of history. His enthusiasm for the subject, his probing questions, his criticism of passages obscure to one of his generation were immensely helpful. Al Richmond, a colleague of more than thirty years, spotted many inaccuracies as to date-time-place and in long conversations reminded me of all sorts of things that I had forgotten.

Being an inveterate pack rat (I cherish and hoard old newspaper clippings, letters, out-of-print books), I had quite a good start on research materials, but many people helped to supply some of the essential ingredients for this book. Graeme Murphy, a student at the University of California library school, performed feats I should never have dreamed possible. Besides retrieving transcripts of the House Committee on Un-American Activities (quoted verbatim in Chapter 9) and contemporary newspaper accounts of those hearings, he was able to procure through the inter-library service microfilm copies of the Jackson, Mississippi, *Daily News* for the whole period of the Willie McGee case. Pele de Lappe and Toya Robinson combed through the back files of the *Peoples World*. Laurent Frantz gave me permission to use portions of his superb essay on the Fifth Amendment, "Does Silence Mean Guilt?", written in the early fifties. Leonard Boudin furnished much information on the Right to Travel cases. Bertram Edises lent me his file on the Jerry Newson case. Congressman Fortney "Pete" Stark kept peppering the FBI with irate letters demanding that they send me my file, as required under the Freedom of Information Act, and he succeeded in prying loose some of the documents just in the nick of time for me to use them at the end of the book.

Ann Golden set up a brilliant filing system for all these items. Patti Williams fought her way daily through snowstorms of paper, old drafts, piles of Xeroxed newsprint to keep the house in order. In fact, she is really the one "without whom this book could never have been written," as authors are prone to say in dedications. The Rockefeller Foundation gave me weeks of peace and happiness at their Bellagio Study and Conference Center in Italy—I must say to my great surprise, as I had said in my application for this tremendous treat that I should be writing a sympathetic account of the Communist Party.

As for bibliography, I found the following books about the witch-hunt of the forties and fifties particularly useful: *Thirty Years of Treason* by Eric Bentley; *The Un-Americans* by Frank Donner; *Inquisition in Eden* by Alvah Bessie; *Scoundrel Time,* Lillian Hellman's bitter and fascinating memoir in which she excoriates the Cold War liberals for their tacit collusion with the witch-hunters; *The Truman Era* and *The Haunted Fifties* by I. F. Stone, collections of his contemporaneous writings that vividly recapture the flavor of those days.

For a peek into the mind of the "I-was-duped" school of ex-Communist, one should scan *The Naked God* by Howard Fast (who has since gone guru, according to the newspapers), a lamentably self-serving wail about his own sincerity and dedication to a cause he believed to be noble versus the flinty-eyed, cold cynicism of Party leaders, among whose major sins, it develops, was giving some of his books bad reviews. (My recollection is somewhat different, as when I first joined the Party it was pushing Howard Fast's turgid historical potboilers on a captive audience. In those days, the witch-hunting committees had coined the phrase "premature anti-Fascist" to identify Communists; I confess to being a premature anti-Fast-ist.)

Among the books directly on the subject of the Communist Party that I consulted, one stands out like a beacon: *A Long View from the Left,* Al Richmond's autobiography, a brilliant, analytical (and often very amusing) memoir that deserves to become a classic. I cannot recommend it too highly for anybody who seeks to learn about that largely sealed-off corner of American radical history, to penetrate "the inordinate obsession and mystification that shroud Communism in the United States," as Richmond puts it in his preface.

For obvious reasons, I have changed the names of many

living persons (although I have tried to preserve the characters intact). My policy has been to use the real names of "identified Communists," as the House Committee on Un-American Activities would say, only with express permission of the individuals so identified in my book.

A Fine Old Conflict

Introduction

As a DISCONSOLATE TEEN-AGER, going for the regulation "nice Sunday walk" in Hyde Park with Nanny or our governess, I often wandered off to Speakers' Corner to listen to the Communist orators on their soapboxes and to join in singing their stirring anthem, the Internationale: " 'Tis the final conflict, / Let each stand in his place, / The Internationale / Shall be the human race . . ." For some years, before I saw the words written down, I thought it began: "It's a fine old conflict . . ." which to me it was then and ever shall be.

I started to write an account of that fine old conflict in 1960, about two years after I had said goodbye to the Communist Party—au revoir but not adieu, for I went on seeing lots of the comrades, giving what support I could to their endeavors.

My intention was to set down some personal reminiscences of the Party, and in doing so to try to exorcise a destructive poltergeist that kept knocking about in the furniture of American politics: the Communist conspiracy, or Red Menace, for decades part of the credo of almost all public figures from elected officials to newspaper editors, from labor leaders to lowly city councilmen, from conservative to liberal. I hoped also to lay to rest some myths created by the "I-was-duped" school of American ex-Party members.

At the time I found it heavy going, perhaps because I was too close to the events I was describing. Henry James once said, "It's a complex fate, being an American"; how far more complex a fate to be an American Communist in the forties and fifties. I was not sorry to be sidetracked by *The American Way of Death* and other work, and did not get on with this book until the mid-1970s.

Today the phrase Red Menace has a curiously old-fashioned ring, and the "dupes" have variously gone to their maker, faded into oblivion, or become American successes in business, letters, the movies. But thanks to the spate of True Confessions by Howard Fast, Whittaker Chambers, Bella Dodd, Elizabeth Bentley, Louis Budenz, and many others, published in the fifties and later, they have left a lasting imprint on American political thinking, and in my view have done much to obscure the realities of life in the Communist Party.

Yet not for me to sort out the tangle of events in the Communist world of the postwar era, to assess the changes in Communist strategy and tactics (or the Party Line, as it is called for short), the rise and fall of Party leaders. My effort will be a good deal less ambitious: merely to reconstruct my own experiences as a part of the Menace during those years and as an ex-Menace thereafter, to describe the fascination, difficulties, and frequent joys of being an "activist" in an embattled, proscribed (and, to me, occasionally comical) organization.

To trace the route that led me into the Communist Party, U.S.A., requires *un peu d'histoire,* as the *Guide Michelin* would say. Much of this has been written about elsewhere: in my sister Nancy's largely autobiographical novels; Harold Acton's memoir *Nancy Mitford;* my own book *Daughters and Rebels,* an account of our childhood and my subsequent life with my first husband, Esmond Romilly; Philip Toynbee's *Friends Apart,* a memoir of his friendship with Esmond. What follows is a brief recapitulation of the cast of characters and events insofar as they relate to the Fine Old Conflict.

In the beginning there were Farve and Muv, drawn to the life as Lord and Lady Alconleigh (or Uncle Matthew and Aunt Sadie) in *The Pursuit of Love,* Nancy's supreme fictional account of our family. In reality they were Lord and Lady Redesdale; the Radlett children were the Mitford children, with some variations.

We lived in a series of country houses in the Cotswolds— "from Batsford Mansion to Asthall Manor to Swinbrook House," Nancy used to say, describing the decline of the family fortune—with occasional excursions to our house in Rutland Gate for the London season. To me Swinbrook, where I spent most of my childhood, had aspects of a medieval fortress prison, from which quite early on I determined to escape.

My parents have been described as eccentric, although I did not consider them so, perhaps because it is impossible to imagine one's own parents being any different than they are.

Farve was a man of violent passions and prejudices, the terror of housemaids and governesses—and of us children, on the not infrequent occasions when one of us might be unlucky enough to trigger an unpredictable outburst.

As a Younger Son (his older brother, who would normally have inherited the title, was killed in the First War) he had received little education, having gone from an obscure public school straight into the usual murky colonial venture—in his case, tea farming in Ceylon—to which Younger Sons were then relegated. Perhaps it was there, shouldering the White Man's Burden, that Farve acquired that extra degree of British jingoism, remarkable even for his class and generation, that has been commented on by Harold Acton and others. "Farve is one of Nature's Fascists!" my two Nazi sisters used to say approvingly, and accurately.

By the time I was growing up, Farve, caricatured by Nancy as the General Murgatroyd of her first novel, *Highland Fling,* had more or less resigned himself to the role in which she cast him—had become, in fact, a successful caricature of himself.

My mother was a far more complex person. After her death in 1963, James Lees-Milne wrote in *The Times:*

Her own personality made her a woman very much out of the common. . . . Her very upbringing was unconventional. Most of her childhood was spent at sea on her father's yacht and until she "came out" she had scarcely set foot on dry land. In consequence she looked at life with the philosophic detachment of a mariner and accepted its vicissitudes with a wonderful fearlessness and robust good sense. . . . One of her peculiar charms was a patrician reserve. . . . She presided over her willful and, be it said, deeply devoted family with imperturbable serenity, pride and sweetness . . . that enigmatical, generous, great-minded matriarchal figure, with her clear china blue eyes and divinely formed, slightly drooping mouth which expressed worlds of humour and tragedy.

This moving description fits my mother as I came to see her towards the end of her life. When I was a small child I loved her, or believed I did. But by the time I was a teen-ager, I am afraid I actively disliked her. Nancy has written that she was "abnormally detached," giving this example: "On one occasion Unity rushed into the drawing-room where she was at her writing-table, saying 'Muv, Muv, Decca is standing on the roof—she says she's going to commit suicide!' 'Oh, poor duck,' said my mother, 'I hope she won't do anything so terrible,' and went on writing."

To me (the poor duck Decca) she seemed cold, strict, unapproachable, a person to whom one could never open one's heart or confide one's dreams. Her "patrician reserve" held no peculiar charms for me.

The dream of my childhood was to go to school. In common with many of our female contemporaries, my five sisters and I were brought up at home, while lucky Tom, our only brother, was sent to Eton. My mother taught us to read starting at the age of five (by the time we were six we were supposed to be able to read the *Times* leader without fault), after which we graduated to the schoolroom, presided over by a succession of governesses, few of whom were able to put up for long with our relentless misbehavior.

To my constant pleas to be sent to school, Muv would respond that it would be too expensive, or that the uniforms were too hideous. When I was twelve, a scheme occurred to me that would circumvent these objections. I had just read a fascinating book on astronomy, Sir James Jeans's *The Stars in Their Courses,* and yearned to follow in the author's footsteps. I would be an astronomer when I grew up, but first I must learn all about science. To this end, I bicycled to Burford, about three miles from Swinbrook House, and there sought out the headmaster of the state grammar school, which was free, required no uniforms, and offered the coveted science courses. Here, I knew, I could prepare for the School Certificate, first step towards college and a subsequent heavenly career as an astronomer, probing the mysteries of the universe.

The headmaster explained that since I had not yet been to school, he would have to give me a special exam based on a reading list he would furnish; if I passed, he would admit me as a student. I biked home, clutching the list, and in great trepidation accosted Muv in the drawing room.

Blushing furiously, I blurted out my plan, which even as I was unfolding it began to sound utterly ridiculous. "Little D. being a scientist! What nonsense, no, of course you can't go to the grammar school," and her face turned to disapproving stone. About this time I began to cherish the notion of running away from home, and started saving up for the purpose in a special Running Away Account in Drummonds, our family bank.

I myself was hardly aware of the depth of bitterness left by the grammar school incident until twenty years later, when Muv came to visit us in America after many years of estrangement. I reminded her of it, and to my surprise found myself in tears, crying with the same rage and frustration I had felt at the time. To her credit, Muv said she had later realized it was a mistake not to let me go to school: "At the time, you see, all my worries were about the older children; you and Bobo and Debo seemed quite safe and happy in the schoolroom."

The older children were indeed a family apart. Nancy was born in 1904, followed in quick succession by Pamela and Tom, then Diana, who was born in 1910. After a four-year gap, during which my mother may well have thought her family complete, Unity (Bobo to the rest of the family, but Boud to me) appeared in 1914, myself in 1917, and Deborah in 1920. Thus we seemed almost like two families of separate generations, the more so as we grew up and became subject to the influences of the outside world.

The older four, who matured in the twenties, bore the stamp of that decade—Nancy, in fact, must have been a potent influence in shaping its distinctive character. In memoirs of the day, and her own novels, we see her darting about in the society of the fashionable and the intellectual like a magnificent dragonfly: "a delicious creature, quite pyrotechnical my dear, and sometimes even profound, and would you believe it, she's hidden among the cabbages of the Cotswolds," as Brian Howard remarked to Harold Acton.

She did not tarry long among the cabbages. In my earliest memories of her she was always the center of some merry, brilliant gathering, many of whom were to leave an indelible mark, distinctly of their period, on English literature—Evelyn Waugh (whose company my parents forbade her after publication of *Vile Bodies*), John Betjeman, who used to entertain us with his renditions of Low Church hymns, Harold Acton—all chattering away in the language of the Bright Young People, as the newspapers called them: "Too, too divine. . . ." "Isn't he too sick-making for words? . . ." "My dear, it was blissikins. . . ."

These were the children of the Great War, as it was then called (for who could surmise that a greater one already was in the making?). Themselves too young to have taken part in the carnage, they had grown up in its shadow, and had witnessed the virtual decimation of the generation of young men just preceding theirs.

Perhaps the sudden release from the grim war years had produced in them a sort of frenetic ecstasy comparable to the St. Vitus's dance of the Middle Ages. The originators of a "generation gap" at least as wide and deep as that of the sixties, they were out to shock their elders in every conceivable way. They gaily toppled the old, uncomplicated household gods—England, Home and Glory, the Divine Right of Kings (and hence of the House of Lords), the axiomatic superiority of the English over all other races; they sacrilegiously called the Boer War, in which Farve was, according to Debrett's Peerage, "thrice wounded," "the Bore War"; they paraphrased Blake's "England's green and pleasant land" to "England's green, unpleasant land." They created an upheaval in standards of behavior, manners, and morality the likes of which England had never seen.

As for their "life style," as it would now, alas, be called—women wearing skirts up to the knee, bobbing their hair, smoking, drinking cocktails—how desperately risqué and improper it all seemed! In Nancy's novel *Highland Fling,* written in 1929, the daring words "Have a sidecar, Sally darling" (spoken to a pregnant woman, no less) must have seemed every bit as shocking to the older generation as talk of pot, grass, speed to the parents of the sixties.

The hallmark of Nancy's contemporaries was a special sort of flippancy and lightness of tone seldom successfully recaptured in the spate of memoirs about those days. Philip Toynbee, in his review of Harold Acton's *Nancy Mitford,* observes that much of the early part of the book "reads like the burbling of semi-idiots, the gossip of nitwits," yet he betrays a certain envy of the Bright Young Things, whose way of life he had just missed, as I had, by being born a few years too late: "Frivolity is usually a term of abuse, but I must confess that I was often fascinated by the cultivated frivolity of these elders. . . ."

To me, they personified Truth and Beauty, a gay and wicked challenge to the older generation. How I longed to be part of their grown-up world! Yet when, after what seemed like an interminable time, I finally did grow up I resolutely turned my face from these undeniable fascinators and all their works —even, for a time, from Nancy herself.

If Nancy was a trend-setter for her contemporaries, she was the more so within our family. Robert Kee, the English television interviewer, who knows my sisters well, once asked me: "Aren't you something of a sport, in the biological sense, among Mitfords? It has always seemed to me that your family regards the rest of the world, and everything that happens in it, as a huge joke put on for their benefit. Yet obviously you have espoused causes which you feel deeply about. Doesn't this set you apart from the other Mitfords?"

Escaping from the private Mitford cosmic joke, originally fashioned by Nancy, into the real world and eventually into the earnest life of the Communist Party was indeed rather uphill work. Yet being her younger sister had its beneficial side in that it was an immensely toughening experience. My mother used to say, "Nancy is a very curious character," and that she was—a hard jokemaster with an uncanny ability to ferret out one's weak spots, to be exploited in unmerciful teasing.

For example, I can see myself now, a stocky five-year-old, cast as First Fairy in a production of *A Midsummer Night's Dream* arranged by the older sisters. Standing foursquare, fat little legs apart, hands clenched at my sides, I resolutely thumped out my lines in a most unfairylike monotone: *"O*-ver hill, *o*-ver dale. *Through* brush, *through* briar." Immensely proud of myself, after the play I sought out my sisters to receive their plaudits for having memorized my part so well. Led by Nancy, they stood in a circle, legs apart, hands clenched, and plonked out in chorus: *"O*-ver hill, *o*-ver dale. *Through* brush, *through* briar." The hot tears that followed! And the hotter shame of being seen in tears.

Once, a few years before Nancy's death, a writer on the London *Observer* rang me up in Oakland; she was preparing a piece on the subject of Sisters, she said. Since there were so many sisters in our family, she wanted a comment from me; she had already spoken to Nancy in Versailles, who had said, "Sisters stand between one and life's cruel circumstances." I was startled into saying that to me, sisters—and especially Nancy— *were* life's cruel circumstances, a remark that did not find favor with her when it appeared in print.

However, one soon learned to give as good as one got, as techniques for teasing were perfected by sister after sister and passed on down the line. There was a popular song in the fifties called "Please Send Me Somebody to Love." Our entreaty to the Almighty could have been "Please Send Me Somebody to Tease," and except for poor Debo, each of us did have a younger sister to practice on. I found the habit hard to kick in later life, although I did try, especially after I came to live in

America; not having been brought up to teasing, Americans (with some notable exceptions) do not take kindly to it.

Debo's children used to call their Aunt Natch "the part-time ghoul"; an apt description, for if Nancy was a pitiless super-tease, she was also capable of marvelous, if intermittent, flashes of amiability and she took endless pains to brighten our lives with moments of high buffoonery.

One day when I was eight, shortly after my father had sold Asthall to a family called Hardcastle and before our move from there to Swinbrook, Mrs. Hardcastle's sister arrived at the front door—a formidable and highly unprepossessing lady with huge bosom, deeply wrinkled face, heavy black mustache. Admitted by Mabel, our head parlormaid, she said she had come to measure the windows for curtains and would like to be taken all through the house.

Mabel led her to the kitchen, where the cook and kitchen-maids politely showed her around, to the drawing room, thence to the nursery, where at Nanny's instruction Boud, Debo, and I stood up to shake hands. "What a *dear* little girl!" said Mrs. Hardcastle's sister, bending down to put her arms around me. The terrible mustache loomed close to my face. Horrors! She was going to kiss me.

The sight of my petrified expression was too much for Nancy. She burst into shrieks of laughter, whereupon the cushions tumbled out of her blouse and the jig was up. Only Nancy, we felt admiringly, would have gone to the considerable trouble of perfecting the transformation, and only she could have successfully deceived Nanny, the servants, and us children.

Paradoxically, the other toughening aspect of being Nancy's sister was what I used to call her "weak-mindedness." Although she made sporadic efforts to assert her independence from Muv and Farve, she remained very much under their domination until her marriage to Peter Rodd at the age of twenty-nine. It seems incredible that in those already modern, liberated times a woman in her middle and late twenties—especially one as brilliantly talented as Nancy—could be so totally subject to parental discipline. The extent of her thralldom comes through in her letters quoted in Harold Acton's memoir: "The family have read *Vile Bodies* and I'm not allowed to know him [Evelyn Waugh]. . . ." "As a list of those forbidden the house now includes all my best friends I foresee more tiring rows with the family. . . ."

Through the eyes of childhood I observed her long engagement, forbidden by Muv and Farve, to Hamish St. Clair Erskine, whom they regarded as a ne'er-do-well. By 1931 the engagement was broken, or rather seemed to have petered out. That year (I was a brooding thirteen, and Nancy twenty-six) we had a conversation that left a deep and lasting impression on me. We had gone for one of those long Swinbrook walks, trudging through the wet, leafy lanes, when the drizzle seemed like one's inner tears of bitterness because of the boredom and general futility of life. To my amazement Nancy, who almost never let down her comedian's mask, confided that she had had a terrible row with Muv, who was furious with her for turning down a proposal of marriage from a rich and eminently eligible young man. "You'll die an old maid if you go on like that," Muv had observed grimly.*

---

* Years after Muv's death I reminded Nancy of this in a letter. *"Did* it happen, or did I dream it?" I asked. "I know it must have, I can almost hear the squelch of one's gumboots as you imparted this odd bit of information. And the certain conviction, in my mind, that one had to get away from that dread place at all costs."

She wrote back: "I think I was telling lies if I said Muv wanted to marry me off. I think I was probably in a blind temper about something else & talked wildly. One of the reasons for my respect [for Muv] is that she never did urge marriage without inclination & I hardly think she knew who was rich and who was not."

Yet Harold Acton quotes a letter from Nancy to Mark Ogilvie-Grant

Was marriage, then, the only escape route from Swinbrook—and at that, marriage to some hearty country squire,
the only type of suitor likely to win parental approval? If
Nancy, already a successful author, was so thoroughly trapped,
what hope was there for me? I hardened my resolve to run
away as soon as I had saved sufficient funds.

If the four older Mitfords were twenties products, Boud and
I were very much creatures of the thirties (Debo was, and is,
unclassifiable). To telescope the events of that decade as they
affected our family, already recorded in *Daughters and Rebels*
and elsewhere:

In 1933 Diana divorced Bryan Guinness and took up with
Sir Oswald Mosley, head of the British Union of Fascists, to
whom she was secretly married some years later in Germany,
with Frau Goebbels, Hitler, and Goering as wedding guests. At
the time of the Guinnesses' divorce, Boud, now an eighteen-
year-old debutante, was a frequent visitor at Diana's London
house. She joined Mosley's Fascist party, then went to Germany, where she lived on and off as a member of Hitler's inner
circle until the war broke out.

My parents accompanied Boud to Germany on one or two
occasions and became ready converts to the Nazi cause. (After
my mother's death I was looking through one of her engagement books, a meticulous record of births of calves and foals,
family happenings, Nanny's holiday, dances, dinner parties.
Sandwiched between these items was an entry for June 1937:
"Tea with Fuhrer.")

Oddly enough, it was I rather than Boud who first became
interested in politics. Before her sudden conversion to Fascism,

---

dated 19 February, 1932: "I never considered it [the marriage in question]
only I was so bored down here and Muv went on at me about it and said
you'll die an old maid and I haven't seen Hamish for months and months so
I toyed with the idea for five minutes."

Boud's main preoccupations had been literary and artistic; she was a talented, if eccentric, artist; she knew by heart quantities of esoteric poetry. She seemed to live in a sort of dream compounded of Blake, Coleridge, Hieronymus Bosch, Henri Rousseau. I, on the other hand, was passionately engrossed with the other world that lay beyond Swinbrook, a Depression world in which students were demonstrating against the Officers' Training Corps, in which great hunger marches protested the treatment of the unemployed.

From within the Swinbrook fortress I watched these developments with avid interest and responded, like many another of my generation, by first becoming a pacifist, then quickly graduating to socialism. I became an ardent reader of the left-wing press, and even grudgingly used up a little of my Running Away Money to send for books and pamphlets explaining socialism. I discovered that human nature was not, as I had always supposed, a fixed and unalterable quantity, that wars are not caused by a natural urge in men to fight, that ownership of land and factories is not necessarily the natural reward of greater wisdom and energy. I read about great movements in England and other countries to divest the rich of their wealth and to transfer ownership of land and factories to the workers.

When Boud became a Fascist, I declared myself a Communist. Thus by the time she was eighteen and I fifteen, we had chosen up opposite sides in the central conflict of our day.

What propelled us in these different directions? The facile, pop-psychological answer would be that we were motivated by "sibling rivalry"—horrid phrase—and this probably did play a part. But I think that so far as I was concerned, a far more potent influence was at work: the *Zeitgeist* of the thirties, that crucial decade.

Just as the sixties in America was a decade of political turbulence in which young people (including my own daughter) suddenly rallied to the banners of black liberation, draft resistance, student rebellion, so in the thirties the cause of anti-Fascism, and the magnet of socialist reconstruction of society, drew many of my generation and those a few years older. My conversion to Communism was not an instant process, nor did it ever have the profound religious overtones often ascribed by ex-Communists to their experience. It developed, I think on looking back, out of the political exigencies of the times.

For another view, in *Unity Mitford: A Quest*, David Pryce-Jones writes: "Out of this childhood, and these ceremonies and safeties, the one evolved as a fascist and the other as a communist: one experience but two outcomes, opposed in externals, though in fact complementary." In other words, two sides of the same coin, a point he makes repeatedly: "Thousands had simultaneously stampeded along the highway to Moscow and Madrid, she [Unity] had taken the turning to Germany, their mirror-image." Mr. Pryce-Jones was born in 1936. Had he been around at the time of the events he describes, I do not think he would have made this equation. Would that there *had* been a stampede along the highway to Madrid, a gathering of the anti-appeasement, anti-Fascist forces in sufficient numbers to compel the governments of England, France, and America to take an early stand against the Fascists—it could have changed the course of history.

At first my political feud with Boud was something of a joke. At Swinbrook we divided up a disused sitting room at the top of the house and decorated it with our respective insignia: her Nazi pennants, photographs of Hitler, Italian "fasces"; my hammer and sickle, bust of Lenin, file of *Daily Worker*s. Sometimes we would barricade with chairs and stage pitched battles, throwing books and records until Nanny came to make us stop the noise.

By the time of the outbreak of the Spanish Civil War in 1936, the joke had turned bitter and my political differences with the family dead serious. I was now officially grown up, having endured the traditional English upper-class puberty rites of a year in Paris and a miserable London "deb" season, consummated by presentation at court. Nancy, probing as ever for one's most shaming weaknesses, called me "the Ballroom Communist," a cut below a "parlor pink." (She was, however, impartial with her slings and arrows: when Boud's friendship with the Nazis was crowned with the supreme honor of an invitation to sit beside Goering as guest of honor at a huge and glittering May rally, Nancy wrote to her: "Darling Stonyheart, We were all very interested to see that you were the Queen of the May this year at Hesselberg. Call me early, Goering dear, For I'm to be Queen of the May!")

I had a comfortable balance of fifty pounds in my Running Away Account, yet escape from home seemed as far away as ever. The war in Spain now became my major preoccupation, and my thoughts centered obsessively on ways of getting there to join the Loyalist guerrillas.

The opportunity to run, when it did come, was afforded by one of those improbable chance encounters that can in one dazzling flash change the course of one's life. In early 1937 I had gone to stay with an aged relation, Cousin Dorothy Allhusen, and there I met for the first time Esmond Romilly, a second cousin of ours whom I had long admired from afar. Esmond had been in the news for some years, ever since he had run away from Wellington, his public school, at the age of fifteen to work in a Communist bookshop, where with other runaways he plotted the editing, production, and distribution of a magazine designed to foment rebellion in *all* the public schools. He and his brother Giles had written a book, *Out of*

Bounds, describing their education and their conversion to radicalism, which had stirred considerable controversy in the press when it was published in 1935.

I had followed Esmond's fortunes with deep interest in the newspapers and through family gossip; shortly before arriving at cousin Dorothy's I had read a dispatch in the *News Chronicle:* "Esmond Romilly, 18-year-old nephew of Mr. Winston Churchill, is winning laurels for his gallantry under fire while serving in the International Brigade, which is fighting for the Spanish Government in defence of Madrid." In a disastrous encounter with the enemy at Boadilla, on the Madrid front, in which scores of volunteers were killed, Esmond and one other member of his unit had been the only survivors. Suffering from a severe case of dysentery, Esmond had been invalided out of the International Brigade and sent to England to recuperate, which is how he came to be staying at Cousin Dorothy's.

That weekend Esmond agreed to take me with him back to Spain, where he had a commission as a reporter for the pro-Loyalist *News Chronicle.* The following Sunday we fled, having devised an elaborate stratagem to deceive my parents into believing I was going to stay in Dieppe with some "suitable" girls of my age. By the time they discovered my defection, Esmond and I were living in Bilbao, capital of the Basque province, and were engaged to be married. In an effort to prevent our marriage, Farve made me a ward in chancery and his solicitors sent Esmond a telegram saying: "Miss Jessica Mitford is a ward of the court. If you marry her without leave of judge you will be liable to imprisonment." We took this as a declaration of total war. Eventually the British consul in Bilbao blackmailed us into leaving by threatening to withhold British aid in the evacuation of Basque women and children from the war zone unless we obeyed his instruction to return to England. This shabby piece of bargaining brought home to me the strength and ruth-lessness of the forces ranged against us. In a stormy session with the consul we capitulated; but not before Esmond had exacted a compromise that enabled us to leave, not for England, but for the south of France, where I should be safely out of reach of judge and family.

After a bitter and confusing row with Nancy and Peter Rodd, who came to meet us in Saint-Jean-de-Luz and who to my dismay had taken the parents' side in the contretemps, we settled in the Hôtel des Basques, a refugee center in Bayonne. From there I wrote to my unknown guardian, the chancery judge, pointing out that he would not be able to extradite me since I had committed no crime; by the time I had reached my majority, and would be out of his jurisdiction, I might have a growing family. I asked his permission to marry, which he promptly gave.

After our marriage we continued to live in Bayonne for several months, while Esmond finished his book *Boadilla,* an account of his experiences in the Spanish war. He was, as I often reminded him, the only person I had ever known who had written two autobiographies before the age of nineteen.

My mother did her best, I realize on looking back, to ex-tend the hand of friendship. Her letters to me in Bayonne, which I have kept all these years, contain many a peace feeler. She even offered to send me an allowance, a gallant gesture as my father certainly would not have approved; Esmond angrily refused the offer.

Although she faithfully kept me informed of family doings and assiduously tried to mend our relationship, her letters sometimes unwittingly widened the rift. We were not amused when she wrote from Germany: "It has been great fun touring around with Bobo. I think the others told you of our tea party

with the Fuhrer, he asked after Little D. I wished I could speak
German I must say. He is very 'easy' to be with & no feeling of
shyness would be possible, & such *very* good manners."

That autumn we returned to London, where we lived in a
friend's house in Rotherhithe, an East End district near the
river, supporting ourselves in the manner of the untrained and
unskilled: Esmond as advertising copywriter and sometime
journalist, myself as market research canvasser.

We saw my mother sporadically and those of my sisters with
whom I was on speakers; these were stiff, uncomfortable occasions, for Esmond did not care for any of them. I never saw my
father again. (He was consistent to the end. In 1955, shortly
before his death, I was planning my first trip to England after
an absence of sixteen years. My mother wrote to me in America
to ask if I should like to visit Farve. He was ill, she said, and
hadn't long to live. I did rather long to see him, yet it seemed
an act of disloyalty to my second husband, who is Jewish, and
Constancia, my fourteen-year-old daughter, Esmond's child. I
consulted them; absolutely, they said! You should, you must go
to see him. I wrote back saying we would love to see Farve
provided he promised not to roar at Bob and Constancia. Muv
replied: "Since you have set impossible conditions, I shall not
arrange a visit with Farve.")

Esmond and I never did join the Communist Party in England (contrary to what my family and the press all thought),
although most of our friends were members. In Esmond's view
the British Party was at that time overloaded with bourgeois
intellectuals, too much off in a corner, isolated from the main
labor movement to be worth the effort involved in being a
member. We were, however, staunch fellow travelers and supporters of the international Communist line: the United Front
against Fascism, collective security of Russia and the Western
democracies against the Axis powers.

Following Chamberlain's capitulation to Hitler at Munich in 1938, an atmosphere of unrelieved gloom settled over England. Further betrayals seemed in the making. There were persistent rumors that powerful pro-Fascists in the British and French governments, having successfully scuttled all hopes of a collective stand with Russia against the Axis powers, might go full circle and maneuver Western Europe into an anti-Communist alliance on the side of Hitler against Russia.

As Esmond wrote at the time, mirroring the despair of a generation that had lost control of its own destiny: "People in England aren't excited or hysterical any more at the idea of the coming war. People are adjusting themselves to a kind of half-life—a life where it's no good making plans, no good thinking at all of the future. . . . People don't talk about politics very much, either. What's the use? No one can feel any more that they have the remotest control over what is happening."

But Esmond was not one to adjust "to a kind of half-life." We decided to go to America on immigrants' visas, to see something of that strangely alluring land, to savor all possible adventures and experiences that the New World had to offer before the approaching war should engulf us. We sailed for New York in February 1939.

This would be an unreal, fantastic interlude, a waiting period, an escape from the political doldrums in which England was temporarily becalmed. When war broke out, we decided, we would join the Communist Party and take our place with the proven leaders of the crusade against Fascism, which, we felt sure, would create the conditions for worldwide socialist revolution.

But when that day came in September 1939, we were still in America, and the American CP, in what we considered a hopelessly wrong-headed response to the Nazi-Soviet pact, was in full opposition to the war, its spokesmen appearing on platforms with isolationists and America Firsters under the slogan "The Yanks Are Not Coming."

In our view, the pact was an inevitable outcome of the Munich betrayal and the intransigent refusal over the years of the Western democracies to respond to the unremitting Soviet effort to establish collective security against Nazi aggression. The role of the Communists in the Western countries, then, we believed, should be to press for vigorous prosecution of the war against the Axis powers—instead of which they were denouncing it as an "imperialist adventure."

We found ourselves in total disagreement with the Party Line. Esmond decided to go to Canada to train for the Royal Canadian Air Force. I remained in Washington, where our baby, Constancia, was born.

Just before Esmond left for England in 1941, the Germans invaded Russia, which changed everything overnight. The Western Communist Parties swung straight behind the war effort; now their cry was for opening a second front against Hitler. And now, we decided, was the time for us to join the Party, Esmond in England and I in America, where I was to stay until the baby was old enough to travel. Whether Esmond ever did so, I do not know. He was killed in action in November 1941. I remained in America and carried out our resolve.

CHAPTER 1

Washington

AT THE TIME of Constancia's birth I was living in the large, disorganized, and animated household of Clifford and Virginia Durr, who lived in the country a few miles from Washington.

The Durrs were Alabama born and bred, staunch Democrats and supporters of Roosevelt. (Their address was RFD 2, Seminary Hill, Virginia, always rendered by Nancy when she wrote to me there as FDR 2.) My long sojourn with them came about almost by accident. In the autumn of 1940, the day after Esmond left for the long months of training in Canada, Virginia took me to the Democratic National Convention in Chicago as a distraction from my misery over his departure. There we met some Texan friends of hers, who gave us delegates' badges so that we could join them on the floor of the convention. I was suffering desperately from morning sickness—the Texans, who chivalrously offered to let me throw up in their ten-gallon hats, said it must be the Democratic donkey kicking up its heels, upon which the unborn babe was nicknamed "the Donk."

After the convention Virginia invited me to stay for a few days until I could get settled in a flat of my own in Washington. Like the Man Who Came to Dinner, I stayed for two and a half years, soon adding yet another member to their already bulging household.

Fascinating as they were and much as I loved them, the Durrs had for me something of the quality of characters in an unlikely novel of Southern life. They had moved to Seminary Hill when Cliff, a former counsel for Alabama Light & Power Company, went to work for the Reconstruction Finance Corporation in the New Deal. He was an uneasy transplant from his native Alabama into the vicious realities of Washington politics. He was in fact the Southerner with a conscience, the home-lover with a deep sense of responsibility, a peace-lover, conservative by nature, eventually flung by history into a radical role.

The company they kept was much to my liking, as they had a wide and immensely varied acquaintance—thanks mostly to Virginia, who adored entertaining and had an insatiable appetite for meeting new people, seeing old friends. Virginia was chairman of the National Committee to Abolish the Poll Tax; her sister Josephine, called "Sister" after the Southern manner, was married to Justice Hugo Black. Thus the kaleidoscopic mix of people who came to visit included judicial dignitaries, Southern legislators—whom Virginia was forever trying to proselytize for the anti-poll-tax cause—New Deal functionaries, earnest young radicals.

Lyndon Johnson, then a freshman congressman, and his wife were familiars; they came out often of a Sunday afternoon to relax with their shoes off on the lawn and chin away with Cliff and Virginia in their (to me) near-incomprehensible patois about the ins and outs of Southern politics. "Ki-i-ssin' cou-ousins," the Durrs called them—and anyone else from the South who was not related by blood. In one of my rare letters to my mother (for we were much estranged in those days) I mentioned that Lyndon Johnson and Lady Bird had come out to tea. She wrote back: "Who is Lady Bird? I looked her up in the Peerage, but could find no trace."

Virginia was also after the higher echelons of the Senate. Once she invited Senator Claude Pepper (pronounced Clohohd, like the sound of a cow in pain) and his wife to dinner. The other guests arrived, eight o'clock came and went, then nine o'clock, but no Peppers. Virginia was vastly annoyed. The following day she took me to one of those huge official Washington cocktail parties in the Mayflower Hotel ("Honey, get your white gloves on; we've got to go and meet the British Tank Commission"); across a sea of heads she descried Mrs. Pepper.

A ship in full sail, her white leghorn picture hat bobbing up and down, Virginia steered a course through the crowd, with me, anxious little tugboat, following in her wake. "Whaa, Mildred," she cried on reaching her quarry, "Ah was most put out that you-all never came last night. What in the world happened?"

Mildred, quailing before the onslaught: "But whaa, Virginia, you never sent me a reminder card." To which Virginia responded, "Whaa, Mildred, you know darn well in that hick town you came from there were no reminder cards."

But Mildred, I felt, had the last word. Shortly before Christmas there was a telephone call from her maid. The Peppers had gone to Florida for the holidays; Mrs. Pepper had left a Christmas present for Mrs. Durr and would she kindly come to pick it up? Virginia, fuming at what she perceived as a deep discourtesy, nevertheless drove over to fetch the present. It turned out to be a horrid little cactus in a pot.

It was under Virginia's auspices that Constancia was born. Like many of her Southern compatriots, Virginia took an uncommon interest in births, miscarriages, and the like, and enjoyed running the show for others. Unfortunately, I was working as a salesgirl/model in Weinberger's Dress Shop throughout my pregnancy and for the purpose procured an extremely tight girdle. As months went on it began to feel like a ring of fire round my expanding belly; after work I would dash over to Cliff's office at the RFC to meet up with our car pool, and ease it off. One day I was standing in a corner of the office, shedding my girdle as usual, when a distinguished-looking white-haired man came in; he turned out to be Jesse Jones, RFC commissioner and Cliff's boss. Virginia complained about this: "Whaa, honey, you know how nervous that makes Cliff. Besides, you gonna have to quit wearing that damn girdle, else the baby'll be born flat."

She made me go to a well-known, very expensive Washington gynecologist for checkups, although I felt perfectly well and could ill afford the five dollars he exacted for the monthly urinalysis. My fury knew no bounds when I discovered the same doctor was treating Sister (Mrs. Black) for menopausal difficulties with injections of the urine of pregnant women—and charging her ten dollars a shot. I went round to his office to denounce him as a crook for selling my urine to Sister and charging me to boot, told him he was fired, and assured him I should spread the story of these fraudulent dealings all over Washington. He offered no defense, merely stared in open-mouthed astonishment.

Thereafter I made arrangements for the accouchement in the nine-bed charity ward of Columbia Hospital. At the time I was reading *In Place of Splendour,* the stirring autobiography of Constancia de la Mora, daughter of a Spanish grandee who fled her highborn family to cast her lot with the Republican army during the civil war. In the flush of tender euphoria that often accompanies childbirth, I thought to name the baby Constancia. Esmond's letter cautioning against this—"she'll be called Connie, a horrid name"—arrived too late, after the birth certificate was filed. As it turned out, Donk was the name that stuck, modified by Virginia's three little daughters to Dinky-donk or Dinky, her nickname to this day.

The regulation hospital stay after childbirth was in those days a fortnight, which gave one plenty of time to make friends with the other patients and to think up ways of exerting pressure on the management to make our lives more comfortable. There was one new mother who was unable to urinate without being catheterized, a painful and revolting procedure over the details of which I shall draw a veil. As her health improved, she often felt she would be able to use the bedpan without the dread catheter, and would ring her bell to summon a nurse. Invariably, the nurses took so long to respond that the desire passed, and she was forced to use the catheter after all.

I became increasingly restive over the callous behavior of the nurses, and devised a punishment to fit their crime, which I unfolded to my fellow patients: "Next time Mrs. ———— rings her bell, I'll count to ten. If a nurse hasn't come by then, let's all wet our beds." It worked beautifully. The bell was rung, I counted, no nurse loomed, and we all swung into action—even Mrs. ————, who in the giggly excitement that swept the ward found herself suddenly able to perform. When the nurse finally appeared, she was faced with changing all nine beds, eighteen sheets. For the rest of my stay at Columbia Hospital, one had but to touch a bell for a nurse to come flying. It was my first successful effort at organizing for mass action; "the bedpan strike," my fellow activists called it, though I suppose that twenty years later it would have been described as a pee-in.

After Dinky's birth, my two main preoccupations were to find and join the Communist Party, and to equip myself to be useful once a member. Somehow I must pull out of the dead-end world of market research, retail selling, and the like, and acquire some training; but in what line? My first choice would have been journalism, and I toyed with the idea of enrolling in the journalism school of Columbia University, which I assumed was in the District of Columbia. By the time I discovered my mistake—and learned that to qualify for enrollment one must have an undergraduate degree—I was thoroughly settled in with the Durrs and disinclined to move. So I enrolled in a private secretarial school to learn shorthand and typing. Possession of these skills would, I believed, transport me into realms of ideas and action. I secretly cherished the hope that one day I might become secretary to a Party leader.

To my distress, I proved to be a phenomenally slow learner. Try as I might, the other students, for the most part recent high school graduates and far younger than I, zoomed past me in the speed tests in the most dismaying fashion.

Eventually I was hired by the Office of Price Administration (the wartime price control and rationing agency) in the cruel category of "sub-eligible typist," at a salary of $1,440 a year—and this in the days when it was said that the wartime shortage of clerical workers was so severe that the applicant for a government job was taken into a room with a typewriter and a washing machine; if she could identify the typewriter, she was hired. The job description for sub-eligible typist was deeply depressing: "Must be able to follow simple directions." I yearned to improve, to qualify as a proper secretary whose job description was "must be able to exercise initiative."

My boss, Marie Berger, a lawyer in the enforcement division, was pleasantly tolerant of my incompetence as a typist. Indeed, she never learned the full extent of it, for I soon discovered a marvelous place called the typing pool, and learned to partake of its life-restoring waters. I used to wander down there, where some twenty crackerjack typists were furiously pounding away, and pretend to be an executive. "I want nine copies of this by noon, please, and be sure it is correctly proofread." (For some reason, everything had to be done in nine copies.) Then I would go off and lurk in the ladies' lounge until my beautiful pages were ready.

Marie and I worked in a huge barnlike room in Temporary Building D, our two desks squeezed in among hundreds of others, for she was not high enough in the OPA hierarchy to rate an office of her own. "It's too noisy to think in here," she would say dispiritedly.

One day I was mooning about the corridors as usual, waiting for my typing to be finished, when I noticed a dear little office fully equipped with two desks, typewriter, telephone— and apparently unoccupied. I kept it under surveillance for a few days to make sure it was really vacant, then moved our stuff in. Most of the private offices, I had noticed, had cryptic designations on the door: SENIOR TEXTILE ANALYST, FIELD SERVICES, and the like. I pondered a suitable one for us, and settled on WHOLESALE-RETAIL COORDINATOR. Through my typing-pool connections I ordered a sign made up, which I affixed to the door. For the first few days other OPA workers would stop by. "You're new here, aren't you?" they would say. "What do you do?" "Oh . . . we just coordinate wholesalers and retailers," I would answer, pointing to the sign. It proved to be a fully sufficient and satisfactory answer.

Marie was so pleased that she arranged a promotion for me, which took me out of the clerical stream ("where your talents are being wasted," she said rather coldly) to the rank of Investigator I: "Must be able to analyze trends, formulate programs, and conduct pilot drives." In addition to this encouraging description of my new duties, the job carried a considerable pay increase; I would be making $1,800 a year.

One obstacle to my certification as an OPA investigator was the Civil Service eligibility requirement of a college degree or two years of business experience, not including retail selling. I studied the application for a while; I had never gone to school, let alone college, and my only "business experience" had been my pathetic ventures in retail selling. I had, however, been sent to Paris at the age of sixteen, and had there taken the "Cours de Civilisation Française," a beginner's course which the Sorbonne offers to foreigners. I paused, but only for a moment, in filling out the Civil Service form, and put down: "Graduate, Université de la Sorbonne." Paris was then occupied by the Nazis; it seemed unlikely that the personnel people would check.

I found it difficult, and embittering, to be living in America at that time. The boring and oppressive American preoccupation with material comforts, the open boasts one often heard in some circles about successful black market dealings (*"My butcher sells me all the steak I want; he never asks for ration coupons"*), filled me with gloom. Seen from these shores the war was a spectator sport, to many a rare opportunity for personal enrichment. The unseemly scramble for affluence was not limited to out-and-out war profiteers; it was in evidence everywhere.

Reality was back in England, where the Nazi invasion seemed imminent, where people were stoically preparing for the onslaught. Yet after Esmond's death it seemed pointless for me to return—I had nobody to return to, and encumbered by the infant Dinkydonk I should not be in a position to be of much help in the war effort.

In these circumstances the OPA enforcement division was, for me, an exhilarating place to work. A war agency, yet unlike the so-called old-line agencies (such as the War Department or the Treasury), it was infused with the crusading New Deal spirit and frequently locked in battle with major business interests. The OPA seemed as close to the front line of the war against Fascism as anything in Washington.

My new-found colleagues—lawyers, investigators, economists, rationing experts—were for the most part young, dedicated, immensely energetic, and hard-working anti-Fascists. It was our job to hold the line against war profiteers, price gougers, greedy landlords, violators of rationing regulations. The press, predominantly anti-New Deal and anti-Roosevelt, was also the enemy, referring to us contemptuously as "slide-rule boys" and "OPA snoopers." *Time* magazine, which led the pack against price control, explained: "A new Washington term for the academicians who used to be called 'braintrusters' is 'slide-rule boys.' Slide-rulers in OPA number well over 100."

As early as 1941, *Time,* in a preview of the McCarthy witch-hunt that would dominate the next decade, reported: "Ever since paunchy Price Boss Leon Henderson, in a particularly tactless moment, blurted that Martin Dies was 'not a responsible member of Congress' the Dies Committee has been out to get him or his staff. The Committee obtained a list of all his employees, 40 of whom have written for Communist publications." Throughout the war OPA continued to be a favorite target of *Time,* with its special flair, forerunner of Spiro Agnew's, for inventing new pejoratives: "OPA's foolish fumblers . . ." "Malice in OPAland . . ." "OPA's 2,700 lawyers, backbone of the slide-rule cabal . . ." "OPA's slide-rule boys, the Leon Henderson carryovers headed by gangling '5 ft. 20 in.' Deputy Price Administrator J. K. Galbraith . . ."

There was also considerable internecine warfare, as the agency had its quota of saboteurs, collaborators with big business, sent in by powerful conservatives in Congress. Richard Nixon worked there for a while in the tire-rationing division, although today none of us remembers ever meeting him. Perhaps he was off conspiring with Bebe Rebozo, who made his first fortune in retreaded tires in the thirties and forties. According to a biographer, Nixon's desk was next to that of J. Paull Marshall, later assistant vice-president of American Railroads, "an intransigent Republican who liked Nixon as soon as they met. 'Most of the OPA lawyers were left-wingers, and it was natural that Dick and I should develop an affinity for each other,' he says. 'We both believed in the capitalist system, but the other lawyers were using rationing and price control as a means of controlling profits.' "*

The Washington office was responsible for establishing rent control, price control, and rationing policy, writing detailed regulations, and conducting "pilot drives" to test the enforceability of the regulations before promulgating them in the Field —which sounded like a huge freezing prairie somewhere in the Middle West, but was actually OPA's term for the rest of the country.

The lawyers shared the investigators. Sometimes I was assigned to work for Bob Treuhaft, an enforcement attorney, among whose many attractions were his slanting, twinkling black eyes, his marvelously funny jokes, his (to me) exotic Bronx idiom and pronunciation. Bob had written the regulation on Pleasure Driving, designed to alleviate the critical gasoline shortage by imposing a ban on all driving except for business reasons—one could drive to work and back but not to a dinner party. He proposed we should conduct a pilot Pleasure-Driving Drive to determine the level of compliance with the new regulation. We staked out a spot near the superfashionable Troika nightclub in the Mayflower Hotel, where we would meet each night under the stars in the freezing Washington winter and apprehend pleasure drivers as they alighted from their cars.

One night we caught the Norwegian ambassador. He stopped his car outside the Troika and we advanced upon him, explaining that he was in violation of OPA regulations. His wife was livid: "Surely you don't expect us to take the bus?" The ambassador diplomatically kicked her in the shins and said, "In the future, my dear, we shall have to." I was pleased by this

* Bela Kornitzer, *The Real Nixon,* Rand McNally, 1960, p. 143.

surprising bit of luck, surely bound to result in nationwide publicity for the Pleasure-Driving Drive. I could visualize Bob and me posing for photographers outside Temporary Building D, sternly displaying the ambassador's confiscated ration book as a warning to all who might be tempted to Pleasure Drive. But alas, he was "too smart for us," as Bob ruefully put it. The next day his picture was on the front page of the Washington *Post,* boarding the bus in some far-off suburb on his way to the embassy, with the caption "Norwegian Envoy Conserves Gas."

For OPA loyalists, fiercely bent on securing compliance with the agency's regulations, any violation of these would be unthinkable. Thus shortly after the pleasure-driving ban was announced, Bob's roommate, Ike, also an OPA lawyer, and a noted womanizer, woke him up at three o'clock one morning to report ecstatically, "Bob! I laid *four* of them tonight, all in different parts of town from Washington to Silver Spring, using only public transportation!"

After the Norwegian ambassador nab, Bob wrote a poem for me, and my heart flipped. It began:

> *Drink a drink to dauntless Decca,*
> *OPA's black market wrecker.*
> *Where there is no violation*
> *She supplies the provocation.*
> *Smiling brightly, she avers,*
> "Je suis agente provocateuse."

But I think I really fell in love over the rape of the OPA Census Building plans. In one of those gargantuan bureaucratic maneuvers for which the government is famous, it was decided to move the entire OPA from familiar, grubby old Temporary Building D to the grander and hence more desirable Census Building, which had been evacuated to accommodate us. For months earnest relocaters had been at work preparing meticulous ground plans and charts, the goal being that on the day of the move everybody would find his desk, typewriter, chair in the Census Building in the exact same juxtaposition to his neighbor's desk, typewriter, chair as it had been in Temporary Building D. To this end, colored and numbered tags were affixed to every movable object.

The evening before the move, Bob and I were working late in our respective offices. He dashed in to the Wholesale-Retail Coordinator's office, gleefully waving a sheaf of papers: "The master plans for the Census Building move! Quick, we haven't much time to spare." He had found them lying around in full view, and swooped them up for the purpose of doing a bit of master planning himself. This was a marvelous chance, he pointed out, to teach a well-deserved lesson to some of the racist, anti-Semitic characters who had infiltrated the OPA.

It took hours of painstaking, meticulous work poring over the charts, removing the sets of colored tags and rearranging them according to the Bob scheme of things, and we staggered out into the night bursting with laughter at the thought of our colleagues' reactions the next day.

We were not disappointed. Arriving early, we observed their expressions change from bewilderment to rage as they sought and found their desks. The frumpy racist mistress of the chairman of the Ways and Means Committee, whose appointment as investigator could, we thought, be attributed only to this alliance, gasped open-mouthed as she found herself surrounded on all sides by Jews and the one black investigator. The office glad-hand was next to the office grump, and so it went. Bob and I, of course, found our desks, now cozily ranged side by side, without difficulty.

Bob's recollection of the beginning of our romance is somewhat different. For the Harvard Twenty-fifth Anniversary Re-

port, a compilation of brief biographies of graduates of the class
of 1934, he wrote: "In the OPA I met a fantastically beautiful
woman* who attracted me not only by her charm and wit, but
by her frugality. I watched with fascination as she moved down
the line of the block-long counter of the cafeteria in the huge
OPA temporary building. As she passed the beverage section,
she would pick up a glass of tomato juice, down it, and set the
empty glass down on a handy little shelf below the counter.
Next she would scoop up a salad and dispose of the plate in the
same way. Then a sandwich. When she reached the cashier, she
had nothing on her tray but a cup of coffee—cost of lunch, five
cents. This, I decided, was the girl for me."

During our long vigils outside the Troika, and in other
pleasurable moments, I learned something of Bob's background, which I found of great fascination—so completely unlike that of anybody I had heretofore known, though as I
gathered later from books like *Act I* by Moss Hart and *Jews
Without Money* by Mike Gold, actually fairly typical of many.

His parents were Jewish immigrants who had come to
America as teen-agers from Lublofürod, a tiny village somewhere in Hungary or Czechoslovakia, depending on the fluctua-
tion of the frontier during various wars and upheavals. His
family surname, too, had changed with the vicissitudes of Jews
in the Diaspora. Generations before, when Hebrew patro-
nymics had to be abandoned in favor of Hungarian-sounding
names, the name was changed from Coin (a variant of Cohen)
to Török, meaning Turk, assigned no doubt by some whimsical
official who noted the slanting eyes of a Bob forebear. Later,
when Hungary became part of the Austro-Hungarian empire, it

* A vast exaggeration, of course. Perhaps a Harvard manner of speech?
Reading other entries in the Anniversary Report, I noted many of his classmates felt constrained to use similar hyperbole in describing their future
wives.

became convenient and advisable to switch to the German-sounding Treuhaft. Today there are many Treuhafts scattered around America, all related and all traceable to the same Lublofürodian origin.

Bob's mother, Aranka, was sent to work in a New York clothing factory at the age of thirteen, married Albin Treuhaft when they were both eighteen, and in a version of the classic American success story, had through a combination of talent, charm, and hard work fought her way up in the predatory clothing industry, eventually to become first a millinery designer, then a custom milliner with her own elegant hat shop. At the time of their marriage, Albin was a waiter; prodded forward by ambitious Aranka, he became a bootlegger and later part owner of a restaurant in Wall Street.

Until Bob was about nine, the Treuhafts lived in a tenement in the Bronx ghetto. They had scraped together money to bring over Albin's parents. Bob remembers them as terrible, narrow-minded old people who spoke no English, their principal function to cook and mind him and his little sister, Edith. By the time Bob reached high school age, the family fortunes had enabled them to move to a house in Brooklyn, where he attended New Utrecht (pronounced Noooootr'k) High School, a vast establishment of some ten thousand students. The student body was half Jewish, half poor Irish and Italian Catholics; no blacks. Bob's only contact with his gentile classmates was an occasional street fight in which opposing groups of Jews and Catholics would square off to throw rocks at each other; until he went to college, he had never met a Gentile socially. "It would have been unthinkable, beyond the pale, to invite one to our house," he explained.

In 1930, his last high school year, Bob and one other boy sat for the Harvard entrance exam. Although the other entrant was a far better student, exam nerves got the better of him and he failed (later to win a Rhodes Scholarship and become assistant secretary of labor in the Truman administration), while relaxed Bob sailed through.

As the first boy from Noooootr'k to be accepted at Harvard within living memory, he was called in by the principal, a legendary, aloof figure who lived at the Harvard Club and was driven to and from work in a chauffeured Cadillac. The principal extended his pleased congratulations, and invited Bob to come to lunch with him at the Harvard Club during spring vacation. But alas, when that time came and Bob went to collect the promised lunch, he was coldly informed by the Harvard Club that his putative host was presently residing in Sing Sing, having been caught stealing money from Noooootr'k's student cafeteria. The chauffeur and Cadillac (and presumably as tertiary beneficiary, the Harvard Club) had, it seems, been financed for years from this lucrative source.

During his undergraduate years, and later at Harvard Law School, Bob was not particularly interested in politics. His radicalization began with his apprenticeship to Elias Lieberman, general counsel for the International Ladies Garment Workers Union in New York. The rank and file of the ILGWU were a fiercely militant bunch, constantly at war with "the boss" and often at odds with the class-collaborationist officers of the union. They streamed through Lieberman's office with a bewildering variety of grievances, and Bob found himself carrying the legal cudgels against the Class Enemy with a zeal that transcended the partisanship of advocacy. "You can't know this feeling," he said, "unless you have represented the wonderful people who form the membership of a union like the Embroiderers, Pleaters, Tuckers, Stitchers and Tubular Piping Workers, Local 66, or Covered Button Workers Union Local 12."

One of the ILGWU's most successful projects was its musical *Pins and Needles*. The cast of this wonderfully funny show were themselves members of the union, whose songs effectively punctured the sacred cows of the day: "Gee, but I'd Like to Be a G-man," a daring spoof on J. Edgar Hoover; "Nobody Makes a Pass at Me," a takeoff on Madison Avenue advertising slogans.

David Dubinsky, the union president, ordered the cast to give a benefit performance for "brave little Finland," then locked in battle with the Soviet Union. They refused to do so without first taking a vote, as required by Equity rules: a ploy suggested by Bob, who, agreeing with many in the cast, had reservations about Finland's Fascist government—whereupon Dubinsky accused Bob of being a Communist. Bob was so astonished that he started to read whatever literature he could find on the subject. This was the beginning of his Marxist education.

When the U.S. entered the war, he was classified 4-F (to his dismay), so decided to seek a job directly connected to the war effort, which brought him to Washington and the OPA.

We discussed joining the Communist Party. It seemed inconceivable that the war against Fascism would not eventually turn into a world revolution against all forms of repression, sweeping capitalism into the dustbin of history, as Lenin would say. Having but one life to live, what could be better than to devote it to this noble cause?

Bob was all for it. In the course of his duties as shop steward for the radical United Federal Workers local in the OPA, he had occasion to meet with many co-workers whom he assumed, from their single-minded devotion to the anti-Fascist cause and their ability as organizers, to be Communists; but in Washington government circles the Party was so far underground, it would be deeply awkward to approach anyone about the matter of joining. So we perforce had to content ourselves with supporting Party causes from the outside: helping with benefits for Spanish Civil War refugees, marching in picket lines calling for a second front, and the like.

Dinky and I had moved away from the Durrs' and were sharing a flat in Washington with one of Ike's girl friends. Throughout the autumn of 1942, the five of us met almost nightly for dinner at our flat or theirs. Dinky was the star of these occasions—she was in fact the one fixed star in my firmament, my constant friend and companion, the only remaining link with my past life with Esmond. In hopes that she would soon learn to talk, I treated her more or less as a grownup, somewhat to Bob's surprise. Actually, he rather approved of my equal-to-equal attitude to Dinky, diametrically opposed to the Jewish-mother routines of his own childhood.

At Christmas time, Bob and Ike concocted an appeal to one of Ike's former girl friends, who had moved away from Washington. It was a song to which they had written the words and music, reproduced by them as a record on one of those do-it-yourself phonograph machines:

> *Dear Joyce, please come to Washington—*
> *Ike wants to marry you;*
> *Dear Joyce, please come to Washington—*
> *No government girl will do.*
> *I think of you night and day;*
> *I think I'm with the REA, the FSA, the CAA,*
> *When I'm really going dopey in OPA.*
>
> *Dear Joyce, please come to Washington*
> *If you have any feelings;*
> *Dear Joyce, come back to Washington—*
> *Think of Henderson's ceilings,*
> *Think of rations, rent, and price;*
> *No need to hoard that wedding rice.*

Dear Joyce, come back to Wash-ing-ton.
Don't think twice, be nice—
Come to Washington!

So pleased were they with this effort, and with the barber shop quartet effect of their out-of-tune voices backed up by a piano accompaniment supplied by a musician friend, that they made several more records, addressed to girls around the country: "Dear Kate, please come to Washington—Bob wants to marry you"; "Dear Jean, please come to Washington—Bob wants to marry you," and so on.

By New Year's, to Bob's and Ike's pleased surprise and my deep chagrin, several of the girls showed up in Washington. I was excluded from their merry revels. It was rumored that Bob had become engaged to at least one of them, possibly more—he was known to be a trifle absent-minded about such matters. For the first time in my life I was assailed by the bitter, corroding emotion of jealousy.

I could not quite understand this myself, but it brought home to me what I had begun to suspect: that my feelings about Bob were in a hopeless muddle. Like Marianne in *Sense and Sensibility*, I did "not approve of second attachments" and indeed had never envisaged forming one (rather to Virginia's annoyance; she was forever producing eligible suitors, whom I would firmly ignore). Thus I had no call on Bob's affections, no right to mind if he took up with others.

The best solution for me, I decided, would be to get out of Washington, as far away as possible, and start a totally new life. There were three transfer possibilities open at the moment for OPA investigators, I was told: Denver, Detroit, and San Francisco. Of Denver and Detroit I knew nothing; they sounded much the same to me. But San Francisco had a special ring to it: the Golden Gate, stellar city of the roaring West, home of Harry Bridges and the militant Communist-led International Longshoremen's and Warehousemen's Union (ILWU). Thither I repaired with Dinky in early February 1943.

CHAPTER 2

San Francisco

BOB, WHO CAME to see us off on the train, was appalled by the sorry state of our luggage, consisting of a large suitcase bound with string, a dozen assorted shopping bags, and Dinky's tricycle, none of it in acceptable shape for checking through. "I didn't expect to see matched luggage," he groaned as he helped me pile it all into our tiny compartment, "but you might at least have gotten matched shopping bags." When the train pulled out of Union Station, Bob was still on it, "to make sure the conductor doesn't kick you off when he sees the mess." I found it immensely consoling that he stayed with us for an hour, then got off somewhere in West Virginia, to return to Washington by bus.

The three-day journey was uneventful except for a brief encounter with a middle-aged man I found in the club car one evening, reading the palms of some women who were clustered about him in great excitement. I went over, and watched him perform with uncanny accuracy. "I see beauty parlor equipment," he would say, and sure enough, the hand he held belonged to a hairdresser. Another palm revealed canine presences, kennels, and leashes; there were oohs and ahs when its owner exclaimed in amazement that she was a breeder of prize poodles.

Then he looked at my palm, long and intently. "You have

one overriding passion—money. That's all you really care about." When I laughingly protested, he became quite serious. "How much are you making now?" "Eighteen hundred a year." "Well, you can have a job in my casino right now for twenty-six hundred a year. People's money is my business, and I need people like you." "Your casino?" "Yes, I'm Harold Smith, and you may have heard of my club in Reno. It's called Harold's."

I regretfully declined; it did sound rather fascinating, being a shill? a dealer? He must have had something like that in mind, but I was set on my course for San Francisco. As it turned out, Harold had charted my immediate future with extraordinary prescience, for within a few months I found myself immersed in fund-raising for the *Daily Peoples World,* West Coast equivalent of the *Daily Worker.* Later, as financial director of the San Francisco Communist Party, I became obsessed with thoughts of money to an extent that Harold Smith would doubtless have found most gratifying.

I spent wakeful nights on the train with Dinky in the clutter of our single berth, squeezed in between suitcases and shopping bags, her trike wheeling from time to time over our faces in rhythm with the train's movements. What were we doing, rumbling across the breadth of America to a strange metropolis where we should not know a soul? Was I running away, not only from Bob, but from the fresh and bitter memory of Esmond's death, blindly putting distance between me and all those past connections? Separated by six thousand miles from my family in England and by three thousand from my nearest American acquaintances, I could be virtually reborn as an anonymous bit of human flotsam in this remote outpost. I was both excited and a bit desolate at the prospect.

My first evening in glamorous San Francisco did little to dispel my sense of gloom. We arrived after dark and checked into a downtown hotel. Finally unburdened of our dreadful luggage, I put Dinky to bed, asked the maid to give an eye to her, and wandered out to have a look at San Francisco night life. There were numerous bars in nearby streets; I cased these joints carefully, chose one that looked pleasant and not too crowded, and made my way to a table. An imposing black-garbed hostess, her every well-combed curl mutely deploring my travel-worn state, came over and said reprovingly, "Have you an escort?" No escort, alas, I replied.

She explained that an emergency wartime measure adopted by the city government forbade unaccompanied women to fre-quent bars. I started to object to "frequent"—after all, I had only just arrived—when a surreal savior intervened in the shape of a brisk, uniformed, thirtyish policewoman who mate-rialized as out of nowhere, dismissed the hostess with a wave, and said, "I'll handle this. It's O.K., honey, you can have your drink." Uncomfortably I did, under her supervision, and we chatted briefly about the problems of delinquency. Having suffered instant disillusionment of all my preconceived notions about rip-roaring, open-town San Francisco, I returned to my hotel, with plenty of time before morning to reflect on my next steps, on what I was actually doing here and why.

The ensuing weeks are a jumble in my memory, com-pounded of finding a place to live, meeting my new colleagues in the OPA Regional Office, getting down to my investigative tasks, joining the Federal Workers Union. I found none of it particularly enthralling. Try as I might, I could not recapture the spirit in which I had departed from Washington; the "new life" would not take shape. I was annoyed with myself, because objectively all the ingredients were there. The boardinghouse into which Dinky and I had settled had its Dickensian side; the Regional Office hummed with political intrigue; the union was clearly a hotbed of radicalism; my co-workers were an excep-tionally promising lot, a good cut above the average run of war-agency personnel. Yet more and more I found my only source of real pleasure and sustenance was Bob's letters.

They were written with what book critics call "economy of style," seldom more than a page or two long, yet crammed with amusing Washington gossip. Some would contain a tantalizing few words that could be construed as a Sign: "I tried to get you on the office phone yesterday, and was told by some fiend in human form that you were home sick. It's no good, Dec, having all those miles of Field between us."

He was assigned by the national office to make a tour of OPA enforcement divisions in the Middle West, and wrote from Detroit: "Between us is the Field. Did you pause to observe while traversing it that it is slushy and dirty and bleak and cold; that it is square and ugly? They offered me a job here which I would have grabbed a couple of months ago, but I said no, how could I with Dec and the Donk hanging around out in S.F. without a man to take them into a bar. How could I indeed."

By a stroke of luck I managed to solve at one blow the problems of housing and Donk care, both of which loomed large because of drastic wartime shortages of apartments and domestic help. Lugging the Donk with me, I trudged in the wake of the FOR RENT ads for a few days and eventually came to Mrs. Tibbs's boardinghouse, on Haight Street near Ashbury. Two decades later this neighborhood would become world-renowned; in 1943 it was just another run-down district of small shops and working-class homes.

Mrs. Tibbs's advertisement, for room and board at forty dollars a month, had not mentioned child care, but one look at her convinced me she was the right surrogate mother for Dinky—earthy, maternal, a dour face masking twinkling eyes. There were two hurdles to overcome: another prospective tenant, there ahead of me, was on the point of taking the room, and Mrs. Tibbs did not want to look after any more children; her own little Ricky and Billy were enough of a handful, she said. In short order I convinced the other applicant that she would be far better off taking lodgings in the East Bay, where she was working, and artful Dinky, using all her two-year-old charm, persuaded Mrs. Tibbs that she needed a little girl to help civilize her boys.

We took our meals with the other boarders, most of whom were Marines stationed in San Francisco. Dinky settled down with her new playmates and learned to say her first sentence: whenever anything naughty happened, such as a breakage of dishes or a flooding of bathroom, she would gleefully shout, "Rickydidit!" or "Billydidit!" spoken as one word.

Mrs. Tibbs, glad of female company after playing hostess to the Marines for many months, told me her curious life story as we did the dinner dishes. Dr. Tibbs was a dentist; before their separation she had been quite well off. But he must have had odd sex habits. "He ruined my bladder," she confided mysteriously. I wrote and told Bob of this peculiar circumstance. He wrote back: "In a fit of depravity he filled the wrong cavity," and: "What's the madder, you ruined my bladder, you took advantage of me," the sort of letter that made my day.

The OPA Regional Office was housed, along with other war agencies, in the Furniture Mart at Tenth and Market, a short streetcar ride from Mrs. Tibbs's. I soon discovered that warfare between the radicals and conservatives raged even more fiercely here than in Washington. At issue at the moment were OPA enforcement policy and the right of government employees to join a union. The conservatives, who dominated the administrative division, worked behind the scenes with the Apartment House Owners Association and other business interests to sabotage enforcement of price and rent controls. They had, we suspected, planted stool pigeons in the union and were constantly calling people in to cross-examine them about union activity.

Among the chief exponents of the radical viewpoint were John McTernan, head of our division and chief enforcement attorney; Doris "Dobby" Brin (later Walker), a young lawyer who was president of the San Francisco local of the United Federal Workers of America; Al Bernstein, an investigator and OPA union shop steward. All these eventually became lifelong friends.

Under their leadership I strove to achieve our enforcement goals, my first assignment being to investigate the prices charged by secondhand-machine-tool dealers in the area. I was furnished with a bewildering schedule showing the "base price," meaning the maximum that could legally be charged, for lathes, punch presses, dies, molds. The schedule was several pages long, as there were different base prices depending on the make and age of the equipment. Attached to this was a list of second-hand-machine-tool dealers in San Francisco, whose shops I was to investigate to determine if they were overcharging.

Since I had never even seen a firsthand machine tool, and had no idea what they looked like or how to appraise their value, I decided to go incognito to one of the listed merchants in an effort to get a general grasp of my subject. I found one in the murkier part of the San Francisco industrial district, near the waterfront, and walked in.

"Could I see a secondhand lathe, please? Oh, thanks, I see, that's it. Looks very nice, lovely. What year is it, actually?"

The owner was a laconic type, and responded all too briefly; I feared I was beginning to sound like my mother inquiring about an early Victorian table in a London antique shop. But I persisted. "I call *that* awfully nice. Oh, it's not a lathe? Even so, I might be interested; it looks jolly useful for its purpose."

I was scribbling down in a notebook the names, descriptions, and prices of these objects as given by the dealer, who squinted suspiciously and answered in monosyllables. He did not seem at all keen about making a sale; perhaps he was a front for a vast secondhand-machine-tool black market ring? If so, here was a marvelous opportunity to work up a major criminal case against this unprepossessing man and his evil confederates.

Back at the office I reviewed my notes, compared them with the OPA schedule, and to my despair could not make head or tail of any of it. I wished I had some invoices, bills of sale for these mystifying secondhand machine tools, giving precise specifications that might coincide with those in the schedule.

Armed with my OPA identification card, I returned to the shop, waited in a nearby telephone booth until I saw the owner go out for lunch, then went in to speak to his secretary. "Will you please fetch out all your sales records for the past month? I'm here on OPA business, and we need them to determine if you're complying with the regulation."

She nervously opened up a filing cabinet and produced sheafs of receipts and bills. "I'm afraid I'll have to take these back to the office," I said firmly, and swept them into my briefcase.

Later that day, as I was poring over this material at my desk—and even making some headway, marking down several overcharges I had detected—McTernan's secretary came over. "Mr. McTernan wants to see you in his office immediately." To commend me for my diligence, no doubt, I thought.

"Sit down, Mrs. Romilly," said McTernan, looking stern. "Let me ask you this: Have you ever read the Constitution of the United States?"

"Well, yes, bits of it. You mean free speech and so on?"

"No, I mean the Fourth Amendment. Here, read *this* bit,"

and he produced the document. I read: "The right of the people to be secure in their persons, houses, papers, and effects, against unreasonable searches and seizures, shall not be violated . . ."

"There was a man in here just now looking for you, and he had a gun," continued McTernan. "He said you terrorized his secretary and stole all his records. He was mad as hell. He says if he ever catches up with you he'll plug you! No, I'm afraid you'll have to curb your commendable zeal for enforcement in the future." I was abashed (although I thought the gun was a nice Western touch), and at McTernan's direction returned the records with an abject apology to the dealer, whose gat fortunately appeared to be parked for the nonce.

Al Bernstein signed me up as a member of the United Federal Workers Union. He and I had adjoining desks, and shared a propensity for sloppiness that was the despair of the administration. The supervisors would come around regularly to complain: "What if a member of the public were to walk in and see this disgraceful mess?" Sometimes we would spread our stuff out on nearby desks that happened to be vacant. Thus it came as no surprise to me thirty years later to find this passage about Al's famous son, Carl, in *All the President's Men:* "At 9 p.m., when Bernstein sat down to write . . . the clutter on his desk was hopeless, so he moved to three vacant desks near his own and laid out three yards of notes." Withal Al was a gifted organizer, and had even managed to organize the guards at Alcatraz into the United Federal Workers.

Joining this union, which had been publicly denounced by the House Committee on Un-American Activities as "Communist dominated" (an accusation that proved, in this case, to be not wide of the mark), was, I felt, a step towards finding the Communist Party. In *Boadilla,* Esmond described a volunteer in his unit as belonging to the category of "Real Communists": "This was a purely personal definition I applied instinctively," he wrote. "To fit it you had to be a serious person of single-aim sincerity, a rigid disciplinarian lacking in any selfish motives."

Applying this definition to my co-workers, I thought I could detect a few Real Communists: for example, Dobby, to whom I was introduced by Al as a new recruit the day I joined. Her first words to me were, "Which committee would you like to work on?" I responded, "Where do you need most people?" Dobby sternly said that was *not* the point of the union, which was engaged in serious struggle on behalf of the working class against the forces of reaction. After a few more mystifying exchanges, it developed that she thought I had said, "Where do you *meet* most people?" While this might not have been an unreasonable question from an unattached newcomer to the area, to Dobby, "a serious person of single-aim sincerity," it must have smacked of irresponsible frivolity.

I threw myself into the work of the union, much of which would not, in normal times, be classifiable as traditional trade union activity. But we were then at war, at the side of the Russians against a Fascist enemy. Conventional trade union demands—higher pay, shorter hours, better working conditions—having been shelved temporarily in favor of all-out support of the war effort, our program now called for tougher enforcement of rationing and price controls, child care centers to facilitate the employment of women in war work, the opening of a second front in Europe. We supported the no-strike pledge and had no quarrel with the law that prohibited strikes of government workers. In OPA we regarded the administrative heads of the Regional Office as our principal adversary, and were constantly on the attack to expose their business connections and their unremitting attempts to sabotage or inhibit effective enforcement.

What with union work, investigating rent overcharges (to

which I had been transferred from the ill-fated secondhand machine tools), dining with Mrs. Tibbs and the Marines, looking after Dinky, my days and evenings were fully occupied and I was constantly surrounded by people. Yet I was horribly, chronically lonely, as though shrouded in a fog of unhappiness through which I could descry but dimly the cast of characters at home and at work. I even developed an illness which I thought might be psychosomatic, attributable to this state of mind. I had stayed in bed with a flaming sore throat, and one morning awoke to find my legs virtually paralyzed. Thinking it might be polio, Mrs. Tibbs sent for a doctor, who pronounced the paralysis a side effect of the septic throat. "Poor Mrs. Romilly, her throat's gone to her knees," I heard Mrs. Tibbs telling the Marines.

When Bob wrote that he intended to come out to San Francisco for his two weeks' annual leave in June, my every thought became focused on his arrival. In anticipation of it, I kept my eye on an apartment beneath Mrs. Tibbs's boardinghouse which was to become vacant. Mrs. Tibbs agreed that I could have it.

It was in truth a very rum dwelling, consisting of two tiny rooms, plus a makeshift kitchen and a boarded-up storefront facing on Haight Street. Access to it was either through the boardinghouse and down a wooden fire escape, or through a pitch-dark alley and up the fire escape. But I was determined to get it in shape before Bob arrived. I bought a quantity of secondhand furniture and ordered it delivered. Mrs. Tibbs telephoned me at the office one day to say the delivery men were there with my furniture, but I had forgotten to leave her the key.

"Couldn't you ask the Marines to climb in through the window and open the door from inside?" I suggested. Mrs. Tibbs agreed, but came back to the phone to report that the Marines had declined this task because they were wearing their good suits.

"Then how about asking them to take off their suits and climb through in their underclothes?"

"Oh, all right, Mrs. Romilly," said Mrs. Tibbs. "But I sure hope they don't make a habit of it."

On the afternoon of Bob's arrival, to calm my nervousness and to pass the hours until his train was due, I went to a movie, *Mission to Moscow,* which I had been particularly anxious to see. Minutes after I came out of the movie theater I realized I had seen and heard absolutely nothing, had no idea what the film was about—I must have sat there in a trance—and I did wonder if Bob was similarly entranced at the thought of seeing me again.

Fortunately he was. We went directly from the train to Izzy Gomez's bar, a famous San Francisco hangout of the day for writers, artists, and radicals, where I was able to point out Harry Bridges sitting in a far corner with some trade union cronies; a fitting welcome to San Francisco, I thought, and how unlike my own!

Deciding the time had come to speak plainly, or at least to elicit some plain talk, I asked Bob what his plans were for the future. "To marry you, and move out here to live" was the inspiring answer. Izzy ordered free drinks all around to celebrate our engagement, and the next day we set off hitch-hiking to Guerneville, a resort town on the Russian River about a hundred miles from San Francisco, where we were married.

The fog now lifted, and everything came beautifully into focus. Bob even warmed up slightly to our Tibbsian living arrangements, having thought when I first led him through the Stygian alley and up the rungs of the fire escape that it was all some sort of elaborate practical joke devised by me to tease him.

Before the end of his two-week leave he managed to secure a job offer from the San Francisco Regional Office of the War Labor Board. The news of our sudden marriage was accepted with good grace by my new friends, especially when they learned that Bob was an officer of the union's OPA section in Washington. Dobby presented us with our only wedding present, a copy of Howard Fast's *Citizen Tom Paine,* inscribed "From your Brothers and Sisters in the Union."

The union took up an inordinate amount of my time, especially after I was elected membership director of the War Agencies local. In this capacity I had to attend the meetings of individual union shops to make sure they were carrying out executive board policy, and was responsible for notifying all shop stewards of executive board meetings. On one occasion I reported that one of the shop stewards had just been married and was absent because she had gone off on honeymoon. "Without first getting the exec. board's permission for absence?" said Dobby, scandalized. She ran the union as a *very* tight ship.

There was a brief flurry of excitement when I was given notice by the OPA regional director that my employment was terminated—the administration had just hit upon a convenient way to get rid of me. Aliens were then generally ineligible for government employment. OPA's budget, however, contained a special appropriation of fifty thousand dollars to enable the agency to hire foreign economists and rationing experts. It was through this loophole that clever Marie Berger had shamelessly engineered my original appointment as "sub-eligible typist" in Washington. I had long since forgotten about that, but the Regional Office personnel people, looking for a way to deal with my increasingly obnoxious presence as a union troublemaker, had at last tumbled to the fact that I was still being paid out of the "alien expert" fund.

The Brothers and Sisters of the union rallied with heartening solidarity. First incredulous, then indignant, they quickly saw that by firing a union officer, management had handed the union a challenge that had to be met. A frenzy of activity followed; emergency meetings, petitions, rallies were skillfully orchestrated by the union's Old Hands, who succeeded in putting the administrators on the defensive by exposing their anti-union motive. Behind-the-scenes calls to our friends in Washington eventually produced a legal opinion from OPA's national office supporting my eligibility for general employment on the ground that I had applied for first citizenship papers.

I was hastily reinstated, and soon all the government offices in San Francisco were blanketed with leaflets announcing: "UNION SCORES DOUBLE VICTORY! We keep our membership chairman! OPA keeps a trained investigator!" It was an exhilarating moment for me, and in my enthusiasm I mailed a copy of the victory leaflet to my mother. She replied: "I wish I knew what the 'union' is, to me it means the Union of South African Republics."

But what did we actually do in the union, aside from attending endless meetings at which we enunciated and reaffirmed our policy of all-out support for the war effort and passed resolutions demanding the opening of a second front? Even at the time I was hard put to it to explain our raison d'être to outsiders. One of Bob's relations asked what the advantages were in belonging to a union in circumstances where wages and conditions were not issues, and the strike weapon was expressly prohibited by law? "Well . . . the main advantage is that if you are fired for union activity, the union will fight to get you reinstated," was my somewhat lame rejoinder.

. . .

DURING MY FIRST MONTHS in San Francisco, I had achieved gratifying success in one of the major objectives of my new life: that of preserving my anonymity. Heretofore anything I or my sisters did was likely to become a matter of newspaper interest. "Whenever I see the words 'Peer's Daughter' in a headline," my mother once remarked gloomily, "I know it's going to be something about one of you children."

Too true. In England throughout the thirties, those headlines had proliferated and from the time Esmond and I arrived in America in 1939, we were tracked by reporters who recorded our every move: BRITISH BEAUTY HATES NAZIS SO SHE'S WORKING IN THE U.S. ("Fancy Little D. being a Beauty!" my mother had written when I sent her the clipping); CHURCHILL'S 20-YEAR-OLD NEPHEW IN NEW YORK; CHURCHILL KIN TENDS BAR IN MIAMI; SISTER OF ADOLF'S PERFECT NORDIC TYPE IS MAKING OWN WAY AS MIAMI BARMAID; JESSICA MITFORD ROMILLY MODELS IN WASHINGTON DRESS SHOP; UNITY "A LITTLE WILD," HER NOT-SO-TAME SISTER SAYS. (An absolute lie; I never discussed my family with reporters, except to confirm that my political views were the opposite of theirs.) Even during my stint as sub-eligible typist the family notoriety followed me; Ike had overheard one OPA secretary confide to another, "She's the girl who danced before Hitler."

It was a blessed relief to get away from all that, to take refuge at Mrs. Tibbs's and the OPA Regional Office, where I was merely an English war widow who happened to fetch up in San Francisco. I longed to be a person considered on her own merits, no longer dogged by the onus (or cachet, depending on viewpoint) of Peer's Daughter. In any event, I thought, it would have been impossible to explain my family to someone like Dobby, born and bred in Texas, to whom the story would have been so far removed from anything in her own experience as to be utterly incomprehensible.

A few years later I felt thoroughly vindicated in thinking that some things are better left unexplained. Dinky, aged four, was still an addicted thumb-sucker—partly my fault: when she was an infant I had recalled our Nanny saying, "A thumb-sucking baby is a good baby," so whenever she cried I popped thumb in mouth. But my San Francisco friends, exponents of the then current theories of child psychology, were horrified at her persistent and voracious sucking; they urged me to take her to the Langley Porter Clinic of the University of California for therapy. Since the clinic was free, and there was nothing to be lost by going, I made an appointment for a psychologist to have a word with Dinky.

To my surprise and annoyance, it developed that I, too, was to be interviewed. A brisk young woman sat me down and read out questions from a form, ticking off my answers as she went. "Your birth date? Childhood diseases? Check which. Migraine headaches, yes or no? Epilepsy? Fainting spells?"

I was getting restive—what could this have to do with Dink's thumb-sucking? She got down to the crux of the form. "Any insanity in your family?" "No." "Any marked eccentricity?" "No." "Any suicides?" "Well . . . one of my sisters shot herself." "Circumstances of shooting?" "She adored Hitler, so when war broke out I suppose she couldn't endure England and Germany being at war."

The brisk one faltered noticeably. "What were you doing at the time?" "I'd run away to Spain before that, to join the Reds, and am now a member of the Communist Party, U.S.A."

She stopped writing altogether. Dinky and I were discharged as cured, or incurable—I am not sure which. Later I was told by one of the Langley Porter psychiatrists, who had become a friend of ours, that Dinky and I were the subject of a staff meeting, which concluded, "Since the mother lives in a fantasy world of her own, and is incapable of giving rational and credible answers to questions, it is impossible to treat the child further."

My terror of discovery by the press was one reason for our decision to be married in rural Guerneville rather than San Francisco, where our marriage might come to the attention of some sharp-eyed newspaperman. The day we got back from Guerneville, Bob, who had gone out to do some errands, returned flourishing the front page of a tabloid newspaper. The headline, in letters four inches tall, read: OPA SNOOPSTRESS WEDS SLIDE-RULE BOY: STUNS S.F. He said later that he literally thought I was going to faint. I turned white and gripped a chair with both hands. So it was with profuse apologies that he admitted he had ordered the page printed up in one of those joke shops that specialize in "personalized" newspaper headlines.

My cherished anonymity was not to last. In November 1943, Herbert Morrison, Britain's home secretary, released the Mosleys from Holloway Prison, where they had been interned as potential traitors since shortly after the beginning of the war. The press reported that in the incomparable style of the Old Boy network, English authorities had treated them with deference and accorded them a private four-room flat in the prison, complete with two female convicts to act as their servants. Their release provoked a storm of furious protest from the English labor movement, recorded in daily headlines in the San Francisco newspapers: 40,000 MEET IN RAIN TO PROTEST MOSLEY RELEASE; MOSLEY RELEASE STIRS FUROR IN LONDON; BRITAIN WARNED 30,000 FASCISTS ARE READY TO RISE; ANTI-MOSLEYITES MARCH ON COMMONS; SIX MILLION MORE JOIN LABOR PROTEST ON MOSLEY RELEASE. *The New York Times* reported: "There is little doubt that the people of Britain are worked up over Sir Oswald's release. Early morning trains arriving here from the Midlands carried large numbers of outraged Yorkshire miners representing 140,000 fellow workers.

Representatives of 10,000 miners of South Wales also arrived, and a telegram signed in the name of 75,000 Sheffield war workers was sent to Mr. Churchill."

The *Times* also noted that "the first German comment on the affair was a masterpiece of putting the cart before the horse. 'The decision of the British Government to free Sir Oswald Mosley is undoubtedly the result of violent reaction against his prolonged confinement,' said the enemy announcement." In a unanimous resolution, the Transport & General Workers Union blasted Morrison's action as "a grave reflection on and insult to the people in the fighting services who are making such great sacrifices in the interests of freedom and democracy . . . an indication that the government is wavering in its adherence to the principles for which we are fighting."

I agreed with these sentiments. But I also read the newspaper accounts with mounting apprehension, an uneasy feeling that it must be but a matter of time before the San Francisco press discovered that Mosley's sister-in-law was living in the area and would track me down as subject for a "local color" story.

One day I was at my desk in the Furniture Mart when I noticed a man with a camera over at the OPA press section, at the far end of the vast open space, erstwhile furniture showroom, where the lowlier employees, investigators and secretaries, worked. I watched him closely; the press section's sole function was to supply the media with mimeographed handouts on developments in price and rationing regulations; it did not ordinarily attract news photographers. He appeared to be making inquiries of the press officer, who consulted a chart and then pointed in my direction.

The cameraman started to make his way through the forest of desks. I got up and walked towards the glass-enclosed offices of the enforcement division executives that ringed the room.

The cameraman quickened his step. I bolted into one of the private offices, which happened to be that of John Porter, chief regional investigator and my immediate boss, where a conference was in progress with a dozen or so district investigators seated around a long table. They looked up in astonishment at this extraordinary interruption. I mumbled breathless apologies: "Awfully sorry—could I just stay in here for a little while?" But the cameraman had darted into the adjacent office and was snapping my picture through the glass partition. In a rage, I dashed out and tackled him, kicking the camera and seizing him by the throat. The whole OPA rose as one man to watch the fight; Porter and his conferees moved in to separate us; the aggrieved cameraman shouted imprecations and vowed that his employer, the *Examiner,* would sue me for breaking his camera.

Porter quieted the hubbub, told everybody to return to their desks, and as the photographer grumblingly departed called me into his office. "Now, perhaps you could explain what that was all about?" I said we had better ask Bob, who was working on another floor in the War Labor Board, to come up and help in the rather tricky job of explaining. Together we unfolded the story to the amazed Porter, who said I could have the rest of the day off to collect myself and avoid the temptation to rough up any more gentlemen of the press who might be lurking in the Furniture Mart.

Bob came home with me. An hour after we got back, Mrs. Tibbs came down to our flat to report that newspapermen from all four San Francisco dailies had been around inquiring for us. She had given them no information, but they were still outside sitting in parked cars. We locked the doors, pulled down the blinds, and prepared to wait it out. The siege continued the next day. Mrs. Tibbs brought food, bulletins about the reporters, who were back at their posts, and the inevitable story in the

Examiner: "SISTER OF HITLER'S 'NORDIC GODDESS' IN OPA JOB HERE. The Hon. Jessica Mitford was discovered yesterday working as an investigator in the OPA office in San Francisco. She is now Mrs. Robert Treuhaft. . . . Mrs. Treuhaft, blue eyed and dark haired, was reluctant to discuss her presence in San Francisco when interviewed at her desk in the Merchandise Mart Building. . . ." The latter a nice journalistic rearrangement of the facts, we thought. It reminded me of the time in 1937 when, shortly after Esmond and I had left Spain, we had discovered an eavesdropping reporter outside our hotel room. Esmond had threatened to punch him in the nose, a remark oddly paraphrased in his story the next day: " 'I am with the girl I love,' Romilly told me last evening."

By the second day the siege was lifted; the reporters had evidently got bored with their vigil and given up. We decided to go back to work, first stopping in at the Whitcomb Hotel coffee shop next door to the Furniture Mart to telephone to John Porter and ask him if the coast was clear. But there, lurking in the Whitcomb phone booth, was my adversary, the *Examiner* photographer, and once more we made a rapid getaway. Our situation was getting pretty ridiculous and clearly the time had come for us to work out a strategy of our own for dealing with the press and so put an end to this time-consuming game of hide-and-seek.

We consulted Dobby, who put us in touch with Morris Watson, editor of the ILWD *Dispatcher,* an adept at press relations. He suggested that I should write a letter to Winston Churchill setting forth my views of the Mosleys' release, and give a copy to the San Francisco *Chronicle* as an "exclusive," thus thwarting my persecutors at the *Examiner,* Hearst's rival morning paper. I did this, and the next day the *Chronicle* ran it as a news story under the headline: JAIL MOSLEY, SISTER-IN-LAW URGES HERE.

My letter said: "Like millions of others in the United Nations and the occupied countries, I have all my life been an opponent of the Fascist ideology in whatever form it appears. Because I do not believe that family ties should be allowed to influence a person's convictions I long ago ceased to have any contact with those members of my family who have supported the Fascist cause. Release of Sir Oswald and Lady Mosley is a slap in the face of anti-Fascists in every country and a direct betrayal of those who have died for the cause of anti-Fascism. They should be kept in jail, where they belong."

Rereading this letter today, I find it painfully stuffy and self-righteous—and also, as Nancy later pointed out in her understated fashion, "not very sisterly." Yet at the time, the freeing of the Mosleys symbolized everything we feared: the possibility of surreptitious negotiations with the enemy by powerful English tories (the appeasement crowd of Munich days were still very much in evidence in high places), an outright betrayal of the anti-Fascist cause. In my case, no doubt, these views—as comes through strongly in my letter—were admixed with deep bitterness over Esmond's death and a goodly dash of familial spitefulness.

The *Chronicle* story caused quite a stir in the union. I reflected that since my hope of remaining forever a "closet Mitford" might anyway have been unrealistic, this particular bit of publicity could prove a blessing in disguise and bring me a step closer to being invited to join the Party.

CHAPTER 3

Joining the CP

THAT AUTUMN Dobby and I were elected delegates from our UFWA local to the CIO state convention in Fresno. Bob came down with us. I had looked forward to this event, but the excitement that took hold from the moment of our arrival at the convention hall surpassed my every expectation. The CIO in 1943 was at the height of its power. The brash upstart that had broken with the AFL in the thirties in the name of industrial versus craft organization was riding the crest of dramatic victories achieved in organizing the vast and hitherto "unorganizable" auto, steel, oil, and electrical industries. Before this meeting my trade union experience had been limited to the white-collar UFWA; in Fresno we met many working-class heroes of the CIO, gathered under the leadership of Harry Bridges, most of them carrying left-wing credentials of the day —the scars of picket line battles, impressive arrest records, service in the Abraham Lincoln Brigade.

We thrilled to the sights and sounds of the convention, the oversize pictures of FDR and Stalin adorning the platform, the strains of "Solidarity Forever" resounding from a thousand throats, and to the feeling that one was part of a great invincible workers' movement. The main thrust of the convention was the drive to reelect FDR, and it was in fact this California gathering that touched off the successful nationwide campaign to draft him for an unprecedented fourth term.

It was there, in a dark corner of the hotel bar, that Dobby popped the question. "Would you two be interested in joining the Communist Party?" We exclaimed in unison, "We *wondered* when you were going to ask us."

For Bob, it was plain sailing. As soon as we returned to San Francisco he was issued a Party membership card and assigned to a Party branch. For me, there was an unexpected hitch: the Party had recently adopted an ironclad policy against the recruitment of aliens. The reason for this was a provision of the Smith Act under which aliens were required to disclose Communist affiliation. Should the alien affirm that he was a Party member, he would be subject to deportation; should he deny it, he would risk a perjury prosecution. The Party met this problem by barring all aliens from its ranks for their own protection.

Since I had come over four years before on an immigrant's visa, and was now married to an American, I found I was eligible for instant citizenship. I had a little trouble answering the routine question in my interview with an Immigration Service officer: "Why do you want to become a citizen of the United States?" As it seemed inappropriate to answer, "So I can join the Communist Party," I conjured up some phrases about the land of freedom and democracy, which apparently satisfied my interrogators, for early in 1944 my citizenship papers came through without a hitch.

Some years later, at the height of the McCarthy repression, there was a concerted drive by the FBI and the Immigration Service to ferret out, denaturalize, and deport foreign-born U.S. citizens suspected of having falsely denied Party membership at the time of their naturalization. We learned that I was a target of this endeavor when friends in various parts of the country—

Miami, Washington, New York, San Francisco—began reporting that they had been visited by immigration officials and questioned about my subversive connections.

I fantasized being brought to trial and presenting my alibi
to a bewildered judge: "But, Your Honor! How *could* I have
been a Party member then? I only joined your country so I
could join the Communist Party, which wouldn't admit me as
an alien." As it turned out, the trial never materialized because
eventually the government, having lost a major test case on the
issue, decided to drop further denaturalization suits.

We joined the Party at a curious moment in its history: the
Browder Period, as it later came to be called in CP parlance. In
1942 Earl Browder, national Party chairman, had enunciated a
policy that called for subordination of all other interests to the
war effort, unqualified support of Roosevelt's foreign and domestic programs, adherence to the no-strike pledge that had
been adopted by the CIO as a wartime measure. In May 1944,
the CP national committee dissolved the Party altogether,
changed its name to the Communist Political Association,
adopted a program of postwar collaboration between labor and
capital, and shelved the goal of socialism for the foreseeable
future.

The *Peoples World,* which carried daily on its masthead the
slogan "Buy War Bonds and Stamps," relayed the Party's program in its columns: "Support all unity measures, war bonds,
USO, war relief, no-strike policy and cooperation with em-
ployers for production. . . ." "Total mobilization for victory is
the Number One job for the CIO. . . ." "Invade Hitler Europe!" "Oleta O'Connor Yates, San Francisco Communist
Party Chairman and candidate for the Board of Supervisors,
declares 'The one election issue in 1943 is winning the war. I
stand for supporting our President and his war policies, and
increasing production in San Francisco by an over-all munici-

pal program that will put our city on a war basis. I shall strive energetically to solve such problems as transportation, child care and civilian defense, and work to improve race relations by ending discrimination.' "

Although in total agreement with the Party's win-the-war program, I was secretly disappointed to discover that its revolutionary goals seemed to have faded away. But the Browder Period was short-lived. In April 1945, Jacques Duclos, a French Communist leader, dropped his bombshell in the form of an article popularly called the Duclos Letter, in which he denounced Browder's policies as "a notorious revision of Marxism, sowing dangerous opportunistic illusions." This clear signal from the international Communist movement resulted in reestablishment of the Communist Party, U.S.A., rejection of Browder's concept of class harmony for the foreseeable future, a reaffirmation of socialist principles, and a return to the strategy of the United Front as originally conceived in the mid-thirties: "a coalition of the working class, the toiling farmers, Negroes, and middle classes against capitalist reaction, fascism, and war."

There was much rejoicing in the ranks at this turn of events. Many comrades had had deep reservations about the Browder policies. The returning war veterans—fifteen thousand Communists had served in the armed forces—had been particularly incensed to discover that in their absence their party had been dissolved.

A word should be said about the changing Party Line. As an observer from the sidelines I had long been aware of the Party's propensity for swift and fundamental policy changes. I had seen the Party switch with the advent of the Nazi-Soviet pact of 1939 from advocacy of a united stand against the Fascist powers to condemnation of the "imperialist war"—a stand with which I totally disagreed. Two years later, when Hitler marched on the Soviet Union, the Party again shifted position and pledged its all to the war effort. But once a member, I do not remember ever questioning "the correctness of the Line," as we would have put it. I was enchanted by the flesh-and-blood Communists we now began meeting, veterans of the 1934 waterfront strike, of the CIO organizing drive of the thirties, of bitter battles between agricultural workers in the San Joaquin valley and hired goons sent in by Associated Farmers. There were, to be sure, a number of bores and misfits in our organization, but even these seemed to be to some extent redeemed by their dedication to our common cause.

In the two big policy changes—the dissolution of the Party under Browder and its reconstitution following the Duclos Letter—did I feel we were automatons, blind followers of the Line as handed down from on high? There was an element of that, but it is not the whole picture. Throughout the Party there were intensive discussions preceding these changes; we held meetings that lasted far into the night to study and dissect draft resolutions from the national office, to scrutinize papers submitted by club members, all of which gave me a strong sense of personal involvement in the Party's policy decisions.

It is hard to convey the sort of alchemy at work in these discussions, compounded of the Party's illustrious history as carrier of the torch against Fascism in Spain, Germany, Italy; the magnetic influence of such persuasive and articulate debaters as Oleta Yates, Bill Schneiderman, Steve Nelson; above all the conviction that the Communist Party, equipped with Marxist-Leninist theory, was historically destined to lead the working class to socialism—it would make mistakes along the way, but these would be corrected through criticism, self-criticism, the testing of theory in day-to-day work. The advent of the Duclos Letter and the reevaluation that ensued seemed a prime example of the built-in corrective factor.

The Party operated on the principle of "democratic centralism," which meant that all members were required to study,
discuss, and vote on all matters of policy; once the decision had
been taken, each member was bound by it, whether or not he or
she personally agreed with it. It was indeed a matter of conform
or get out, but this did not particularly bother me. I had regarded joining the Party as one of the most important decisions
of my adult life. I loved and admired the people in it, and was
more than willing to accept the leadership of those far more
experienced than I. Furthermore, the principle of democratic
centralism seemed to me essential to the functioning of a revolutionary organization in a hostile world.

In those days, until the postwar repression set in, the Party
was a strange mixture of openness and secrecy. Its organizational structure had undergone some changes in the United
Front era. The basic membership unit was no longer the con-
spiratorial-sounding "cell" of three to five members, abandoned
in the twenties. In its place we had "branches" or "clubs"—a
nomenclature deemed more consistent with American political
tradition—some with as many as a hundred members, which
met weekly in rented halls. Over these were the Leading
Bodies; the County Committee, presided over by Oleta O'Connor Yates; the State Committee, with William Schneiderman as
chairman; and highest of all, the Central or National Committee, with headquarters in New York on the legendary "ninth
floor."

Bob and I were at first assigned to the Southside Club, one
of the few "closed" or secret branches, reserved for government
workers, doctors, lawyers, and others whose occupations could
have been jeopardized by open identification with the Party.
Our weekly meetings were held in rotation in the homes of
members, and invariably followed a set agenda which would
have a comfortably familiar cadence to anyone who had at-

tended trade union local meetings or fraternal meetings of Elks
or Bisons: Minutes of Last Meeting, Membership, Lit., Education, Good and Welfare.

A typical meeting would go like this: In line with democratic centralism, each executive board member would have
met with his or her counterpart from other clubs and would
report back to us from these county-wide meetings. Thus the
club membership director, responsible for recruiting, might give
a brief pep talk: "Comrades, at the county membership directors' meeting we discussed concrete proposals for Party-
building." These would then be outlined. "The recruiting drive
is half over and several of you *still* haven't turned in your list of
contacts." A contact was anybody who might be a likely prospect for recruiting; there were "neighborhood *contacts*" (meaning neighbors), "job *contacts*" (fellow employees), and "mass
org. *contacts*" (members of non-Party organizations doing
community work).

The lit. director was generally considered low man on the
totem pole in the club exec. As the job consisted of fetching
cartons of books and pamphlets from the Party bookshop, selling them at the meeting, keeping track of the money received,
and returning unsold merchandise the next day, the chief requirements were a car, a strong back, and a head for figures.
We in the Southside Club were fortunate in having a lit. director whose unobtrusive scholarship made his sales pitches a
pleasure to listen to. In his brief talk he managed to convey his
own enthusiasm for the Marxist classics, greeting them as old
friends, and spoke so perceptively about the Party's current
publications that we eagerly bought his wares and soon acquired an extensive Marxist library.

The Educational had an honored place on every agenda;
usually at least an hour would be devoted to it. (Why the adjec-
tival-noun form was used to designate this portion of the meet-

ing I never learned. A friend who claims to have researched the subject tells me the only other example of this construction is the word "urinal.") It would consist of a talk by one of the comrades on a previously assigned subject: "The Significance of the Auto Workers' Negotiations"; "The Communist Role in the Forthcoming Municipal Elections"; "The Mexican-American Minority and the Struggle for Negro Rights."

Quality of the Educationals varied greatly. A well-prepared Educational would be illuminated with references to the Marxist classics as they applied to current political problems, and might give rise to heated debate. Or we would be treated to a discourse that alternated between massive generalizations—"Our Party must give ever greater attention to the Negro struggle in the South"—and nit-picking, as somebody would rise to say, "Comrade, I think it would be more correctly put if you included in your formulation the struggle of the mass of poor white agricultural and industrial workers." Assignment of Party tasks "flowed out of" the Educational, the objective of which was to lead to political action, thus "linking theory with practice."

The neighborhood club to which Bob and I were transferred after the Duclos Letter was called the Twin Peaks Club, pronounced Tween Picks by the Russian-born comrades, of whom there were not a few. Frequently, especially during recruiting drives, we held public meetings advertised by posters and leaflets at which Oleta, Bill Schneiderman, or some other member of the Leading Bodies would speak.

Our ed. director, Daisy Rossman, was the wife of one of the leading Communist lawyers, Clarence Rossman. She and I, armed with pamphlets and leaflets, often went door to door in the Tween Picks working-class districts trying to drum up attendance for these meetings.

Daisy, a learned Marxist scholar and economist, was a very snappy dresser. She had a vast and enviable collection of hats—

chic porkpies, floppy straws, velvet berets, silk toques, flowered chiffon turbans—and always appeared in one of these superb creations when we set forth on our neighborhood visits. She was also horribly shy, and would begin to shake visibly as we approached some worker's front door.

"Good evening," she would say in low, trembling tones to the householder who answered. "Let us introduce ourselves: I am Daisy Rossman, educational director of the Twin Peaks Club of the Communist Party, and this is Comrade Decca Treuhaft, one of our members."

I would then spring to her rescue and start rattling on about the forthcoming meeting: "It's going to be absolutely marvelous and frightfully interesting. Oleta Yates, our county chairman, has just got back from a terrifically important meeting of the Party's Central Committee in New York, and she will report on the whole thing. *Do* come; I'm sure you'll simply *love* it."

Now it was Daisy's turn to stammer out a few words about the Party's historic role and the concrete tasks before us, which she did with her Dresden-blue eyes fixed on the ground, her abundant blond hair escaping from under toque or turban like the Madwoman of Chaillot. We were generally received politely enough—few doors were slammed in our faces—although often with a degree of astonishment; the two of us must have seemed unlikely representatives of the Communist Party.

Although Daisy went through evident agony mustering fresh courage for each encounter, whereas I on the contrary enjoyed our forays into the neighborhood, it was always I who flagged first. "Do let's knock off. I bet Bob and Clarence have got dinner ready by now."

But Daisy, her mind's eye fixed on a future proletarian dictatorship, and beyond that to the time when the state would wither away as Lenin had predicted, was always for plowing onward. "Decca, don't you realize that the very next leaflet we hand out might change somebody's whole life?" Our lives as Communists were informed by a supremely optimistic view of the human potential. One never knew behind which door we might discover an embryonic Lenin, a fledgling Rosa Luxemburg.

The club Educationals were supplemented by a network of special classes. In 1945, after the Duclos Letter, Bob and I attended an intensive eight-week course in Marxist economics given by Claire Stark, who was then state ed. director and one of the leading Party theoreticians. She was a brilliant, incisive thinker with the square, no-nonsense physique of a girl scout leader and a foghorn voice developed over years of soapbox oratory. A dozen of us gathered in the ed. office at Party Headquarters for the first meeting, at which Claire, in her precise, staccato style, laid down the rules for the class. We were going to study Marx's *Capital;* anybody who failed to do the required reading between classes would be dropped.

She handed out the reading assignments, which, to my horror, came in chunks of as many as 150 pages a week. Actually, it was a well-devised plan. While *Capital* is a difficult book to read, it is well worth the trouble. The daunting portions are in the beginning, where the theory of surplus value is laid out in mathematical form. The later chapters, however, which deal with the historical development of capitalism, contain sizable pockets of compelling and sometimes lyrical prose. If one were to poke along with it at a more normal speed it would be easy to get hopelessly bogged down; but forced to dash through as we were, we did at least finish the job and get a fair smattering of what it is all about.

Dead tired from the round of work, housework, and meetings, Bob and I would read aloud to each other until three in the morning to finish an assignment, and then quiz each other to test our comprehension:

"Explain the equation 'C equals c plus v.' "

"The capital *C* is capital, isn't it? Means of production and the like?"

"So what's the small *c*?"

"Raw materials and so on, I should think."

"No, no—*commodities,* silly, but I suppose it amounts to the same thing."

"And *v*?"

"Oh, *v* is for variable capital, such as vages."

"Roughly right. Oh, dear, I see it says here that the ratio of surplus value to the sum total of the capital advanced is economically of very great importance. And 'we shall, therefore, in the third book, treat of this ratio exhaustively.' "

"I'm exhausted already."

One of our fellow students, the editor of a labor newspaper, tried to monopolize the meetings and forever had his hand up. Perhaps because of his relatively exalted position in the labor movement, Claire at first allowed him a certain amount of leeway, listening tight-lipped as he prefaced each comment with "Well, I haven't done the reading, but as *I* see it . . ."

At the third meeting, Claire opened by asking, "Now, Comrades, what is meant by the absolute and relative impoverishment of the working class?" The labor editor was on his feet. "I haven't done the reading, but this is the way *I* look at it." This time Claire was ready for him. Beaming cherubically, she interrupted. "Just a minute, Comrade. We're not here to find out how *you* look at the question of relative and absolute impoverishment, but how *Marx* looked at it." Utterly demolished, the poor fellow slunk off that night, never to return.

The point of studying the Marxist classics was, of course, to enable us to apply the theory contained therein to contemporary conditions in the United States. It was Claire's role, as our teacher, to explore the connections between Marx's eloquent descriptions of early industrial England and the present-day conditions of the American working class. She often brought to class a current issue of the *Wall Street Journal* or the financial pages of *The New York Times,* to illustrate the direction she felt our economy was now inevitably taking: a trend towards a major depression like that of the thirties, a manifestation of what Marx predicted would be "the chronic crisis of capitalism."

Theory, in turn, was to indicate the direction of sound Marxist practice; the abstract must be translated into the concrete. Consequently, at the end of our illuminating course of study with Claire, Bob made an appointment with a San Francisco stockbroker for the purpose of translating theory into practice. Convinced by Claire's lectures that another great depression was impending, he decided to make a killing on the market by selling Sears Roebuck stock short. He reasoned that the first businesses to be hit in the downturn would be the great retail outlets; besides, we hated Sears because of its anti-labor policies, and we thought it would be a good thing to help drive down its stock.

Sears stock was then selling for thirty dollars a share. The stockbroker, receiving Bob's three-hundred-dollar order to sell short ten shares, expressed some surprise. He pointed out that the outlook for the market was bullish, and that his house was particularly recommending Sears to its customers as a growth stock. He was even more astonished when, in the face of a rising market, the stock dropped three points right after Bob's order was placed. He went over to Bob the next time he saw him in the office. "This simply doesn't figure," he said. "Do you know something we don't know?" Bob just stood there, hands in pockets, looking wise. "Do you play a system?" the broker persisted. "Well, yes," Bob conceded. "What system do you use?" Bob told him that the name of the system was Marxism-

Leninism, and that its secrets could be learned in several books and pamphlets that he would be glad to furnish. "Never heard of that one," said the stockbroker. "I must write it down," and he did.

When the drop in Sears stock proved to be merely temporary—for it soon rose again and continued to rise, wiping out our three-hundred-dollar investment—we complained bitterly to Claire. "How *could* you?" I said. "And we were going to give all the profits to the Party. Now we've gone and lost the lot." Claire was contrite. "But, Comrades," she said earnestly, "this is the first time in fifteen years of teaching this course that the comrades have taken it so literally. I was speaking, don't you see, in terms of an inevitable historical *trend*. I—I—" She was at a loss for words, and broke into her hearty "Ha-ha-ha."

WITHIN A FEW MONTHS of joining the Party, Bob and I rose in the ranks. He was elected to serve on Oleta Yates's campaign committee, and helped to draw up the Party's municipal election platform; his chief contribution, as I recall, was to propose a plank calling for Free Garbage Collection, for which innovative idea he was highly commended by the Party leadership.

I was elected club *Peoples World* Drive director. The drive, an annual fund-raising campaign through which the paper was financed, was to me reminiscent of the London season. The three months of the drive were a frenetic, nonstop round of social activities—dinners, dances, benefit performances—at which admission would be charged. There were, of course, subtle differences: whereas the high point of the London season was presentation of the debutantes to the King and Queen, the culmination of the PW Drive was marked by presentation of awards to those comrades who had by individual effort raised a hundred dollars or more, entitling them to the coveted prize of a lifetime subscription to the PW.

In my role as drive director, I began out-Dobbying Dobby. One of my jobs was to collect a day's pay from each club member. Since many of them were self-employed lawyers with fluctuating incomes, the computation of their day's pay was more flexible, and gave more scope for creativity, than that of a worker on fixed salary. I would wait until I learned through the legal grapevine of some particularly lucrative settlement of a case and demand the pay received on *that* day: "and be sure you figure it before taxes, please, Comrade."

Determined to win our lifetime sub, Bob and I gave a PW fund-raising party in our flat at Mrs. Tibbs's, at which we charged fifty cents admission and fifty cents per drink, phenomenally steep prices for those days. Since the attendance was small, and I feared we should fail to raise the sum we had hoped for, I started improvising more rules: fifty cents a drink, but twenty-five cents to *refuse* a drink; ten cents for use of lavatory, five cents extra for toilet paper; a seventy-five-cent exit fee for those leaving before 1 a.m. This terrible party became the talk of the town, and word of it soon reached the county leadership. Shortly thereafter, I was called in by Oleta, who informed me that I had been nominated for the full-time job of county financial director.

CHAPTER 4

Every Body
a Contact

LIKE ANY GOOD AMERICAN ORGANIZATION, the CP was a great believer in forms and charts. There were forms for new members, seeking data on Class Origin, Age, Extent of Marxist Reading, Activity in Mass (meaning non-Party) Organization; there were forms for dues payments and Monthly Sustainers; there were even forms for requesting temporary withdrawal from activity. Eventually the information derived from these forms would be collated, charted in triplicate, and forwarded to the national, state, and county offices. There they became the raw material from which conclusions were drawn, criticisms launched, campaigns mounted. Also, sad to say, they frequently found their way into the files of the FBI, who in turn fed them to various congressional investigating committees and thence to the press.

From time to time, out of some hot discussion in the County, State, or National Committee, demands for more specialized data would emerge. It would suddenly be discovered, for instance, that in the New York region the median age of Party members was a ripe forty-five. Where, then, were the Youth? Forms would hurriedly be devised to search out the Youth Contacts of members in the area and, more important, to ascertain what the Youth Comrades themselves were doing to remedy the situation.

A big blowup in the San Francisco County Committee resulted in a form of really daunting proportions. A number of malcontents (factionalists, we called them) had discovered to their joy that the full-time leadership was overloaded with ex-lawyers, ex-social workers, and other bourgeois elements of that ilk. The factionalists seized on this issue and launched a full-scale campaign aimed at Effectuating Change, i.e., ousting the old leadership and substituting proletarians—themselves, in fact. The leadership countered with its genealogical form, something like a family tree, designed to probe in depth the Class Origins of not only the full-time staff members, but that of their parents and grandparents.

This was a clever move, for in a frontier state like California one does not have to search far into the background of even the pillars of bourgeois society to find ancestors of lowly origin. Thus the county chairman, Oleta Yates, a main target of the factionalists, was able triumphantly to identify among her forebears not only a minor AFL official, but a genuine laborer as well.

It was my bad luck that this form should have made its appearance just as I was being considered for the post of full-time financial director of the San Francisco Party. Other considerations, I knew, would fade into insignificance—my ignorance of bookkeeping, indeed even of rudimentary arithmetic.

The form went something like this:

Paternal Grandmother

Occupation_____ Union Affiliation_____
Class (check which): Industrial Worker____ Agricultural
      Worker____ White Collar ____ Intellectual____ Petit
      Bourgeois____

and so on, for the rest of one's forebears.

I thought back to Grandmother Redesdale, whom I could barely remember. There were stories about her, of course, the usual family legends: that out of fastidiousness she refused to touch any coins until they had been scrubbed clean and polished by the footmen; that she had once laid a booby trap for King Edward, when, invited by Grandfather to stay at Batsford, he had brought his current mistress along and disapproving Grandmother had arranged for strings of slop pails to be placed strategically each night between the bedrooms of King and mistress. . . . But occupation? Union? Class? Alas! I could dimly conjure up a picture of her, shortly before her death, no doubt, a huge, black-garbed figure slowly stuffing down enormous quantities of food while the parlormaids hovered nervously nearby, perhaps fearing for the fate of a soufflé deteriorating in the kitchen. "Petite bourgeoise" would hardly do; there was nothing petite about Grandmother. And I did hope the comrades would not find out about the blood of Charlemagne, which Grandfather, in his book, *Memories,* by Lord Redesdale, had taken pains to prove was coursing through our veins.

A sympathetic co-worker to whom I confided my predicament suggested, "In a case like yours it's customary to put down 'intellectual.' " An amusing idea, I thought, remembering the scorn in which intellectuals were held by my parents, but one that would hardly solve the problem. I had noticed that the term "intellectual" was used loosely, to say the least, in the Party, probably because to be bourgeois but intellectual, like Lenin, Engels, Marx, was O.K., whereas to be bourgeois *tout court* was not. However, the thought of having to live up to the implications of being descended from a line of intellectuals was pretty terrifying.

Remembering that my father had a small gold mine in Canada which he occasionally dug about in, and that Grandfather's Japanese gardens at Batsford had been a renowned tourist attraction, I thought fleetingly of listing them as "miner" and "gardener" respectively. "Domestic" would do nicely for all three females, I reflected (for they were a domestic lot in the adjectival sense), and for my mother's father, who had owned a yacht, "Sailor."

In the end Clarence Rossman, county ed. director, spared me the agony of coping with the form and steered my application through the County Committee without it. A few dissenting voices were heard, but it was decided that the thing should be given a try provided that I, in turn, would do all in my power to overcome the handicaps of birth and upbringing.

"Oh, for a shipment of Moscow gold!" I often moaned while struggling with the problems of meeting the ever-expanding budget of the Communist Party of San Francisco. At the beginning of my tenure as financial director I rather assumed (for I was still a relatively new member of the Party) that such shipments might be expected from time to time. Surely there could not be quite so much smoke about the sinister foreign financing of our activities without at least a tiny, saving flame of fire. To my disappointment, I soon learned that the Moscow gold myth was just another piece of bourgeois propaganda. We could not look to that quarter to finance the very considerable work that would be needed to bring the Proletarian Revolution to the U.S.A.

I shared an office with Clarence Rossman, who had recently forsaken his lucrative law practice to become a full-time Party "functionary," as we called the staff members, at a wage of forty dollars a week. In some ways typical of the best and most effective of the CP professionals, Clarence had as a lawyer earned a nationwide reputation for his championship of radical causes. Bob and I had heard of him, and admired him from afar, long before we came to San Francisco. He had graduated from law school at the time of the longshoremen's strike of

1934, and became the nucleus of a small group of young Communist lawyers who set up shop in a waterfront loft to serve as counsel for the ILWU at subsistence wages. In this capacity he represented Harry Bridges in two successive deportation proceedings brought by the government, and in the successful appeal to the Supreme Court.

As the fortunes of the ILWU rose, so did those of its lawyers. By the time Bob and I got to San Francisco, Clarence's law firm represented virtually all the CIO unions in California, and the law partners were enjoying corresponding affluence. Yet despite his burdensome financial obligations (he and Daisy had two small children, not to mention her millinery bills, which must have been considerable), he doubtless considered it a privilege to be called upon to serve the Party at a tiny fraction of his former earnings.

Clarence, as he demonstrated in his support of my appointment, was a great believer in Bold Cadre Promotion, a concept much stressed by Stalin and other Communist theoreticians. His stubborn determination that I should make a success of the job grew, not out of any petty desire to prove himself right to those County Committee members who had opposed my appointment, or out of friendship and consideration for me, but rather from his truly selfless, single-minded devotion to the Party. It was the ruling passion in his life.

Clarence was my mentor, often my inspiration, the source of an endless flow of grandiose fund-raising schemes. If these plans could realize but a fraction of what he projected, they were well worth trying, and although he sometimes dazzled me with the splendor of his vision, I faithfully and enthusiastically tried to tread the path he charted. Gifted as he was in raising money, Clarence was even better at spending it. He was alternately friend and foe in the uphill battle to keep the office solvent, now cherished ally, now exasperating adversary.

He tended to see everything, causes and results, in simple mathematical terms. If 1,000 leaflets could be said to influence, say, ten votes in an election campaign, then 100,000 would bring a corresponding 1,000 votes; by the same reasoning, if we could muster the funds to print a million campaign leaflets for a Party candidate running for the San Francisco Board of Supervisors, the election would be in the bag.

He applied the same logic to his special field, Marxist education. If one session of a study class improved a new member's understanding of the class struggle by 2 percent, then ten classes would bring an increase of 20 percent; attendance at fifty classes must, then, produce a full-fledged Marxist. If Clarence never expressed these convictions in so many words, his actions made them apparent. I can see him now, solid back bent over his desk in rigid concentration, true-blue eyes in which still lurked the unwavering optimism of childhood, scanning the latest batch of New Members Attendance forms, which provided the clue to success or failure of the Recruits Orientation Classes.

The results as revealed by the forms were always disappointing. Out of several hundred new members who were supposed to be attending, seldom had more than thirty or forty shown up. The Waterfront Section was particularly delinquent, and Clarence determined to make this a point of concentration. "Dear Comrade, it is most important—no, it is essential—no, it is absolutely essential. Underline the words 'absolutely essential,' " I heard him dictating.

"Why don't you put it more simply? *'Dear* Comrade, *do* come,' and underline the 'Dear' and the 'do,' " but my helpful suggestion fell on deaf ears. Clarence was off on another tack; the hundreds of mimeographed letters having brought such extremely slim results, he decided that a more personalized, hand-typed appeal must be tried.

Our office secretary, a thin, tense young woman, efficient and self-effacing, was a devoted and immensely disciplined Party member. For two weekends, from dawn until midnight, she labored over the typewritten letters—not short notes, but single-spaced two-pagers in which were outlined the Rossman theory of Marxist education. As I predicted, the enormous work of hand-typing proved unproductive; the average horny-handed longshoreman, arriving home half-dead from fatigue after a grueling day's work on the waterfront, was hardly likely to notice this particular refinement as he ripped open his mail.

Twisting and turning in his predicament, Clarence, over my furious remonstrances, sent out the next batch of notices by first-class mail at three cents postage instead of the standard un-sealed, precanceled one cent, for which I had taken consider-able trouble to get us a permit. Once more, no noticeable change was recorded in the New Members Attendance forms.

Clarence's final move proved his downfall as far as this particular battle was concerned. I guessed he was up to some-thing. There was a look in his eye—preoccupied rather than crafty. Clarence, the least crafty of men, had, I am sure, no wish to deceive; he wanted only to forestall an unproductive and wearisome row with me, to present a *fait accompli* after the ends had triumphantly justified the means. "I didn't have *time* to argue," would have been his explanation.

He waited until I was out of the office, emptied my box of petty cash, and dashed to the post office. When I returned, the deed was done; all two hundred New Members' notices had gone out—special delivery, at ten cents a letter, for a total of twenty dollars, half of a staff member's weekly wage.

I decided the time for comradely criticism had come. At the weekly staff meeting I flourished the latest batch of attendance forms. The turnout had been worse than ever. With what I hoped would be recognized as fine sarcasm, I proposed that future New Members' notices should be delivered by Western Union as singing telegrams: "Happy Marxist classics / Next Wednesday at six. / Read 'em carefully, dear Comrade, / Even though they're prolix." Or alternatively, the notice of time and place might be concealed in a bouquet of flowers delivered by Florists' Telegraph Delivery association. With a stab of remorse, I realized that Clarence was sitting forward listening intently to my every word; he even started to say that "prolix" was pejorative, we should have to rewrite that line. However, wiser (if stodgier) heads prevailed, and a resolution was duly passed forbidding any further expenditures on this project without clearance by the finance committee.

The actual job of raising the money was at times nerve-racking, at times fun, always hard work. I found it fascinating. We laid Firm Foundations, Clarence and I, we Drew in New Forces, we Developed New Perspectives, we Evaluated and Estimated and Tested the Correctness of Our Policies in Life Itself. At least Clarence did. I was more interested in getting the money in, and seeing that once in it was properly protected from the ever-vigilant, ever-grasping state and national offices and from Clarence's exuberantly lavish schemes.

We started pretty much from scratch. These were the relatively lush postwar years, and there was plenty of money around. Left-wing lawyers who had starved along with their clients during the Depression years were now quite prosperous. Even the small businesses into which some members had waywardly drifted were flourishing. Nevertheless, Party finances had been sadly neglected. Most of the full-timers were bored by the subject, and only occasionally took time out from their arduous labors to wring their hands over the enormous debts and vanishing bank balance. Payless paydays were commonplace for the seven-member San Francisco staff, and our monthly commitments to state and national offices were a joke.

They hadn't been met for years. Into this mess I enthusiastically stepped. Somewhere in them thar hills on which San Francisco is perched there must be gold.

Traditional ways of raising funds were outlined to me by those in the know. Our cut of monthly dues payments was negligible, and must be supplemented by Members' Sustainers, Outside Contacts' Sustainers, Proceeds from Mass Meetings, and Affairs. I balked a little at the latter. "How could one actually raise money out of them?" Before I had time to expose my ignorance further (for to me this expression connoted romance), it was explained that an affair was any social event, from a dinner to a picnic to a dance, at which contributions were collected. Banquets, as one comrade put it, were also a form of struggle.

"And then there's the whole question of *wills*," my interlocutor mysteriously continued, lowering his voice to a characteristic, faintly spine-chilling whisper. Not Clarence this time, but Moody Bramlett. Moody was in all ways the complete opposite of Clarence. Whereas Clarence was solid, real, straightforward, human, and American as apple pie, Moody was rather an eerie one, wraith- to corpselike in appearance; although actually pure Californian, he seemed somehow foreign. He was above all conspiratorial in both mentality and manner. A now aging comrade, he had over the years set something of a style which was consciously or unconsciously imitated by certain of his juniors. As the mannerisms of a company president will eventually find their way down to the underlings, or the tricks of speech of a successful actor will be copied by neophytes, so it was in our organization.

Two influences seem to have led to the Bramlett style of speech and conduct. Since this style was encountered so often among the membership, it may be worth a digression to attempt an explanation of its genesis.

Moody's history was much like that of many of his contemporaries. He was a veteran of innumerable encounters with the Class Enemy. These included major battles—the resistance to the Palmer raids of the twenties, the pioneering CIO organizing drive of the thirties—as well as everyday skirmishes, ranging from the discovery that a trusted friend was in fact a paid FBI informer to the uncomfortable awareness that his car was often followed and his home telephone tapped by the FBI. His wife had spent two terrible years in the Tehachapi prison for women because of a very slight infraction of the California election law: during a signature campaign to qualify the CP for the ballot, she had been trapped by an *agent provocateur* into signing a voter's petition affidavit, affirming she herself had gathered the signatures which had actually been collected by the agent. Moody himself had frequently been the target of the House Committee on Un-American Activities and other subversive-hunting committees. It would have been a rare individual who could have survived a lifetime of such real persecution without some peculiar reaction. The cumulative effect on Moody was to invest him with a noiseless walk, a low, measured, at times almost inaudible voice, and a general air of mystery.

But the guiding influence that had shaped Moody throughout his adult life was the Party. A factory worker in his early teens, he had had almost no formal education. Later the Party undertook to educate him, and it was in Party classes that he had learned vocabulary, spelling, syntax as by-products of the theory of the class struggle, political economy, the history of the U.S.S.R. Thus he spoke as though translating from Russian or German (at least, that is how I supposed his idiom to be arrived at), only occasionally, when upset, letting loose a stream of purely American curse words that had remained stored in his mind from his factory days.

In view of his unusual and checkered background—unusual, that is, in terms of the average American, though not in terms of the average long-time Party member—Moody's particular idiosyncrasies were not only understandable; their innocuousness was even laudable. A lesser man might have been driven over the brink altogether.

The question of wills. Fixing me with a searching, mournful look, Moody explained that wills were to be handled with discretion "coupled with" flexibility, with understanding "coupled with" boldness. Moody was a great "coupled with" man. In fact, this was one of the curious stock Party phrases. No matter how many thousands of times I heard and read it over the years—"the China Lobby coupled with Wall Street interests"; "the problems facing the Youth coupled with those facing the Mexican American and other minorities"—it evoked for me two anxious greyhounds tugging at a common leash.

The wills sounded marvelous, but a bit long-range. Boiled down to the readily obvious essentials, the idea was to get people to bequeath their money to the Party.

"Couldn't we have . . . an affair?" I suggested, flushing a little. "Just to get in some ready cash, you know," I added hastily. Moody agreed. In fact, a suitable opportunity immediately presented itself; a number of Party members were returning from the war and a banquet to honor the CP veterans would be most appropriate. Moody explained how to go about it. He listed several possible halls with adequate cooking facilities, told me how to get in touch with the chairman of the Culinary and Marine Cooks Union branches, how to get our waning credit extended by the printer who would prepare the invitation.

"Then there are certain comrades in . . ." He wrote the word "Petaluma" on a piece of paper. Although in those days the Party operated very much in the open, uninhibitedly using the mails to communicate with the membership and holding branch meetings in rented halls, certain older comrades like Moody seemed incapable of shedding disciplines acquired in an earlier period, when it was assumed that all Party activities must be conducted in utmost secrecy. A hidden bug in the office picking up our conversation, G-men lying in wait for a car headed for Petaluma, and all might be lost. I got the message. Moody was suggesting that the comrades in Petaluma, chicken farmers all, might supply gratis the main course of the banquet.

"Do you think the chickens should be . . ." I wrote "broiled or fried" on the piece of paper. Moody, who loathed being teased, replied stiffly that the method of preparation should be left up to the Culinary Union comrades.

Feverish activity ensued. There were meetings with the Petaluma chicken farmers, who were mostly foreign-born, and proved to be a delightful lot, if a little out of touch with the current Party Line; they opened our discussions of the chicken dinner with a rendition of the revolutionary song "Comintern":

> *The Comintern calls you:*
> *Raise high Soviet banner,*
> *In steeled ranks to battle*
> *Raise sickle and hammer.*
> *Our answer: Red Legions*
> *We raise in our might.*
> *Our answer: Red Storm Troops*
> *We lunge to the fight.*
>
> *From Russia victorious*
> *The workers' October*
> *Comes storming reaction's*
> *Regime the world over.*

*We're coming with Lenin
For Bolshevik work
From London, Havana,
Berlin, and New York. . . .*

There were sessions on the Bolshevik work of the banquet with the Culinary comrades, whose dialectical approach to the Question of Seasoning resulted in seemingly endless debates before a consensus was reached as to the quantities of spices that would be required. The Artists and Decorators branch was mobilized to transform the gloomy hall into a paradise of beauty for the night of the banquet. The thing was shaping up to be a great success, and I was very pleased with myself, at how quickly I had learned the ropes and what an excellent organizer I was becoming. My first really important Party assignment, and it was going too swimmingly for words. Furthermore, I felt I was even developing a cadre or two along the way. The chairman of the Culinary branch was a charming middle-aged Italian, head chef at the Palace Hotel, Giulio by name. He often roared with laughter during our meetings, which I took as a significant sign of development, as he never let out so much as a giggle at County Committee meetings.

The ticket sales were coming along most satisfactorily under what I felt to be an excellent slogan: PALACE HOTEL MEALS AT A FRACTION OF THE COST AND WELCOME CP VETS TO BOOT. I was busy, busy, busy. A hundred threads were gathered in my hands: ticket sales to branches, ticket sales to Outside Contacts, publicity, decorations committee, waitresses committee, door committee, cooking committee, Petaluma chicken farmers. . . .

It was too good to last. The only task that had fallen to me alone—my fault, as I should have assigned it to the publicity committee—was the drawing up of the invitation. It was a lovely invitation, I thought, and I had spent considerable time over its preparation. One day, soon after it had been distributed to the branches, Moody beckoned me gravely into his office. "Two comrades from the Women's Commission wish to meet with you," he announced curtly. Much rattled, I followed him. Logically enough, the two Women's Commission comrades turned out to be two women. *Tricoteuses* flashed through my mind, for one was actually knitting, and both their faces were tumbrelish. However, they greeted me pleasantly enough; I gathered I was about to be developed, rather than devastated.

"Ideologically," one of them began, "this leaflet is full of weaknesses." I stared at the invitation, suddenly seeing it in a new light. My objective had been to fill it with what I hoped would be the spirit of the occasion. What would a lonely GI long for, dream of, while stranded on some lone Pacific atoll, in some drear English port, or boiling African desert? "CHICKEN DINNERS LIKE MOTHER USED TO MAKE. FREE-FLOWING LIQUOR. 20 BEAUTIFUL GIRLS 20," the leaflet read. I had designed it to resemble an old burlesque poster, flaming red on cheapest newsprint.

As I examined this monstrosity the telephone rang. It was the chairman of the Petaluma branch. Did I want the chickens delivered dressed or undressed? "Oh—undressed, by all means," I answered, glancing uncomfortably at my visitors, hoping they would not misunderstand and think I was answering an inquiry about the 20 BEAUTIFUL GIRLS 20.

The *tricoteuses* warmed to their theme. Actually, they were very nice, hard-working women, with a slightly inflated sense of their own importance, perhaps, but undeniably sincere. Patiently they explained that women had for too long been relegated to the role of mere playthings for the amusement of men.

The "20 BEAUTIFUL GIRLS 20" was an outrageous, unforgivable boner. "Coupled with" the plaything aspect was the implied degradation of women to the status of cooks in the phrase "like Mother used to make." Coupled (or tripled?) with all that was my insensitivity of the role played by those enemies of the working class the Liquor Interests. Granted the Party was by no means dry, and that the liquor sales at the banquet would bring much-needed funds to our treasury, there was no need to emphasize it in the leaflet. I was given to understand that my leaflet had placed in jeopardy the gains won over the years by the Women's Commission.

Reluctantly, however, my visitors bowed to the financial exigencies and agreed not to recall the leaflet if I in turn would promise to study Lenin's pamphlet on the Woman Question.

Giulio roared with laughter when I shamefacedly told him of the contretemps. "You tell 'em I myself joined the Party because I heard there were lots of *free women* in the Soviet Union!" he chortled. "In Italy we were proud of our beautiful, *well-developed* women. Why, there even used to be a song, 'The Girl with the Popular Front.' "

But Giulio was soon laughing on the other side of his face. The day before the banquet, a large pickup truck drew up before our office, holding up Market Street traffic and causing much commotion. "O.K., now where do you want 'em?" asked the driver, pointing to a mountain of crates filled with freshly killed, fully feathered chickens. I was horrified. "But I asked the farmers to be sure they were *undressed*," I wailed. "Not very comradely of them." Soon Giulio arrived, in response to my anguished call for help, only to confirm my dawning dreadful suspicion that in the world of chickens, "undressed" meant the opposite of what it would to the Women's Commission. Giulio soon got himself under control and assembled a crew who worked through the night at the mammoth job of plucking and, yes, dressing those hundreds of chickens. Despite vicissitudes, the banquet was a stunning success.

COLLECTION of the Outside Contacts' Sustainers was a time-consuming job yet rewarding, both in terms of amounts of money realized and for the occasional glimpse afforded into the odd byways of human behavior.

One had to be careful about the approach, as some of the Outside Contacts were pretty skittish, and constantly had to be reassured that their contributions would be kept absolutely secret. Moody was privy to the names of the best contributors. He went over the list with me, explained how and when to make appointments ("Always use an outside pay phone"), and told me how much each Contact should be good for. While I had to make out receipts for record-keeping purposes, most Contacts, he said, would flinch from accepting receipts and would be very alarmed if their names were on the duplicates; the sum received should be entered but the space for the name left blank.

Some of the Contacts lived in extremely plush circumstances. One of these, a rich businessman, met me in his lavish Montgomery Street office. Moody had said he generally gave about a hundred dollars, so I was pleasantly surprised when he peeled off ten lovely crisp twenty-dollar bills.

"I'll just make out a receipt for our records, but I'll leave your name off it," I said. "No, no," replied the Contact. "I want my name clearly spelled out in full, and be sure to write 'Received by Communist Party of San Francisco' on the bottom." He unlocked a drawer in his desk and showed me hundreds of receipts, some dating back to the thirties.

"It's a kind of insurance," he explained. "One never knows what twists and turns politics may take. Someday you people may come to power. I'm keeping these, just in case."

Aside from those who gave regular Monthly Sustainers, there were certain Contacts who could be counted on for very substantial lump sums in real emergencies. One in particular, a divorcee who lived in a splendid house with a swimming pool, was a devoted Party sympathizer and could be touched for up to a thousand dollars. During the election campaign our resources had been badly drained, so I went to see her. She apologetically explained that her tax lawyer, who supervised her financial affairs, had absolutely forbidden her to make any contribution for several months. But after listening to my impassioned appeal, she impulsively took a large emerald ring off her finger. "Take this. It was my engagement ring, but since my divorce it has no sentimental value to me. I want the Party to have it. It's insured for twelve hundred dollars; you should get a good price for it. Don't take less than a thousand."

Thrilled by this generous act, I dashed back to the office and flashed the precious booty for all to see before setting out to get it appraised by a jeweler. The jeweler peered at the stone through his loupe and pronounced it made of glass. I was shaken but not defeated; he must have got it wrong. I visited two more jewelers, who confirmed the diagnosis. The cruelty of life! Of course I could never tell the divorcee, it would be too much of a blow; she would live to the end of her days thinking she had enriched the Party's treasury by a thousand dollars. But I did confide in Oleta. "Well, I'm not too surprised," she said dryly. "That woman's ex-husband is a Trotskyist. What a typical Trotskyist trick!" In the end, we sold the ring for $2.50 at the Party's annual rummage sale.

THE STATE FINANCE DIRECTOR was an ex-Youth by the name of Frank Carlson. The term "ex-Youth" may seem to some readers merely an awkward way of describing any person past his twenties. Such readers may never have been asked, "Weren't you once a Youth?" or have heard someone declare hotly during a meeting, "Well, I'm glad to say *I* never was a Youth—I got right into the Party when I was eighteen."

Frank was one of the Red Diaper Babies, a member of the Young Pioneers from the age of five and later of the Young Communist League. He often went about his work singing one of the Young Pioneer anthems, as familiar to graduates of that organization as "London Bridge Is Falling Down" to the ordinary adult: "We're Pioneers born, and YCLers bred; / And when we die we'll be Party Members dead!" Frank was something of a follower in the footsteps of Moody. He seemed congenitally incapable of addressing one in a normal tone of voice. Many is the time he slid silently into my office, treading almost on tiptoe, making me jump violently as he leaned over my desk to ask in tones fraught with revolutionary secrecy, "How are the raffle ticket sales coming along?"

Like almost everyone except me, Frank found the day-to-day job of raising money extremely tiresome. He would far rather be working on a memo dealing with "The Role of Democratic Centralism in the Party Today" or "For an End to Bureaucracy!" (titles of Party leaflets and articles frequently followed this odd construction, with an exclamation mark at the end) or "The Present Situation and the Next Tasks"—an all-purpose heading. The memos were called Educationals, and they were passed out to the branches to become the basis of discussion. Once a Carlson Educational turned up in our branch, provocatively titled "Relations with the Leadership," and to the annoyance of the Women's Commission member present, I was startled into exclaiming, "Well, *really!* I can't say I ever looked on them quite in *that* way!"

The state office, with its full-time staff of eight, was financed largely through Sustainers from the various county organizations, of which San Francisco was then the only solvent one; thus Frank had a vested interest in seeing that I left no avenues unexplored in my search for money. Bob made up a ditty to the tune of "Reuben, Reuben," commemorating the Sustainer system: "Decca, Decca, I've been thinking / What would Marx and Engels say? / If the county don't sustain us / Then the state will wither away."

Unlike Moody, Frank did have a sense of humor and it was occasionally possible to pry an unwilling guffaw out of him so long as he considered the subject matter suitable. He was imaginative and clever in producing ideas for the finance committee to work on, although there was nothing he hated more than stirring his own stumps to bring in the money.

"Blood, Decca. Have you ever given it any thought?" He had crept up on me in his usual way, giving me quite a turn. "I'll tell you who can give you all the information. Bill Gordon, over in Oakland. There are two possible places to sell it: Irwin Memorial Blood Bank pays twenty-five dollars a pint, and Cutter Lab has a place on skid row that pays four dollars. It's one of those rackets; they bleed the winos and never check up on how often they come back for more, so stay away from Cutter."

As usual there was a financial crisis, triggered this time by the sudden need for several hundred dollars to send some Party delegates to a conference back East. I got Gordon on the phone. He was most helpful, and told me exactly how to go about signing up members for various blood banks. "Oh, and we finally got some money out of Permanente," he continued. Permanente was Kaiser Industries' innovative, brand-new health plan clinic, at which we had been casting sheep's eyes for some time, in the hopes that among the forward-looking and community-minded young doctors on the staff some, at least, could be persuaded to contribute.

"Really? Did the doctors come through?"

"No, dear, the pain test," Gordon explained. "They are conducting research to find out how much pain the human body can stand. We just send the members up there, and they get ten dollars for taking the test."

"Oh, Gordon, how could you. I suppose they record their screams and groans on a seismograph?"

"No, it hardly hurts at all, dear. I really think you should consider it."

But another idea was germinating in my mind. As Marx once said, "Theory becomes a material force as soon as it has gripped the masses."

How to get this particular theory to grip the delegates due to leave next week for New York? I had the details in mind, having looked carefully into the matter, and, screwing up my courage, crossed the hall that separated county from state offices. There I sought out Bill Schneiderman, revered state chairman, hero of the landmark deportation case that the Party had successfully fought all the way up to the Supreme Court.

"Now, Bill, you know bodies," I began carefully. Schneiderman was sitting across from me, not deliberately looking imposing, but nevertheless creating that general impression. He *was* imposing. Tremendously sharp, noted for his cutting repartee, often target but always winning champion in innumerable inner-Party fights, Bill was a magic one. He was by no stretch of the imagination a personality kid. A major and recurrent complaint against him was that he was too cold and impersonal, he took no interest in the comrades' personal lives. I always thought this was rather a good point in his favor, not wishing my own private life subject to comradely scrutiny. Bill was a tough nut, to be respected and approached as such.

"When people die far from home and have to be transported back for burial," I continued quickly, "a live one has to accompany the corpse. The funeral parlor will pay the transportation of the live one. Wouldn't it be a marvelous idea if we could line up a few bodies for the delegates? Free transportation one way. Do be for it!"

Bill indicated he was not going to be for it by a characteristic gesture, an annoyed wriggle of his shoulders which never failed to remind me of Nanny when I had misbehaved as a child. "No, Jessica!" Movement of shoulders. I had gone too far again, she would add.

"Such a mode of transportation would hardly lend dignity to the occasion," Bill started to say.

"But neither would it detract," I cut in. "The bodies are kept in a separate part of the train, and you don't even have to take them into the diner with you; I've checked all that. Think of the savings!"

"Well, I'll discuss it with the comrades, but I think it most unlikely they would agree." Wriggle wriggle. I knew I had lost the day.

The pain-test and blood-bank business was coming along nicely. Its success even led me to wonder out loud whether members of the Seamen's branch could not be persuaded to contribute to a bank that product, homonymous with the name of the branch, which they of all people were so well equipped to produce. "Think again, Decca," warned Frank. "I'm not sure the Women's Commission would take kindly to a plan of action from which they were so obviously to be totally excluded."

"How about getting the comrades to will their bodies for scientific research, then? I understand medical schools pay about seventy-five dollars per corpse in good condition. If we got everyone to do it—after the Leading Bodies had set the example, of course—it would soon bring in a nice lot."

Frank and I drew up an elaborate program on paper, complete with goals and slogans: "5,000 Bodies in the State of

California! Sign up your Outside Contacts! Every Body a Contact, every Contact a Body!" A good theme song to launch the campaign would be "When a Body Meets a Body." Giulio was all for it. "I'll pledge my wife's body right away," he promised.

Once more the Leading Bodies proved disappointingly conservative, and our plan was filed away under Motions Defeated by County Committee.

CHAPTER 5

Oakland

MOST OF THESE HIGH JINKS came to an end when we moved to Oakland in 1947. After the war Bob had joined the firm of Gladstein, Grossman, Sawyer & Edises (Gallstones, Gruesome, Sewer & Odious, as they were affectionately called by their intimates), labor lawyers among whose clients were the CIO, the Communist Party, the ILWU. They had earned an illustrious national reputation in their defense of Harry Bridges against the numerous and unremitting efforts of the government to deport him to Australia. Many were the rallies we attended to protest the threatened deportation and to join with the white-capped longshoremen in singing Woody Guthrie's "Ballad of Harry Bridges":

> *Oh, the FBI is worried,*
> *The bosses they are scared,*
> *They can't deport six million men, they know;*
> *We're not going to let them send Harry over the seas,*
> *We'll fight for Harry Bridges and build the CIO.*

Dinky, who was learning something about the economics of labor law practice, always rendered the last line as "We'll fight for Harry Bridges and *bill* the CIO."

At first Bob commuted from San Francisco to work with

Bert Edises in the firm's Oakland office. From this vantage point he watched the development of the unique general strike of 1946, first (and so far as I know last) of the postwar period in which a whole city was shut down tight.

The strike started in a small way with a walkout of retail clerks at Kahn's, one of the big department stores. Teamsters respected the picket line, refusing to take their delivery trucks through. One morning a battalion of armed police appeared to escort a convoy of scab-driven trucks through the line. This had an electric effect. The dissension which had characterized the labor movement in the immediate postwar era—the bitter enmity between the old-line AFL craft unions and the newly organized, left-led CIO unions—was forgotten in the wave of indignation set off by the police action. Union after union called its members out on strike in an unprecedented show of unity, and by the following day the shutdown was total.

After three days Kahn's capitulated and the strike was over. But the various factions that had formed the victorious alliance held together long enough to mount a successful electoral challenge to the ultra-conservative Knowland machine, which until then had had a total stranglehold on Oakland's political structure.

Four out of five labor coalition candidates for city council won seats in the next election, their slogan: "Take the Power Out of the Tower!"—meaning the Tribune Tower, an Oakland landmark and headquarters of Joseph R. Knowland's all-powerful newspaper, the Oakland *Tribune*.

Bob and Bert Edises were in the thick of it. Of evenings, Bob would regale me with accounts of their work on the Joint Labor Committee, a classic United Front operation in which leaders of the CIO unions, many of them Communists, held the uneasy coalition together with incredible tenacity, bringing to bear all their organizing skills to make it work—for a while.

It was not to last. All traces of the general strike and its political aftermath have long since vanished. The Tower soon regained (and to this day retains) its power. But at the time it looked like the dawning of a new era, the beginning of a worker-led rebellion against the established order that might spread through California and ultimately throughout the nation. Oakland, we decided, was the place for us.

Our new life in the wasteland of Oakland across the bay from glamorous San Francisco was by no means the purgatory that our Washington friends thought it would be. Anxious letters came, questioning our decision. It's like moving from Manhattan to Jersey City or Newark, one friend wrote; you'll change your mind soon enough.

The camparison was apt. San Francisco was sophisticated, cosmopolitan, a labor town with an established and politically influential union base, Oakland backward, provincial, a small town suddenly grown large, its population swollen in the thirties with the construction of the San Francisco–Oakland Bay Bridge, and now once again bursting its bounds with the huge influx of war workers.

Oakland was San Francisco's industrial appendage, unable to assimilate its surging population, its cultural barrenness the butt of jokes to San Franciscans. Gertrude Stein, once escaped from Oakland, had said of her home town (when safely away in Paris): "There is no there there."

We thought otherwise. And our sage friends, who had predicted that we would long to return to Eden, were wrong. Oakland was still at the frontier, where the issues were sharper, the corruption cruder, the enemy more easily identifiable—for years we enjoyed what almost amounted to a personal vendetta with the Oakland police chief and the Alameda County district attorney. There was nothing abstract about the class struggle in Oakland.

The Party organizations reflected the differences in the two areas. In San Francisco, Party leaders tended to move in a rather elite circle which included higher-ups in the labor movement, Party lawyers, architects, writers, and other professionals. The East Bay Party, under the leadership of Steve Nelson, a carpenter and veteran of the Spanish Civil War, was younger, less stratified, and made up largely of workers, many of them blacks, who soon formed the bulk of our acquaintance. Besides Bert we knew not a soul in Oakland when we moved there. But within a week, when we had made contact with the East Bay comrades, we felt that we knew, or would soon know, everyone worth knowing.

We bought a house on Jean Street, in a middle-class neighborhood hard by the Oakland Municipal Rose Garden. We were as usual fairly close to the edge of poverty; Bob, not as yet a partner in the firm, drew a salary of sixty dollars a week as a junior associate. One of my first moves was to apply for unemployment insurance. Having as financial director meticulously complied with the government requirements for social security deductions from the wages of our San Francisco staff, I was bent on recouping some of this good Communist money.

To qualify for unemployment benefits one had to prove that one was actively seeking work in one's trade or occupation. I explained to the caseworker to whom I was assigned that there *was* no work in my particular field; the Communist Party of Alameda County already had a financial director, and I had ascertained that the Republican and Democratic Party offices had no openings for me. Rather to my surprise, I was put on the rolls and I collected for several weeks. Eventually a supervisor called me in and said I was holding myself in too narrow a category; had I no other work experience? Yes, I had been an OPA investigator, but the OPA was all washed up after the war.

She offered me an opening at Kahn's department store, where my job would be to check, as an undercover investigator, on the loyalty and honesty of the sales force. I said I thought that was a shocking proposal; surely she realized that as a Communist my principles would prohibit me from spying on fellow workers. This seemed to muddle her effectively and I continued to draw benefits for some weeks, when despite my vehement protests she cut me off for not actively seeking employment. "My husband's law firm will appeal this all the way up to the Supreme Court!" I threatened. Nothing doing, said Bob and Bert, who were far too busy battling the real estate interests, the Oakland police department, the district attorney.

Their practice was primarily in the field of labor law; they represented all the CIO unions in the East Bay and some state-wide unions. The only left-wing lawyers in the county at that time, they were constantly in court fighting labor injunctions and defending oil refinery workers, warehousemen, auto assembly line workers in the postwar wave of strikes. They also served as unpaid counsel for the newly organized Civil Rights Congress, whose twin objectives were defense of civil liberties of Communists and other radicals, and the struggle for Negro rights.

At the beginning of our life in Oakland I watched these activities from the sidelines, being preoccupied with the birth of our son Benjamin, a lovely fat jolly creature whose upbringing was quickly assumed by Dinky, now aged six. A firm religious believer in those days, she had been praying for a baby. "Your prayers have been answered," I pointed out. "Here it is, so be an angel and look after it." Dinky watched over the adored newcomer, fed him his breakfast, rushed home after school to play with him, and taught him his first words: "Dinky's always right. Benjy's always wrong."

For the first time in my life I was faced with serious house-work, having hitherto clung to my amateur status in this respect by having a full-time job outside our home. Bob never ceased to marvel that I could have reached the age of thirty without mastering the rudiments of cooking, without gaining some minimal understanding of the properties and uses of various cleaning materials. He himself had from earliest childhood watched his grandmother and mother go about their household tasks, had absorbed the various techniques as by osmosis, and later applied them to practical advantage when sharing bachelor quarters in Washington.

But in *my* culturally disadvantaged childhood (I kept explaining) one did not actually see the housework done, as it would all have been finished early, before we came down in the morning. As Nancy said in *The Pursuit of Love:* "Housemaids are notoriously early risers, and can usually count upon three clear hours when a house belongs to them alone." After my precipitate departure from this way of life, Esmond and I had lived either in furnished rooms where the landlady did all or with friends who were adept homemakers, as the ladies' mags call them.

For a few depressing months I stayed at home trying to cope with the tidal wave of washing and cleaning that daily threatened to engulf us. Bob bought me some texts on the subject, my favorite of which was Mrs. Beeton's *Book of Household Management,* a two-thousand-page tome published in 1871. It was full of riveting information: "Menus for a Servants'-Hall Dinner for 12"; "Duties of the Butler"; "How to Select a Wet-nurse"; "To clean ribbons: Mix together ½ pint gin, ½ lb. honey, ½ lb. soft soap. . ."

Too often the end of the day found me curled up on the sofa poring over these instructions, so full of mystery and imagination, while the unwashed breakfast dishes lay drearily in the sink. Or, stimulated by Mrs. Beeton, I would try my hand at inventions for Bob to patent: "Blueprint for the One and Only Bedmaking Machine," in which iron arms protrude from a large pot labeled "Machinery in Here," with levers attached marked "Tuck," "Strip," "Top Sheet Only," "Bottom Sheet Only," and an intricate "Pillowcase Changing Attachment." "Woman's work is never done," I would murmur sadly when Bob got home in the evening, to which his rejoinder was, "You can say that again, in this house."

I copied out and hung above our kitchen sink a stirring passage from Lenin's essay on the Woman Question: "You all know that even with the fullest equality, women are still in an actual position of inferiority because all housework is thrust upon them. Most of this housework is highly unproductive, most barbarous and most arduous, and it is performed by women. This labor is extremely petty and contains nothing that would in the slightest degree facilitate the development of women." Dinky and I would recite this together as we pottered about the kitchen.

A perennial complaint of some wives we knew was that their husbands kept them tied to unproductive, barbarous, arduous, petty housework and so prevented them from taking their place beside men in the world of work and careers. Not so Bob, who, declaring himself in fervent agreement with Lenin, positively drove me from the nest. He implored me to seek some outside employment and put the running of the household in more competent hands.

The opportunity to do so arose early in 1949 when a member of the State Committee came to call. "Comrade, we think it's time you got some experience in mass work," he said gravely. There was need for an assistant to Hursel Alexander, a black organizer* who was executive director of the East Bay Civil Rights Congress. "The last comrade who had this assignment found it too demanding; in fact, he had a nervous breakdown and tried to jump off the bridge," said the State Committee member. Later I thought I saw why.

Hursel was a terrific charmer and a prodigious worker, with a mesmeric ability to wring the last ounce of effort from those within his orbit. He would get carried away with his own eloquence and fiddle around with the English language in the most innovative fashion: "We must move on this case before the Limit of Saturation runs out!" So much more descriptive, I thought, than Statute of Limitation. Or: "The defendant was tried *in abstemia.*" It was my job to follow in Hursel's wake and act as midwife to the innumerable projects he spawned, to investigate cases, raise money, organize meetings, and put his leaflets into more conventional English.

Our office secretary was a white woman in her early thirties called Kathleen Robinson (pronounced Kat'leen by Hursel), not quite pretty, for her young face was haggard from perpetual overwork, but with ineffably sweet eyes like a saint's. She was an absolute whiz at office work, producing daily miracles from our battered old mimeograph machine. From a background of working for insurance companies she knew all sorts of extraordinary tricks about the folding and stuffing of mass mailings. *"Not* one at a time, Decca," she would patiently enjoin me, and

* A word about terminology: in the days of which I am writing, there were two acceptable designations for Americans of African descent: colored and Negro. The older folks generally preferred to be called colored; younger and more militant people considered it a matter of race pride to be called Negro. Until the advent of a new wave of black militancy in the sixties, "black" would have been unthinkable, a pejorative comparable to "nigger." Thus when I am recording conversations of those times I use Negro; when speaking in my own voice of today, I use black.

under her skillful hands great mounds of beautifully folded letters would fall into place in a twinkling, like something in a speeded-up Charlie Chaplin movie. Sometimes her very speed would get the better of her. "But, Kat'leen, you've put 'Untied Front' instead of 'United Front' on all these thousands of leaflets," I pointed out on one occasion. "Oh, Kat'leen, Kat'leen, whatever shall we do wit' you?" Hursel chimed in, rolling his eyes heavenward in mock despair. "What sort of a loose-livin', loose-moraled joint will they think we're runnin' here? Lordy, Lordy . . . Untied Front indeed." Patient, devoted Kat'leen was a perfect foil for Hursel's high-spirited clowning.

Under Hursel's guiding hand, the East Bay CRC was transformed from a small, sterile committee of aging, foreign-born whites into a dynamic, predominantly black organization with some five hundred active dues-paying members—this at a time when the NAACP chapter in Oakland could muster no more than fifty.

The black population of the East Bay was sharply divided between the old inhabitants, many of whose families had lived and to some extent prospered there for generations, and newcomers from the South, who had flocked in with the advent of World War II seeking jobs in war industries.

During the war the Kaiser Corporation sent its agents into rural areas of the South to recruit men to work in the shipyards. The response was tremendous, and soon black workers by the trainload, many of them sharecroppers with no experience of city life, were pouring into the area. The AFL shipyard unions were segregated, with the blacks in special Jim Crow auxiliaries, essentially vast dues-collecting organizations in which there was no semblance of union democracy or job security. After the war the black workers were relegated to menial jobs or flung into the ranks of the unemployed, and imprisoned in the decaying temporary war housing projects of the West Oakland, Berkeley, and Richmond ghettos.

There had been a parallel migration of Southern whites into East Bay war industries. These now found employment in the building trades and other skilled occupations controlled by old-line craft unions, from which blacks were excluded; many joined the Oakland police force.

Thus parts of Oakland seemed a microcosm of some Alabaman or Louisianan town, replete with white prejudice in its most savage form. The transplanted blacks, having shaken the dust of the South off their feet, were in a mood to fight back. It was they who formed the backbone of our organization.

In deference to my recent motherhood, it was agreed I should work part time and draw five dollars a week to help pay for somebody to look after the children. Remuneration in Party assignments was roughly set on the principle of "to each according to his need"; since Bob was now a full partner in the law firm, he agreed to subsidize me in my new job. As it turned out, after drawing the five dollars for a couple of weeks I relinquished any further claim to it, every penny of our treasury being needed to finance the myriad campaigns embarked on by Hursel. Likewise, any illusion about part-time work was soon dispelled and I began devoting virtually all my waking hours to the absorbing exigencies of CRC.

Before I started working in CRC I had read much about "the Negro question," as we used to call it, and thought I understood it fairly well. Wage differentials between black and white workers, the profits reaped by the real estate industry from both black and white because of segregated housing—I could hold forth quite knowledgeably on this sort of thing. From books like Herbert Aptheker's pioneering work *A Documentary History of the Negro People in the United States* I had learned something of the unceasing struggle carried on by blacks against their oppressors since slavery days. In CRC, thanks to Hursel and his entourage of young black militants, ghetto ministers, and churchwomen, I began to fathom the real-life implications of the statistics and the studies, to know black people as individuals, to breach the near-impenetrable barriers that separated whites from blacks, to be accepted into black homes, black churches.

In spite of the gaiety and energy with which Hursel infused the organization, his restless *joie de vivre* and nonstop optimism, horror underlay our work. At the time I joined his staff Hursel was in the process of accumulating a dossier on brutal police practices in Oakland, with a view to demanding an official investigation by the California state legislature. Complaints poured in at the CRC and at Bob and Bert's law office. I was often sent to get statements from witnesses, or from the family of the victim, which I would then incorporate into an account of the case for leaflets or mailings.

I found it hard to describe adequately the monstrous beastliness, authority clothed in nightmare garb, that our investigations disclosed. We discovered that on Fridays, payday for most workers, police would regularly lie in wait outside the West Oakland bars that served as banks for the cashing of pay checks, arrest those emerging on charges of drunkenness, and in the privacy of the prowl cars beat them and rob them of their week's pay en route to the West Oakland police station.

How to get this across to people? My leaflets, of which I was then moderately proud, have a pretty trite tone as I now reread them. Typical headlines such as "Thugs in Uniform"; "Defenseless Negro Victims of Police Brutality"; "It *Can* Happen Here" would be followed by a distillation of the facts: "Leroy Johnson, 26-year-old Negro worker accused of drunkenness, beaten into unconsciousness and robbed by six Oakland policemen . . ." "James Washington, 15, assaulted and badly injured by Oakland cops on his way home from his newspaper route, charged with 'loitering' . . ."

To gather the information I spent endless hours in West Oakland, or out at the county hospital, where the more seriously injured were sometimes sent. I shall never forget the appalling accounts I heard. The colorless, almost monotone recitation of Mrs. Washington in her tiny, crowded sitting room: "James never been in no trouble before, and then this law, he stop and say, 'Watcher doin', nigger,' real ugly, and then some more law they come and they beat up on him, and they carry him down to Juvenile, and when I seen him he was bleedin' it look like from just about everywhere, his ribs broken and all bandaged up."

Or Leroy Johnson, in the prisonlike atmosphere of the county hospital, his head enclosed in a wire contraption that looked like a beekeeper's helmet—a surgical device to hold his broken jaw in place—his voice coming painfully through clenched teeth in a barely intelligible murmur: "I guess I *had* been drinking. Went out to get some air. Them law come up in a police car with them night sticks and I don't remember what happened until I woke up in here."

Armed with this evidence, we led innumerable delegations of ministers and trade unionists to the chief of police, incongruously named Divine, to be met by this singularly glib, smooth-tongued individual with blanket denial that any transgressions had occurred in his department. How I grew to loathe him! And to long for his downfall. (It did eventually happen, some years later. Two of Divine's lieutenants, whom Bob was suing for damages in a police brutality case, were caught receiving stolen goods. Divine hastily resigned "for reasons of health.")

Bob and Bert assiduously brought each case to the attention of J. Frank Coakley, district attorney of Alameda County, demanding that he prosecute the guilty policemen. This was done simply for the record, as there was no hope of redress from that quarter; the D.A. was strictly a creature of the Knowland machine, a far-Right-winger whose reelection every four years was assured by the unqualified support of the Oakland *Tribune* and by the fact that for twenty-one years no lawyer had the temerity to oppose him for office, except for Bert, who ran against him in 1951, and Bob, in 1966.

Likewise, not another lawyer in the county could be found to handle police brutality cases. Bob and Bert harried the self-styled liberals of the bar with pleas for help in the proliferating cases that threatened to swamp their small office—and to drive it into bankruptcy, as there was no expectation of fees in these cases. While many lawyers expressed in private their sympathy for the victims and disapprobation of the police department, they frankly admitted that they dared not risk antagonizing police and district attorney; "I have to preserve a working relationship with the D.A.," was the recurrent theme. To add insult to injury, frequently these lawyers would refer black clients of their own who had been assaulted by police to the Edises, Treuhaft law firm. "That's the one kind of case where they never ask for a split of the fee," Bob observed bitterly. (Today the picture has changed. By the mid-sixties, this unseemly timidity no longer pervaded the bar. A new breed of lawyer was emerging from the law schools: gifted and able young men and women championing the oppressed, fighting the legal battles of welfare recipients, minorities, prisoners; but this was still far in the future.)

Hursel, with the backing of the more militant black churches and such Left-led unions as ILWU and United Electrical Workers, was hammering at the door of the state assembly's Committee on Crime and Correction, headed by Assemblyman Vernon Kilpatrick, a liberal Democrat.

We did succeed in bringing the committee to Oakland—as the *Peoples World* reported, it was "the first time in the history of the nation that a specific probe has been conducted into the over-all practices of a major police department toward minority groups." To our frustration and fury, the *Tribune* and Hearst's evening paper, the *Post-Enquirer,* gave this historic event the silent treatment, printing not a line about it. CRC countered by distributing thirty thousand leaflets headlined: "Unholy Alliance Between Police Department and Oakland Tribune!"

The committee's investigator, Robert Powers, was a former police chief of Bakersfield. This sounded most inauspicious: appointing the fox to guard the chickens. Most of us in the Party would have reacted in reflex fashion, denouncing the committee for acting in bad faith by appointing such a person and dissociating ourselves from its deliberations. Not so Hursel, who had an extraordinary ability to work with all sorts and conditions of people, to see beyond labels, to extract the best from them. Judging Powers to be an honest man, he closeted himself with him for hours on end, feeding him information from our voluminous files, guiding the course of the investigation.

In retrospect, I discern a pattern in that three-day hearing that with variations was to be repeated over and over again in the course of our work over the next several years:

Bob and Bert testified, as did a number of police victims whose cases they had investigated. Chief Divine, predictably, declared his department was "clean as a hound's tooth." The NAACP, which had stood on the sidelines throughout our year-long campaign, sent a representative, who testified in generalities and called for cooperation between the police and responsible groups in the community. The committee eventually issued a wishy-washy report finding "some degree of truth" in the charges. Powers was fired on the initiative of Republican

committee members for having cooperated with CRC, a subversive organization.

To put it in context, by 1949 the Cold War was already
three years old (Churchill had made his "iron curtain" speech
in 1946, shortly after Roosevelt's death) and we were heading
into what is loosely called the McCarthy era. Actually, although in the aftermath of Watergate it has become fashionable
to look back with fond nostalgia on good old liberal, honest,
decent Harry Truman, a more accurate designation for that
grotesque period in American history might well be the Truman
era.

The soil for the noxious growth of McCarthyism had been
well prepared by the Truman administration, and the anti-
Communist crusade was well under way long before the junior
senator from Wisconsin himself appeared on the scene. Joseph
McCarthy was virtually unknown outside his home state until
February 9, 1950, when he made his celebrated speech alleging
that the State Department was in the hands of Communists,
which catapulted him into the national limelight he enjoyed
for the next five years.

Some signposts on the road to McCarthyism: 1947—Truman establishes the federal loyalty oath, barring alleged subversives from government employment. States and universities
follow suit. The Attorney General, under authority of a presi-
dential executive order, publishes a list of subversive, proscribed organizations. 1948—Ten Hollywood screenwriters
sentenced to a year's imprisonment for refusing to testify before
the House Committee on Un-American Activities about alleged
subversion in the film industry. Mundt-Nixon bill introduced in
Senate, requiring registration of Communists and members of
"Communist fronts." Senator Hubert Humphrey proposes concentration camps for subversives. Henry Wallace's campaign
for the presidency on the Progressive Party ticket, into which

The Mitford children at Asthall, 1926, flanked by Muv and Farve. Back row: Nancy and Tom; middle row: Diana and Pam; front row: Unity, Decca (Jessica), and Deborah

Decca and Esmond Romilly,
New York, 1939

OPPOSITE:

Left: Aranka in one of
her famous hats, 1956

Right: Muv at Inch
Kenneth

Decca and Dinky in
Washington, 1942

Bob Treuhaft at law school,
1937

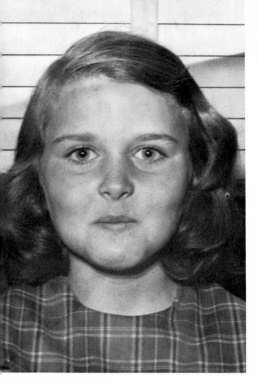

Dinky, aged eight, bursting with excitement as she poses for her passport photograph

Decca, aged five

Decca teaching Benjy to type

Dinky and friends listening to Leadbelly

Paul Robeson, Dinky (right foreground), and friends

Terry François, Jerry Newson, Bert Edises, and Bob working on Newson's defense

Permit to publicize police brutality worded by Decca and signed by Chief of Police Divine

Form 11

Police Department, City of Oakland, California

PERMIT

No._____   This Permit expires January 7, 1950

To operate a loud speaker on an automobile to publicize Police Brutality in Oakland, California, over the streets of the City of Oakland outside the Central Traffic District, on Thursday and Friday, January 5 and January 6, 1950, between the hours of 10:00 A.M. and 6:00 p.m.

Mrs. Decca Treuhaft, Field Representative,
Permission is hereby granted Civil Rights Congress, 675 Jean Street, Oakland, Calif.
PROVIDED, the above is conducted in conformity with the laws and ordinances governing the same. This Permit is not transferable, and is valid only at the location herein designated.

Dated this 5th day of January, 1950

(Signed) Lester J. Divine

CHIEF OF POLICE.

Willie McGee campaign: Decca with poster by Pele

Mob outside Wilbur Gary's house, March 1952

Debo and Decca in California, 1950

Inch Kenneth

Decca and Bob on ferry to Martha's Vineyard

the CP had thrown all its energy and forces, ends in disastrous defeat signaling the final rupture of the New Deal coalition. 1949—Twelve top Communist leaders found guilty under the Smith Act of conspiring to advocate the overthrow of the government by force and violence. Alger Hiss tried and convicted of perjury. Several of the largest Left-led unions expelled from CIO.

Four months after McCarthy's opening salvo, the Korean War broke out, bringing Truman's foreign policy into harmony with his domestic drive against the Left and furnishing McCarthy with more ammunition for his anti-Communist crusade.

In this climate most liberals turned tail. Senator Hubert Humphrey proposed "an emergency interim detention system," and declared on the floor of Congress: "We would pick up the . . . dangerous Communists and put them in internment camps, and protect the safety of the country at once. . . . I want them removed from the normal scene of American life, and taken into custody."* The American Civil Liberties Union, supposed guardian of First Amendment rights, instituted its own loyalty purge, excluding from its activities those suspected of harboring subversive ideas.

The NAACP at its 1950 convention passed a long anti-Communist resolution, denouncing left-wing infiltration and calling for the formation of a committee to "investigate and study the ideological composition and trends of the membership . . . and if necessary to expel any unit which, in the judgment of the Board of Directors, comes under Communist or other political control and domination."

Compliance with this resolution was by no means universal; in many parts of the country, particularly the South, local NAACP branches blinked it and welcomed the participa-

* *Congressional Record,* September 11, 1950.

tion of the Left. But in Oakland the NAACP was a small and on the whole do-nothing organization, its membership a fraction of that of CRC. It was dominated by the old inhabitants of the black community who had attained a degree of prosperity, and, having worked out a modus vivendi with the whites, resented and looked down on the clamorous hordes of recent black immigrants. It would have nothing to do with organizations labeled subversive.

The CRC occupied a prominent place on the Attorney General's list of subversive, or Communist front, organizations. CRC's relationship to the CP was, in fact, symbiotic. It had been created in 1946 at a meeting of Communist leaders and close Party sympathizers from the National Federation for Constitutional Liberties and the remnants of the International Labor Defense, which in the twenties and thirties had led the fight to free the Scottsboro Boys and organized the defense of embattled trade unionists, Communists, foreign-born victims of the Immigration department's repressive ministrations. The Party "assigned forces" to the fledgling CRC, that is, it appointed Party members to assume positions of leadership in the organization and to guide its various campaigns. In line with United Front policy, our every effort was bent towards involving non-Communists, recruiting for CRC from the churches, the trade unions, the neighborhoods, and promoting these recruits into positions of responsibility.

The East Bay chapter executive committee of about twenty members was largely made up of non-Communists: black ministers and church mothers, white Unitarians and Quakers, recruited in the course of the police brutality campaign and other local CRC activities. Our president was a black member of the Laborers' Union, our recording secretary a young Unitarian woman. Among the Communists on the board were Buddy Green, black reporter on the *Peoples World;* a white doctor and his wife; a black housewife. Either Bob or Bert would generally attend as ex-officio members, to report on the legal status of various cases. We strove to make the CRC a living example of racial integration and equality.

Did we mislead the non-Party members as to the genesis and leadership of the CRC? This was a perpetual dilemma, for much as some of us would have liked to proclaim our Party membership from the housetops, to do so in the charged atmosphere of the times would, we felt, scare people off and destroy our effectiveness.

It was the same dilemma faced by Communists in the trade unions, the professions, the "broad" organizations, and one that we solved pragmatically, by confiding only in those non-Party members whom we felt to be trustworthy, unflappable, and likely to be sympathetic to the Party's aims.

Our motive for dissembling was not only to save our own skins; rather it grew out of the whole concept of United Front and the political realities of the time. By 1950 the Party had been virtually outlawed by the Smith Act prosecutions and passage of the McCarran Internal Security Act (successor to the Mundt-Nixon bill), requiring Communists to register. Nobody knew how far, or how fast, the government was prepared to go. *The New York Times* speculated that Smith Act prosecutions might mount into the thousands; there was documented proof that the FBI had concentration camps in readiness to accommodate up to 100,000 subversives.

In any event, the CRC membership was well aware that the organization, and many of us as individuals, were frequently and prominently labeled Communist in the press. Whenever the Oakland *Tribune* had occasion to mention Bob or Bert, no matter what the context, the words "lawyers who represent Communists" would appear after their names. After Bob and I were subpoenaed by the House Committee on Un-American

Activities in the early fifties, the words "identified Communist" always followed any reference to either of us in the *Tribune,* a policy of that newspaper that ended only after publication of *The American Way of Death* in 1963. If this tended to isolate us in the white community, it had the opposite effect in the black. It was not that these relative newcomers from the Deep South were knowledgeable about or sympathetic to the Party as such, but that they empathized with us as members of yet another persecuted minority.

Looking back, it seems that in the forties and fifties the Party had become essentially a self-defense organization—had been maneuvered into that position by the unremitting attacks on it. By the time Bob and I joined, the glorious days of the CIO organizing drive and the San Francisco waterfront strike, when the CP was on the offensive, had receded into history; with few exceptions, Communists had been effectively driven from union leadership. This sense of being beleaguered and embattled created a "fortress mentality," in which the Party became increasingly turned inward. The morale and élan that marked its days of achievement and growth during the thirties were gone; morale was sustained by faith alone, and inevitably in this circumstance faith became dogma.

While there was much exhortation to "broaden out," to seek contacts among the masses (and in CRC we had to some extent succeeded in this), Bob and I found that our circle of really close personal friends was becoming more and more limited to other Party members. This was partly due to the successful efforts of the government to isolate us, but it was also partly our own fault: we tended to drop our friends and associates from pre-Party days because we now had so little in common with them. Furthermore, I fear we were tiresomely self-righteous (or should it be leftuous?), taking a superior and patronizing attitude to those of our acquaintance who had not seen the light as we had.

And yet . . . what other organization was responding seriously to what seemed to us the urgent issues? The liberals (with a few shining exceptions such as I. F. Stone, Alexander Meiklejohn, Clifford and Virginia Durr) had fallen back in disarray, had in effect joined the Cold Warriors. Despite all evident drawbacks, I can hardly imagine living in America in those days and *not* being a member.

CHAPTER 6

CRC Secretary

SHORTLY AFTER the police brutality hearing, Hursel left the Bay Area for a statewide CP assignment and I replaced him as executive secretary of the East Bay CRC. To ensure that Hursel's strikingly successful work in the black community would not suffer from his departure, and that continuity of black leadership would be preserved, the Party assigned Buddy Green to assist me and give general political guidance to the organization. As a member of the CP State and County Committees he was above me in the Party hierarchy, hence our working relationship would have been roughly the equivalent, in a capitalist enterprise, to that of myself as foreman and Buddy as plant manager. In accord with the principle of democratic centralism, Buddy reported on our work to the Leading Bodies (the company board of directors, as it were) and was responsible for carrying back to CRC collective decisions arrived at in these high-level discussions.

Buddy, still in his twenties, was a dazzling example of Bold Cadre Promotion. Born in Mississippi and raised in Memphis, he had escaped from the South at the age of seventeen by jumping freight trains, and had come to Oakland with his teen-age wife, Mary, shortly before the war. He had worked variously as middleweight prizefighter, longshoreman, shipfitter, merchant seaman.

His route into the Party brought to mind Daisy Rossman's oft-repeated injunction: "Remember, the next leaflet we hand out might change somebody's whole life." In 1944 he and Mary were running a small café in the main thoroughfare of the West Oakland ghetto, where the Party frequently held street-corner meetings. "They'd come in and ask if they could plug their amplifier into our electric outlet," he told me. "They had some really eloquent speakers. Mary and I would listen, and read their leaflets. After the speeches they'd come in for coffee and we'd sit and talk with them. At first they'd pay me a dollar or so for the use of the electric juice, but I soon got so interested I'd let them have the use of it free." Eventually one of the black comrades in the group took him aside and to his extreme gratification asked him to join the Party.

Buddy had left his Memphis school in the sixth grade, about equivalent to the third grade in California schools. He had never read a full-length book until he was twenty. "I was hungry for information. The Party threw at you a whole batch of reading, gobs of material—books, pamphlets, international stuff—and the reason why blacks are oppressed began to link up with history and the world economic scene. We were brought here in slavery for profit, and kept in oppression for profit. For the first time it became clear in my mind."

In the Party, his development from a semiliterate into a highly able newspaperman was meteoric. The leadership had spotted him as a talented organizer with a gift for writing. Al Richmond, editor of the *Peoples World,* called him in to a staff meeting and asked if he would like to work on the paper. "Gee, it was *frightening,*" Buddy said. "I told them I hadn't the background for that sort of job. But Al told me, 'You've got more qualifications for a job on *our* paper than most graduates of journalism school.' " With the painstaking help of Richmond and other seasoned PW writers, who taught him the elements of journalistic technique, Buddy became one of the best reporters on the paper, his vivid, idiosyncratic style in refreshing contrast to that of some of his stuffier and more verbose colleagues.

Buddy's assignment as "Party leadership cadre" to CRC dovetailed well with his regular job on the PW, since many of the major PW news stories originated with CRC campaigns. Thus as a reporter he would have the inside track—indeed, he would often have initiated the action that led to the story.

Our slogan might have been "No Job Too Big or Too Small," for the scope and variety of the causes we espoused grew month by month. There were national cases to which our chapter had commitments, such as the Rosenberg case and the defense of William L. Patterson, black national executive secretary of CRC charged with contempt of Congress for refusing to turn over CRC records to a congressional committee. There were California statewide cases, such as the Los Angeles Smith Act trial of eleven of our state Party leaders. Above all there were innumerable local campaigns, ranging from defense of blacks falsely accused of capital crimes to demonstrations against black-face minstrel shows sponsored by the Oakland Elks Club to the physical protection of blacks moving into all-white neighborhoods.

We chalked up some significant victories and saved some lives. At the height of the police brutality campaign we undertook the defense of Jerry Newson, an eighteen-year-old black shoeshine boy accused of murdering a white pharmacist and his assistant in their West Oakland store. This case had all the classic elements of a police frame-up: a forced confession, faked ballistics evidence, police intimidation of Newson's teenage friends, prosecution collusion with the Oakland *Tribune,* which in headlines virtually pronounced Newson guilty the day he was charged. It also marked the beginning of our vendetta with the district attorney, J. Frank Coakley, a mutual enmity that flourished and grew over two decades.

Coakley's endless collection of dirty tricks included the planting of a concealed microphone in the jail visiting room where attorneys met with their clients. The microphone was spotted, and yanked from the ceiling where it was hidden, by a prominent local criminal lawyer who was interviewing a defendant. The lawyer indignantly taxed Coakley with eavesdropping on him, whereupon Coakley assured him, "That mike wasn't put there for you—it was meant for Treuhaft!"

With the help of the PW and the Party, CRC campaigned unceasingly throughout the Bay Area to expose the nature of the Newson frame-up. Buddy wrote a pamphlet on the case, which received enormous circulation; we sold over ten thousand of them, which surely put it in the best-seller class for the Oakland area. Great mass meetings were held in the ghetto churches. To this day the Newson case, which became a *cause célèbre* in West Oakland, is remembered in the black community; in the early seventies Huey Newton, then head of the Black Panthers, told us he recalled hearing all about it as a small child. Bob and Bert, he said, were among his boyhood heroes.

Needless to say, there was no fee in the case—Newson's only relatives, his aunt and uncle, were on welfare—and all the defense investigation was done by CRC volunteers. I was assigned to track down Newson's alibi witnesses, who would substantiate the pivotal fact that he was nowhere near the drugstore on the night of the murders. This proved to be no easy task: Newson's social life, like that of many drifting eighteen-year-olds, was, to put it mildly, free-wheeling.

"I was out with ol' T-Bone and the guys that evening," he told Bob. What was T-Bone's last name? Where did he live?

Who were the other guys? Jerry hadn't a clue. So day after day, with little hope of success, I trudged through the pool halls and bars of West Oakland, with my plaintive refrain: "Do you know T-Bone? Anybody here seen ol' T-Bone?" Amazingly, my perseverance paid off, for on one of these forays I found not only ol' T-Bone himself, but some of the other guys, who agreed to testify—a brave decision, as to testify for the defense in such a case was to become a police target thereafter.

Bob and Bert sweated through three trials over a period of three years. In the first trial Newson was found guilty by an all-white jury and sentenced to death. They successfully appealed the conviction to the state supreme court. After two subsequent trials ended in hung juries, Coakley, declaring in open court that he was convinced of Newson's guilt but was unable to prove it, was obliged to dismiss the charges. (I wrote to my mother about this circumstance. "I'm so glad you had a victory in the Newson case," she replied. "What is a hung jury? It seems the tables were turned.")

Deprived of an execution, Coakley turned the full force of his frustration on Newson and on us. Newson had received the statutory indeterminate sentence of five years to life for an amateurish robbery to which he had readily confessed and which had no connection with the murder case, a crime for which the ordinary first offender is paroled after two or three years. Annually he came before the parole board for his parole hearing; annually Coakley sent a letter to the board stating that Newson was guilty of the murders, was "one of the most vicious, calloused killers" he had ever encountered, and castigating "the brazen tactics of the Civil Rights Congress, *Peoples World* and other subversives" for thwarting justice in their defense of Newson. As a consequence, despite his excellent prison record, Newson spent fifteen years in San Quentin for the robbery until finally paroled at the age of thirty-three.

Nowhere but in the tirades loosed by undertakers in response to the publication of *The American Way of Death* have I encountered rhetoric to match Coakley's for sheer color and vehemence. In what Bob called "pure triple-distilled Coakley," he denounced us to a California state assembly committee hearing on the indeterminate sentence where Bert testified, illustrating through the Newson case the inequities of that law. Coakley threatened to have Bert disbarred, and branded our CRC fact sheet on the case as "the most unfair, despicable Communist propaganda I have ever seen, a tissue of lies spawned by the twisted mentalities of persons who for years have been actively, fanatically and admittedly identified with the Communist movement."

Again, when Coakley was subpoenaed in habeas corpus proceedings seeking Newson's release, he spotted me in the courtroom audience. Pointing at me from the witness stand, he shouted, "That woman's a Communist! She's been spending the last five years thinking of ways to torment me!" Thus addressed, I rose and mildly replied that I wished it were true, but regrettably other matters had come up to occupy my time and distract me from this undeniably worthy endeavor.

At the height of the vendetta, we quite fortuitously fell into an opportunity to pull off a spectacular Coakley tease. A well-to-do black family, the Guitons, had approached Bob about finding somebody to "front" for them in the purchase of a house they wished to buy in the exclusive all-white Oakland lake district. Although racially restrictive housing covenants had been declared unconstitutional by the Supreme Court some years before, in practice barriers against black occupancy in many parts of the town were as solid as ever. Bob had participated in "fronting" for black home buyers before, but the Guitons' transaction posed a special problem. Because of a bungled first effort on their behalf, the seller, an officer of the

Bank of America, had been alerted and would be on guard against any prospective buyer who might seem suspect. Moreover, because of the cost of the house and the size of the loan, an intermediary with special qualifications, financial and social, was needed. No ordinary wage worker would qualify, nor even a professional with an already mortgaged house.

We persuaded Henry Saunders, a young associate in Bob's law firm, and his wife to assume the role. They seemed ideal; they were living in a rented apartment, and although Henry was earning but a lowly wage in Bob's embattled firm, as a lawyer on the threshold of his career his prospects could be expected to improve. Their decisive qualifications, I thought, were their upper-class Southern antecedents (Henry's father was an Army colonel) and their thick, unreconstructed Alabama accents. Given these assets, they were unlikely to arouse the suspicion of the seller.

The Saunderses and I went over to see the house. Wearing my best Aranka hat, I played the part of their English aunt, who, anxious to see these worthy young people suitably settled in a nice neighborhood, would provide the down payment and co-sign the loan.

We were greeted by the owner's wife. Clearly enchanted by the three of us, she showed us all through the house, agreed to my proposal that as the kitchen linoleum was a little worn she should knock two thousand off the price, and offered to leave all the wall-to-wall carpeting and floor-to-ceiling drapes in place for the Saunderses. Over tea, which she cordially pressed on us, she told us about the neighbors. They were the highest-type people, she said, bank managers, business executives; "and our district attorney, Mr. Coakley, lives right across the street." My heart leapt.

On the day of the move, I accompanied the Guitons to help them get settled and to observe the neighborhood reaction—

violence might erupt, and I wanted to be on hand to call in help from CRC if need be. We arrived at the Guitons' new home early in the morning. Within an hour, dozens of neighbors had emerged from their houses and were gathering up and down the street, staring at the new arrivals. Suddenly the seller's wife appeared at the front door, all her former cordiality vanished, her face contorted with tears of pure rage. To my cheery "Good morning!" she replied with a stream of invective: I had betrayed her trust in me; how could I do such a terrible, underhanded thing? I asked why, since she had moved out of the neighborhood, it could conceivably make any difference to her whether her house was now occupied by the Saunderses or the Guitons. Because, she said, the neighbors, such lovely people, would feel she had let them down; she would never be able to hold her head up again in decent society. I coldly replied that she and her lovely neighbors were contemptible bigots, and that if she did not leave immediately, I should be obliged to summon the district attorney from across the street to arrest her for disturbing the peace.

Coakley's reaction to his new neighbors was swift and predictable: he immediately put his house up for sale, letting it go for a sum substantially below its worth, thus precipitating a general white exodus from the neighborhood. He confided to an acquaintance of ours, "That pinko Treuhaft outsmarted me this time!"

There is a footnote to this incident. In 1966 Bob ran against Coakley for the office of D.A. It was a thrilling campaign in which, despite the expected avalanche of redbaiting, Bob got 30 percent of the votes. (After the election, Coakley remarked, "I had figured Treuhaft's vote would be about thirty thousand, but he got seventy-five thousand. I didn't realize there were that many Commies in Alameda County.") Our precinct map, on which we had shaded in the areas where Bob had got the majority of votes—the flatlands of Oakland, the black districts, the student community of Berkeley—showed, amid a sea of Coakley precincts in the Oakland lake district, a small shaded oasis which Bob had carried: Guiton's precinct, now almost entirely inhabited by black lawyers, doctors, businessmen.

The Party leadership, whom we had consulted at every stage of the Guiton transaction, was somewhat divided over our role in it. Some thought it was "a diversion from our main task of organizing Negro and white workers for the class struggle," since the Guitons were of the black middle class. Buddy, and other black comrades, vehemently opposed this viewpoint, taking the position that as Communists we were morally bound to assist in *any* action that extended the democratic rights of blacks, no matter what their economic class.

Similar differences arose from time to time between me and the leadership during my CRC tenure. From my point of view as both a Communist bound by Party policy and an ardent CRC worker, the relationship between the two organizations was at once a liability and an asset. The difficulty would arise when I was called on the carpet by the Party leadership, which was often the case, for our chapter's failure to pay sufficient attention to national cases such as the Smith Act trials. While the non-Party CRC executive committee members were in sympathy with these causes, and saw the Smith Act prosecutions as yet another example of government oppression, most of them had been recruited on the basis of the local police brutality and Jerry Newson campaigns, hence tended to put considerably more energy into these matters than into defense of the Smith Act victims.

As executive secretary, I argued with the Party leaders, was it not my job to carry out the wishes of the board, and particularly of those black board members whose positions of leadership in their own community constituted our major strength? Or sometimes I would avoid the issue altogether by developing a diplomatic cold on the day of the Party meeting.

I had an ally in William L. Patterson, who often came out from New York on a national tour to meet with CRC chapters around the country. Pat, then in his late fifties, was a formidable figure in the black Party leadership. The son of a slave, he was a practicing lawyer at the time of the Sacco and Vanzetti case, which had led him into the Party. As a leader in the International Labor Defense, he had organized the mass defense of the Scottsboro Boys in the thirties. Although Pat operated on a national and international level—one of his many dazzling achievements was presentation of the CRC petition "We Charge Genocide: The Crime of Government Against the Negro People" at a United Nations meeting in Paris—he always had time for the lower-echelon CRC workers, and took a deep interest in the day-to-day organizational problems that beset us.

In his view it would be an act of white chauvinism for me, a white person, to try to dominate or manipulate our predominantly black membership, to deflect their attention from the very issues that had led them to join the organization. Then what to do? I asked. I couldn't very well go against Party discipline. "Darling, where principles are concerned, you must learn to fight. You may have to fight all the way to expulsion." "Oh, Pat, it's all very well for *you* to say that," I grumbled. "You know they'd never expel you. But how about poor me, cast into the outer darkness, the weeping and gnashing of teeth?" Which is exactly how I should have felt about expulsion from the Party.

Once expelled, the former member was "put on nonassociation," meaning that at one blow he or she was severed forever not only from the organization and all its activities, but from a whole circle of long-time friends and acquaintances. To continue to see a person on nonassociation was itself one of the most serious breaches of discipline, and cause for expulsion. This would have been bitter indeed, in my case, for in those embattled days the only close friends we had were Communists. And what of Bob? Would he have followed me into the abode of the damned, or should we have had to get a divorce? Fortunately we were never put to this harsh test.

If the Party's intervention in CRC's affairs was sometimes irksome, our strength and ability to mount campaigns out of all proportion to our size lay in the Party's genius for organization, and its loyal ring of sympathizers. In many a crisis, with the help of the Party leadership we could call upon a veritable army of comrades in trade union branches, neighborhood clubs, professional clubs, who would spring into action in disciplined Party fashion to enlist their "broad contacts" and perform any number of tasks, from leaflet distributions to offering resolutions in their unions to raising money among their professional colleagues.

One example, among dozens that could be cited, of this kind of concerted effort illustrates how the Party functioned at its best, both in supplying the troops and guiding the political strategy—carrying out, in fact, its "vanguard role."

One morning in 1952, we read in the San Francisco *Chronicle* that a cross had been burned on the lawn of a black veteran, one Wilbur D. Gary, who had bought a house in the all-white housing project of Rollingwood, some fifteen miles from Oakland. Buddy and I raced out there, past the sign that said "Welcome to Rollingwood" and into the maze of neat pastel bungalows. We had no trouble identifying Gary's house, where a huge crowd of white men and teen-agers was gathered (four hundred according to Buddy, expert crowd estimator), chanting "Out, niggers!" and hurling stones at the windows, one of which was shattered. It was the first time I had witnessed the horrifying sight and sound of a mob in action; one could almost feel the adrenaline (or perhaps it was the blood of Charlemagne) coursing through one's system at this revolting spectacle. Two uniformed sheriff's deputies stood idly by watching the scene.

We made a dash for it through the mob to the front door; seeing Buddy's black face, Gary readily admitted us and led us into the kitchen, where his wife and children were huddled behind makeshift barricades, the chairs and table pushed up against the doors. Buddy explained we were from the Civil Rights Congress and were prepared to put our entire organization at the disposal of his family for defense of their home. With Gary and his wife, we quickly worked out a many-pronged approach: physical protection of the house, trade union resolutions demanding police protection, leaflets to be drawn up by CRC and distributed throughout the Bay Area.

A few judiciously placed telephone calls to Party and CRC leaders brought within an hour a dozen carloads of black and white volunteers prepared to doss down for the night in the Gary living room. They were the first contingent of more than eight hundred who in the next few days poured into Rollingwood to keep vigil in the house, to patrol the streets in cars, to furnish protective escorts for Mrs. Gary and the children on their way to work and school. The defenders achieved a sort of stand-off with the attackers, who continued to gather in menacing knots at a safe distance from the house, but ceased throwing rocks.

At times like this, one hardly slept. The defenders had to be organized into round-the-clock shifts, in itself a formidable job; in line with policy, we strove for a careful balance of blacks and whites, of men and women. While the Party through its connections in the labor movement and other organizations had mobilized this great outpouring of Gary supporters, only a fraction of the volunteers were CP members. In this dangerous, explosive situation which might attract *provocateurs,* we considered it essential to assign to each shift a certain number of trusted Party cadres, who could be counted on as front-line soldiers to direct the defense, keep a watchful eye out for hotheads, and, in consultation with the Garys, to make on-the-spot decisions.

Simultaneously we had a dozen other activities going in an effort to mobilize support for the Garys throughout Northern California. Kat'leen and a volunteer office crew worked far into the night cranking out leaflets, sending mailings to hundreds of unions, churches, PTAs, civic organizations, drawing up petitions to the governor, the mayor, the board of supervisors demanding police protection for the Garys and action against the mob leaders. The Labor Youth League (formerly the Young Communist League) dispatched its teen-age members to distribute leaflets denouncing the rock-throwers at Richmond High School, where Gary's seventeen-year-old son was a student and a football star. Buddy gathered all these multiple strands and wove them into daily front-page stories in the PW.

Buddy and I consulted throughout the crisis with the Party leadership on the complex matters of strategy involved. Our primary goal, it was decided, should be to seek out whites in Rollingwood who would come forward to condemn the mob violence and would themselves undertake defense of the Gary home. To this end we deployed volunteers to go door to door in the housing project and bring the issue directly to the white residents.

We met with instant success. Eight white families responded and agreed to maintain a twenty-four-hour patrol around the house. Faced with this show of opposition by their own neighbors, the attackers ceased their harassment and we withdrew our forces. A clear-cut victory had been won. (As of August

1975, the Garys, now retired, still live in their once-belea-
guered house. Mrs. Gary tells me that over the years nine more
black families have moved to Rollingwood; there has been no
further trouble from the racists.)

The Gary defense also illustrates the perennial difficulties
we faced, as a proscribed organization, in our dealings both
with the principals involved (in this case the Gary family) and
with other organizations, particularly the NAACP. Gary was a
building contractor—in days when such occupations were virtually closed to blacks—and a vice-commander of a black
American Legion post, that patriotic organization then being
strictly segregated. One of our major concerns was to avoid
leading him and his wife unknowingly out on a limb, into a
situation where they would be vulnerable to redbaiting and
harmed either in their business or in their social life. At the
same time, we naturally wanted people to know that CRC had
organized the defense, or to put it more baldly, we wanted to
take credit for the victorious outcome. In consultation with the
Party leadership, we agreed on a plan that we hoped would
satisfy both objectives. Buddy went out to see Gary, and together they drew up an open letter to the community, to be
signed by Gary and distributed by CRC. The tone of the letter,
with its references to "hundreds of democratic minded Americans" and "our beloved Constitution," exemplifies what we
called Broad Coalition Work, meaning the effort to draw the
greatest number of people and organizations into any given
battlefield.

"Dear Friends," it ran, "I wish to express deepest thanks to
the many hundreds of democratic minded Americans, both
Negro and white, who have come to the defense of my home
and family within the last few days, and to those of my white
neighbors who have pledged their support." There follows an
account of the KKK cross, the threatening mob, the dereliction

of the sheriff's office. "For the sake of our beloved Constitution, I urge you and your organization to do all in your power to convince the Contra Costa Sheriff's department, the governor and attorney general of our state, that they should take the necessary steps to guarantee our safety. You have my full permission to duplicate this letter and to make copies available to your membership and to the public. Sincerely, Wilbur D. Gary, Vice-Commander, American Legion Post."

(The style, unmistakably Buddy's rather than Gary's, gives rise to a fanciful speculation: how would the letter have been phrased in the sixties, had Buddy been a New Left activist instead of a Party and CRC leader? Probably something like this: "Dear Comrades, I wish to salute the many hundreds of revolutionary brothers and sisters who put their bodies on the line against the fascist mob. For the sake of our beloved revolutionary cause, I urge you to stick it to the pig sheriff's department, the filthy fascist oppressor governor and attorney general. Seize the time!")

As usual, the trickiest question of strategy involved our relationship with the NAACP. Throughout the emergency they had been, as Buddy put it, "dragging their feet," confining themselves to issuing press releases and resolutions in support of Gary's right to live in the home of his choice. We had tried, and with some success, to recruit individual NAACP members to join in defending the house against the mob. Since it was our fondest desire to enlist the NAACP's support, this participation was built up in Buddy's PW stories to make it appear that CRC and NAACP had jointly organized the defense, whereas in fact had it not been for the swift, concerted action of CRC and CP, there *would* have been no defense and Gary's house might well have been burned to the ground. We mimeographed twenty thousand of the Green/Gary letter under the heading "Issued by the East Bay Civil Rights Congress as a Public Service," and used these to announce a victory mass meeting in Richmond, halfway between Oakland and Rollingwood. The NAACP, not generally noted for such militant activities as leaflet distributions, gave out leaflets at the meeting that read:

KEEP YOUR EYES WIDE OPEN
DON'T GET SUCKED IN!

These groups, organizations and publications are attempting to MISLEAD the NEGRO COMMUNITY:

CALIFORNIA LABOR SCHOOL PEOPLE'S WORLD (Newspaper)
CIVIL RIGHTS CONGRESS (CRC) POLITICAL AFFAIRS (Magazine)
LABOR YOUTH LEAGUE

- They say they are "working for your civil rights," but they work among us in the interest of the Communist Party or other subversive and un-American movements.
- Check and double-check BEFORE you sign petitions, attend meetings, serve on "DEFENSE" committees or join or contribute to questionable organizations.

The charges in the leaflet were, of course, familiar: that the Party and its front organizations "used" issues like Rollingwood, police brutality, the Newson case to extend their influence among blacks, that it exploited these issues for its own ideological purposes.

Were these charges true? My answer would be "Yes, but so what?" The crux of our method was to use these issues to identify the economic and political roots of racial bigotry. We endeavored to show that the cases of police brutality we had uncovered were not random, isolated instances of a few sadistic cops brutalizing helpless victims; rather, police terrorism in the black community was a deliberate, conscious policy of Oakland's political rulers to keep the blacks in a state of subjugation. Likewise, the mob violence against the Garys could not have occurred were it not for the collusion of the authorities, who by their inaction tacitly condoned it—there had been no semblance of police protection until, thanks to CRC's publicizing of the case, organizations all over the state joined the protest.

As to the accusation "They say they are 'working for your civil rights,' but they work among us in the interest of the Communist Party," to me the two seemed indivisible and complementary. One had but to look around the country to discover that where the Party was strongest, where it had the largest enrollment of blacks, there the movement for black liberation was most advanced. Speaking from my own observation, in the 1950s the Communist Party and its numerous sympathizers really were "in the vanguard of the struggle for Negro rights," as we would have put it. This was no empty, self-aggrandizing slogan. Until the sit-in movement of the early sixties triggered the formation of SNCC and CORE, there were *no* militant, racially mixed membership organizations on a national scale devoted to this cause, in which black/white unity was practiced as well as preached, except for the CP and such Left-led organizations as CRC, Labor Youth League, the Progressive Party, and the few trade unions in which Communists still had influence. The FBI and Immigration department took official cognizance of this. Their agents, seeking evidence of Communist affiliation, would routinely ask a suspect's neighbors and co-workers, "Do Negroes visit their home for meetings or social gatherings?"

As we saw it, the day-to-day fight for elementary democratic rights—the right of blacks to a home in the neighborhood of their choice, of trade unionists to organize, of professors to teach according to their conscience, of working mothers to send their children to state-subsidized child care centers, even Bob's favorite, the right to Free Garbage Collection—all led in one direction. Through these assorted struggles, the participants would (could we but find the key to their minds and hearts) become radicalized, would develop a common hatred of capitalism as their common enemy, and would eventually join together to embrace the goal of socialism.

Thus a Communist Party leaflet, issued at the height of the Rollingwood crisis, urged letters to Governor Earl Warren "demanding a full investigation and prosecution of the parties guilty of violence and terrorism at the Gary residence," and followed this up with a smidgeon of anti-capitalist ideology: "The big real estate interests and banks demand outrageously high rents wherever discrimination has forced people to live concentrated in ghettoes. When white working people and small home owners support the just demands of the Negro people for equal rights in housing, the profits in slums will fall." All indubitably true.

Such leaflets, in which the "face of the Party" was revealed, were a rarity in those days; in fact, a countercriticism has been made that by the early fifties the Party, forced on the defensive, did all too little in the way of education for socialism, confining itself to causes that in normal times would be espoused by liberals, the ACLU, the left wing of the Democratic Party.

AT THE TIME of the Rollingwood campaign the Party was entering a strange moment in its history: the Underground Period. With the advent of the Korean War and the concomitant anti-Red hysteria that swept the nation, the Party leadership concluded that a full-scale Fascist takeover was imminent. In anticipation of a sudden FBI crackdown, in which all known Communists would be rounded up in concentration camps, the Party moved to establish an alternative Underground leadership that would continue to function illicitly if Fascism should come to power. Needless to say, every facet of this operation was conducted in deepest secrecy. We of the rank and file would occasionally learn that some trusted comrade, who had mysteriously dropped from sight, had been assigned to the Underground apparatus; thereafter, one never mentioned his or her name.

My only experience with the organizational setup of the Underground occurred when our county chairman signified that a member of the State Security Commission wished to come over from San Francisco to see me. Such appointments were never arranged by telephone, nor was the person's name spoken. The chairman handed me a piece of paper with the comrade's name, a time and date, and the place of meeting—a vacant lot near the CRC office. I committed these to memory, burned the paper, and repaired to the lot at the appointed time.

There the Security Commission member divulged the reason for our assignation. I was to get in touch with a black comrade and CRC member who lived in Vallejo, and arrange for him to procure a social security card and driver's license in the name of Horace Allen. I felt honored to be entrusted with this clandestine errand, especially as I deduced that the false identity papers were intended for the beloved Hursel, who had disappeared from the scene some months before; the initials H.A. were the same as his, and the Vallejo comrade, light-skinned, short, and stocky, looked very much like him.

An assignment from the Security Commission was always considered urgent and took absolute precedence over anything else one might be doing. That night I returned home from a CRC meeting about 10 p.m. and told Bob I would have to go straight out again; he should not expect me home before one o'clock. "Security," I mouthed silently. I did not tell him more, nor did he ask. It was understood that one did not confide in anybody, even a spouse, about such matters.

I drove to Vallejo, an hour's drive from Oakland, losing my way in the labyrinthine roads of the black housing project until I found the right house. It was now close to midnight; all the houses were in pitch darkness, their occupants asleep. I banged repeatedly on the door until eventually the comrade's wife answered, clearly annoyed at being disturbed; but she went to awaken him. When I revealed the purpose of my visit, he immediately agreed to procure the social security card—but, to my consternation, explained that he would not be eligible for a driver's license as he had *never learned to drive*. This posed an unforeseen dilemma. As security rules would prohibit me from involving a third party in the endeavor, it meant that I would have to teach him. In that case, I said, there was only one thing for it: he would have to come by bus to Oakland every day for lessons, until he could drive well enough to pass the test.

This turn of events was most annoying, I reflected as I drove home. Any revolutionary glamour that might have attached to the original assignment would surely be dissipated by the mundane job of teaching the fellow to drive. What with Rollingwood and dozens of other concerns, I was far too busy to take it on. Besides, what if he smashed up my car? I was determined to shed this task if possible.

A way to do so without jeopardizing security occurred to me. CRC shared its shabby suite of offices, in a low-rent district of downtown Oakland, with the Independent Progressive Party, whose director, Marge Frantz, was a superdedicated comrade of unquestionable, total reliability in any circumstance. I do not doubt she would have cheerfully jumped off the Bay Bridge if the Party instructed her to do so. Marge was (and is) one of my favorite people, so it was with a slight twinge of guilt that the next morning I beckoned her to follow me into the vacant lot.

"Security assignment," I said. "Top priority. I was instructed to tell you they want you to teach a comrade to drive;

he'll be here this morning. You're to keep at it until he can pass the test for a license." Poor Marge. Being a Southerner, endowed with the insatiable curiosity and propensity for gossip of that race, it must have been far harder for her than for most people to refrain from asking the obvious questions: "But why? Who is he? What for?" I had accurately gauged that her sense of revolutionary discipline could be counted on to outweigh her native inquisitiveness. She looked very surprised at my odd command, but offered neither comment nor resistance. The comrade proved to be a remarkably slow learner. For three weeks he appeared daily; feeling a little remorseful, I would watch Marge as she reluctantly emerged from her office (she was every bit as busy and hard-working as I) to resume the lessons. At the end of it her car was a mere shadow of its former self, its fenders scarred and dented, its clutch barely working. But the mission was accomplished, the false papers safely on their way.

It was not until 1956, when the Underground apparatus was dissolved and the comrades began to surface from their hiding places, that I admitted to Marge that I had put one over on her. To this day, I do not think she has quite forgiven me.

CHAPTER 7

Intermission: Happy Families

DURING THE EARLY YEARS of our marriage we saw little of Bob's mother and, of course, nothing at all of my family. I had looked forward to meeting Aranka, to being clasped to the warm and loving bosom of a Jewish family, as I inferred from Jewish literature would be my good fortune. Bob was far from sanguine about this prospect—a *shiksa* of radical persuasion with a two-year-old child, he suggested, was arguably not the ideal bride for the apple of Aranka's eye.

Her first visit, when we were still at Mrs. Tibbs's, was a total disaster. Bob and I both happened to have flu at the time and were lying in bed in the chaotically cluttered sitting room which doubled as our bedroom. Aranka arrived via the Tibbs boardinghouse, descended the wooden fire escape burdened with furs, hatboxes, luggage, and a little yapping black dog on a lead, took one look at us, and burst into tears.

The dog, it turned out, was a present for Dinky. Mrs. Tibbs, trying to be helpful, offered to put it out in the backyard. "In that filthy place? I should say not!" exclaimed Aranka. Mrs. Tibbs, with saintly restraint, refrained from calling her attention to the trio Rickydidit, Billydidit, and Dinky, who just then were romping happily in a state of undress in a corner of the yard.

After this inauspicious beginning things did not improve. I tried to be a good daughter-in-law, to fall in with Aranka's ideas about the proper care and treatment of Bob, yet I seldom succeeded in pleasing. She confided that Bob, "like his father, may he rest in peace," suffered from a lack of ambition, that he was not sufficiently motivated to rise in the world, to get ahead, to earn more money. My role as a wife should be to instill these aspirations by being more demanding. I should insist on having a fur coat, a better car, costly objects that would compel him to set his monetary goals ever higher.

The next morning as Bob, slightly late as usual, set off to catch the Haight Street trolley, I leaned out of the window and, with Aranka's injunctions in mind, bellowed, "Get to work, you lazy good-for-nothing bum! How do you think you'll ever amount to anything? I want a new coat! I want a car! Off with you!" It was quite effective; Bob, grinning uneasily, broke into a run, pedestrians stopped in their tracks and craned their necks in my direction, up and down the street neighbors popped their heads out of windows. But my performance did not find favor with Aranka, who in fact seemed quite put out by it. "I can't seem to do right," I sighed to Bob. "Really, there's *no* pleasing your mother."

When she next came to stay—her visits were sometimes, to my annoyance, unannounced—Bob was out of town. "So where is he?" In Phoenix, I explained, on a case for the union. Aranka looked at me accusingly. "Always for the union he is doing things. Isn't it about time he did something for himself?" (A typical Aranka *malentendu;* the union in question happened to be one of the law firm's more lucrative accounts.) No doubt deep down she blamed me bitterly for Bob's involvement with notoriously left-wing unions like the ILWU.

As time went on, Aranka, although never reconciled to our political attachments, more or less abandoned any hope of converting us to respectability. More enduring, however, was her unremitting and vociferous disapproval of the way we were bringing up the children.

Our household arrangements were makeshift. After we left Mrs. Tibbs we generally contrived to have a built-in baby-sitter, somebody who would keep house and mind the children in exchange for room, board, and a pittance of pay. The three bedrooms in our house were put to maximum use, sometimes accommodating a couple in the spare room, and their children, who shared a bedroom with ours. The turnover was fairly rapid: a pleasant Midwestern family—a GI, his wife, and two children—was succeeded by a Japanese couple, recently released from a wartime internment camp, with their two little girls. That is, we thought there were two until four older children materialized, sleeping star-scattered under Army surplus blankets on the living room floor. They were a delightful lot, subtly Orientalizing our household; while they were there we lived principally on rice, fetched in by Bob from a wholesaler in hundred-pound sacks. Our children would cup their hands Japanese style and say "Chow-da!" to ask for a helping. Bob hoped their next instruction would be in suitably reverential ancestor worship. However, both the Japanese family and we began to note that the place was getting a wee bit crowded, so to our mutual regret they departed for other quarters.

After they left I was temporarily in despair, hoping against hope that something would turn up. It did, in the shape of a former strip-teaseuse whom I had met at a PW party, and who moved in the very next day with her baby. Bob was skeptical about this choice, but I thought she might be ideal; as a burlesque artist she must surely have seen plenty of the seamy side of life, I pointed out, and what could be seamier than housework? She was nursing the baby; Bob complained of her habit of greeting him when he got home from work by flipping a breast in his direction. He was proved right—even I could see that she was fairly slovenly. One day she decamped, simply vanished without a word. We noticed a large brown paper bag out by the garbage cans, which upon investigation turned out to be our unwashed plates and cutlery, put out for the scavenger by the faithless stripper.

There was also a great deal of comradely sharing of child care. On one occasion two of our club members, a longshoreman and his wife, had been elected delegates to a Party convention in Los Angeles, and we agreed to look after their children, aged three years, two years, and five months, while they were gone. It was a pretty ghastly few days, and to make matters worse, Aranka happened to be staying with us. As Bob rushed about the kitchen making formula and changing diapers, she exploded: "I sent my son to Harvard he should baby-sit for a longshoreman's children?"

Absorbed as we were in political work, family life and political life merged into one. Dinky and Benjy, loyal supporters of the cause, accompanied us on many a demonstration. Their weekend treats would consist of picketing the Oakland police department of a Saturday morning, turning out on Sundays with CRC contingents for leaflet distributions to churchgoers in West Oakland, canvassing in the neighborhoods during election campaigns—diversions highlighted by an occasional PW picnic, a CRC evening songfest, a Paul Robeson concert.

In this scheme of things Bob and I spent far more time with our children than our own parents had spent with us when we were small. So far as possible we tried to treat them as equals, partners in all our endeavors. They called us by our first names, fairly unusual in those days; Aranka frowned on this. When Bob was a child he had been required to call his parents Mother

Dear and Daddy Dear, as befitted a genteel upbringing, a practice she insisted upon until he was well into his twenties, when
wishing not to call attention to her age, she instructed him to
call her Aranka. In sum, as Bob pointed out, the element of
Gracious Living, so highly prized by Aranka, was conspicu-
ously missing from our ménage.

Somehow the timing of Aranka's visits seemed always to be
unfortunate. Once she arrived when Leadbelly, the great blues
singer, had come to stay for a fortnight. "But, Aranka, we've
only got one spare bedroom. I do hope you won't mind sharing?" Aranka, not amused, elected to sleep on the living room
couch.

Leadbelly was already a legend. He had sung his way out of
a Louisiana prison, where he was serving a life sentence for
murder, by addressing musical pleas for clemency to the governor, whom he charmed into granting a pardon. His real name
was Huddie Ledbetter; he had adopted Leadbelly as his *nom de
théâtre* in nostalgic recollection of the numerous gunfights of
his youth.

He was very large and very black. He would come down to
breakfast wearing a long stark-white nightshirt, from which
protruded his sable limbs and head; the visual effect was spectacular. Soon the house would ring with his wonderful music,
daily concerts for the children, for whom he improvised special
songs.

He and Aranka were ill-assorted houseguests; they would
circle one another warily, with little to say. "Oh, Decca"—
Aranka sighed wistfully—"I wish I was black like Jerry
Newson and Leadbelly. Then you would love me."

Bob, always loyally on my side in my altercations with
Aranka, accused me nonetheless of striking back in my letters
to her: "Thank you *so* much for the perfectly heavenly coats
from Best's, the children look *too* lovely in them, just the thing

to wear on the picket line next Saturday. . . ." "Bob and I
have been subpoenaed by the House Committee on Un-American Activities on account of being subversives, so could you be
an angel and send me a smart hat from your shop to wear at the
hearing?"

Perhaps I did tailor the family news a bit when relaying it to
Aranka. Shortly after we moved to Oakland, Bob and Bert split
off from the Gladstein firm, having quarreled with the partners
over the large fees extracted from trade union clients—a rapac-
ity, they thought, unbecoming in a law firm supposedly dedicated to revolutionary goals. I wrote to tell Aranka about this
development: "Bob's left the Gladstein firm because they were
making too much money."

Later, when we decided to move from Jean Street to North
Oakland, on the fringes of the black ghetto, so the children
could go to a mixed school and have black playmates, I wrote:
"We've sold the Jean Street house. We hated to leave, it was
such a pretty little house, but the neighborhood was too good."

Poor Aranka! She never failed to rise to the bait and would
respond with long wails: "Decca, how can you do this to me?" I
can see now that I was rather beastly to her. Her own life had
been one of unremitting struggle against fierce odds, clawing
her way up in the dog-eat-dog New York millinery industry to
achieve the height of her ambition, her own beautiful hat shop,
Madame Aranka's on Park Avenue. And now, after a lifetime
of upward striving crowned by her son's graduation from Harvard Law School, to be saddled with this preposterous daughter-
in-law! I must have appeared to her as the wrecker of all her
dreams and hopes for the adored Bob. Once, when I was showing her some photographs of Chatsworth, Debo's vast domain,
she turned on me in exasperation: "So why couldn't *you* marry
a duke like your sister?" "But, Aranka, then I should never

have met you," I said, laughing. Which, I surmised, was the unspoken wish behind her outburst.

Yet after long years we became firm friends and grew to love one another dearly. Gradually I came to value and admire her boundless, restless vitality, the extra spark of life that was one of her most attractive qualities, and gradually she became reconciled to me. She even dimly began to see the joke of herself through my eyes. Once, in New York, Bob had gone to fetch some delicatessen for a party we were having in her apartment. Opening up the package of cold cuts, she exclaimed, "This he sold you for three dollars a pound? You should take it back and throw it at his head!" Thereafter, whenever we bought food I would say, "Aranka, shall we nip back to the store and throw this at his head?" And far from minding, she would let out an appreciative giggle.

As FOR MY OWN FAMILY, relations even with those with whom I was on speakers, tenuous at best, had gone downhill as a result of an episode that occurred in 1945. One day in the spring of that year, during my tenure as financial director, a curious document arrived for me, parchment done up in red ribbons and sealing wax, which to my astonishment proved to establish my title to a one-sixth share of Inch Kenneth, a tiny island off the coast of Mull in the Inner Hebrides, which had been my parents' home since 1939. I had never seen Inch Kenneth, acquired by my father two years after I had run away from home. My mother told me the circumstances of its purchase. Apparently Farve was sitting in his club when he overheard one venerable codger ask another, "I say, dear boy, do you know anybody who wants to buy an island?" "I do," said my father, shattering tradition by breaking into their conversation. Shortly thereafter he sold Swinbrook and moved the family up to Inch Kenneth.

How did I come by one-sixth of it? My father, I knew, had taken pains to cut me out of his will, each clause of which ended with the phrase "except Jessica." He had deeded Inch Kenneth to my only brother, Tom, on the assumption that Tom would outlive him, a common dodge by the English rich to escape death duties. Tom had been killed in the war, leaving no heirs.

The document was accompanied by a letter from my father's solicitors, who intimated there had been some mistake which they were sure I would wish to rectify by signing over the power of attorney to my parents. After some quick research in the law library, Bob unraveled the tortuous legal situation. Under English law, the property would, on Tom's death, have reverted to my father, but under Salic law, which obtains in Scotland, it passed to us sisters as "co-parceners." I shuddered delightedly to think of the fate of the odious solicitors, arch-enemies since the time they had threatened Esmond with imprisonment, for overlooking this legal quirk when drawing up the deed of gift to Tom. In this country, said Bob, their appalling error in conveyancing would have them nailed to the wall for malpractice; "but I expect your father just gave them a good caning."

Having established that I was indeed the owner of a share of the familial estate, we discussed how best to use this windfall to advance the cause of World Revolution. My motives were not unmixed with baser considerations; here was a heaven-sent opportunity to perpetrate a tease of epic proportions on my father. Should we deed my share to the Soviet Union for a naval base?

A more practical idea occurred. The founding convention of the United Nations was then under way in San Francisco. Among the worldwide assemblage of journalists who had flocked to cover the proceedings was Claud Cockburn, representing the London *Daily Worker.* We would make over my share to him, as a gift to the Communist Party of Great Britain.

Claud was an almost legendary figure of the Left whom Esmond and I had known in London before the war. In the early thirties he founded and wrote a mimeographed political muckraking journal called *The Week,* which, in the period immediately preceding the war, had become extraordinarily influential. *The Week* was packed with riveting inside stories garnered from undercover sources throughout Europe—at one time Claud's principal informant in Berlin (his Deep Throat, so to speak) was the secretary of Herr von Papen, a member of Hitler's cabinet. Claud had coined the phrase "Cliveden Set" to describe the powerful clique of Nazi appeasers whose frequent meeting place was Cliveden, Lady Astor's house; the sobriquet first appeared in *The Week* and subsequently became a catchword used in the English and American press, from the *Daily Express* to *Time* magazine.

A man of great energy, wit, and imagination, Claud was obviously the perfect emissary for us. We unfolded the scheme to him over drinks at the Palace Hotel's Happy Valley bar, a favorite hangout for journalists covering the convention. Claud seemed delighted with the idea, so we amended the document to give him power of attorney and had it all duly sealed at the British consulate, expecting that as soon as he returned to London we should be inundated with praise and gratitude by the English comrades.

It did not work out that way. Months went by and we heard nothing; my repeated letters to Claud brought no reply. Eventually I got fed up and revoked his power of attorney. Only years later, in 1960, did I learn what had transpired, when I read Claud's version of the episode in an article in *Punch* entitled "Island Fling: A Souvenir of the Mitford Country." Describing my proposal for disposition of my inheritance, he wrote:

She thought that it would be nice indeed for the Communists to have a few square healthy, heathery miles of a Scottish island to disport and relax in, a kind of miniature Caledonian Sochi.

She had, however, a light in her eye. And when she said, not once but again and again, that of course it was a *very small* island, and a bit of it was occupied by a house where—I understood—her parents liked to retire and relax occasionally, I had rather more than a suspicion that she had in mind something a little more spicy than just the welfare of ozone-starved Communists. What could possibly be more delightful to this lifelong enemy of the grown-ups than the mental picture—however unrealistic—of a horde of unbridled Reds cavorting Marxistically on the beaches, rattling the windows of "the Big House" with nightly renderings of "Hurrah for the Bolshie Boys" and the "Internationale"?

Knowing the Communist Party of Great Britain possibly rather better than did Mrs. Treuhaft, I doubted whether this picture would ever really get painted. . . . The Communist leadership, as I had vaguely surmised, was not enthusiastic. Peering into the mouth of the bizarre gift-horse, these men asked "What in hell does anyone think we can do with a small little bit of a desolate island somewhere off the coast of Scotland?"

Eventually my father summoned Claud to tea at the House of Lords. Arriving there, he was approached by a policeman on duty:

"Lord Redesdale's waiting for you. Seems a bit nervous. Asked me to keep the two of you in view all the time."

"Why on earth?" I asked.

"Never know with Bolshies," said the policeman, "thinks you're going to bomb him or do him with an ice-pick, I shouldn't wonder."

Claud, alas, proved to be a most unsatisfactory envoy. According to his account, he ended up in virtual accord with my father:

Lord Redesdale said, "You do realize it's a *very small* island, don't you, Mr. Cockburn? I mean I don't know that any of us—I mean we and the Communists—would be very *happy* in the circumstances." When I assured him that on this point the Communist Party saw eye to eye with him he sighed in almost incredulous relief.

My sisters were deeply annoyed by this caper, but Muv took it with her customary equanimity. "I see you want to give your share to the Communist Party," she had written. "We must get in touch with the editor of the Daily Worker."

In all the years since I had left England she had kept up a steady, although often one-sided, correspondence, writing at least once a week with news of the weather, the births, marriages, and deaths of cousins, family friends, cows, and horses. She scrupulously avoided any mention of politics—just as well, for had I known the extent of her conversion to the Führer's cause I might never have been able to bring myself to speak to her again.

Years later, Nancy gave me an extraordinary account of a row she had with Muv while staying at Inch Kenneth in 1939. They heard on the wireless that war had been declared, and Nancy told Muv that she would have to return to London immediately, as she had signed up for war work. On the drive across Mull in Muv's car, Nancy, half thinking out loud, murmured some derogatory comment about Hitler; I believe the word "fiendish" was used. Muv stopped the car and said furiously, "Take that back or get out and walk!" "Which did you do?" I asked Nancy. "Well, darling, you know it's about twelve miles to the ferry dock and I had masses of luggage. I couldn't very well walk, so I took it back."

Every Christmas and birthday, parcels would arrive from Muv for the children—presents that took me back to my own childhood: nineteenth-century books by Mrs. Molesworth, E. Nesbit, Charlotte M. Yonge, lumpy hand-knit jerseys, old-fashioned card games like Old Maid and Happy Families. These were objects of great fascination to Dinky, though a far cry from the magnificent electric trains, elegant bride dolls, and suits from Best's that Aranka lavished on her grandchildren.

By Christmas of 1947, Dinky had learned to write and laboriously composed her own thank-you letter: "Dear Granny Muv, Thank you for the lovely book. I wish you would come to see us in Oakland one day." To my profound consternation, a telegram arrived the following week: "Have accepted Dinky's invitation. Arriving San Francisco in a fortnight." This intelligence threw me into a strange turmoil. In the nine years since I had seen Muv, she had receded further and further into the background of my life and thoughts, out of sight and almost out of mind; it would be like seeing a phantom suddenly materialized out of the dim past. I was at once immensely excited at the thought, pleased and touched that she would make the long, expensive journey, and deeply apprehensive that the visit would be a disastrous failure. How would she get on with Bob? And the children?

For the next two weeks I was in a state of high nerves. I remembered that as a putative Communist aged fifteen, bursting with new ideas just acquired from reading Party tracts, I had taxed Muv with being an Enemy of the Working Class.

"I'm *not* an enemy of the working class!" she had retorted. "I think some of them are perfectly sweet." I could almost see the visions of perfectly sweet nannies, grooms, gamekeepers that the phrase must have conjured up in her mind.

But the Party had a prohibition against personal or political relationships with enemies of the working class. I sought out the chairman of the East Bay Party to tell him that one was coming to visit us; would I risk expulsion? He replied dryly that the prohibition did not apply to one's immediate family: "If it did, many comrades would never see their parents."

On the half-dreaded, half-longed-for day of Muv's arrival, we dressed up the children in all their Aranka finery and set off for the airport. Should I even recognize her after all this time? I wondered. But I need not have worried. She tottered down the ramp in a state of exhaustion, having flown direct from London (in those days a fifty-hour journey), and we gazed at each other over the long years of separation. In the car we became tongue-tied, and drove for miles in a sort of embarrassed silence, finally broken by Dinky, who, wishing to get right to the nub of family relationships, asked solemnly, "Granny Muv, when are you going to scold Decca for running away?" This effectively broke the ice and set us all to shrieking with laughter.

Actually, it was not an inappropriate question; I myself had wondered to what extent old antagonisms would be revived. Would our domestic arrangements, our ceaseless political work, our odd social life evoke the stony, implacable disapproval I remembered so well from childhood? But it soon became apparent that Muv's mission to Oakland was one of unalloyed reconciliation, that she had come with the purpose of making friends at all costs. It was during this visit that she began to exhibit that impartial loyalty to all her children that was to become a salient characteristic of her old age.

She was a marvelous and accommodating guest, praised everything ("Clever Little D., to make such a lovely meat loaf!"), relished the unfamiliar delicacies such as hamburgers and waffles prepared by Bob, was completely uncritical of the children, wild and unmannered though they doubtless seemed to her.

The language barrier gave a little trouble here; shopping in the Safeway, Dinky was shouting in her Californian accent, "Penny! I want a penny!" "Oh—*panier,*" said Muv, pointing at the shopping carts. "She wants one of those little baskets."

Appointing himself Tour Leader, Bob asked Muv what she would most like to see in California. Her requests were modest: she wanted to visit a supermarket, a women's club, and a funeral parlor—*The Loved One* had just come out, and she was eager to see the curiosities described by Evelyn Waugh. The women's club was beyond our capacity, but we managed the supermarket and funeral parlor, both of which she found fascinating. She immediately sat down and wrote a letter to *The Times* extolling the supermarket system of self-service: "So sensible and practical, I thought." When a few years later the supermarket invaded England, she triumphantly claimed credit in a letter to me:

"There actually are a lot of super markets now in London (I wrote to the *Times* ages ago to describe the one in Oakland & say why don't we have them here) so now there are a lot, & a great success I think with those clever little *paniers.*"

To Bob, her directness and lack of guile were baffling and a constant source of wonder. I had five hundred pounds in my account at Drummonds, left to me out of Tom's estate, a small fortune which we could not lay hands on because of the English currency restrictions. When I learned that Muv was coming to stay with us, I wrote to ask her to find out if there might be some way to get the money out. She reported that she had gone to see the manager of Drummonds, who explained that while the law was quite strict on this point, exceptions could be made. Was there any special reason, he asked, why the money was needed—for the children's education, perhaps, or because of illness in the family? "I said yes," Muv told us, "I think there *is* a special reason; I expect my daughter wants to give the money to the Communist Party." The manager replied that he thought the Exchequer would take a dim view.

We laughed through our tears, but it was impossible for me to convince Bob that this was not, as he supposed, her crafty way of paying me back for past transgressions like the Inch Kenneth affair. She couldn't be that naïve, he insisted. I on the other hand knew that she was incapable of dissembling, and had merely told the Drummonds manager what she believed to be the fact.

Bob was also constantly thrown off balance by what he called the "non-Jewish-motherishness" of Muv. "Why are you wearing those hideous spectacles, Little D.?" she asked one day. "Because I can't see without them." "Oh, yes; I remember you never could see much as a child," said Muv vaguely, sending Bob into fits of laughter.

Never once did she cast aspersions on our political views or on the company we kept; she seemed to take it all in stride as just the way we happened to choose to live. Bob told her about the then imminent passage of the Mundt-Nixon Communist registration bill; should it pass, he said, there was a real likelihood that we would all be hauled off to prison or concentration camp. "Oh, dear, yes, I suppose you will," she said imperturbably. "What a pity. But of course I'm quite accustomed to my children going to prison." (Bob had tried this out on Aranka during her last visit, hoping to extract a cash contribution for the fight against the bill, but had only succeeded in triggering one of her emotional outbursts: "Ai! Ai! How can you do this to me?")

By common consent, Muv and I avoided certain subjects, particularly that of Boud, as both too potentially contentious and too painful to discuss. On the day that war was declared, Boud, who was staying in Munich, had shot herself in the head with a gun she had bought for the purpose. For months she had been near death in a German hospital. Eventually Hitler had arranged for her transportation to England in a private train. Thereafter my mother had devoted her life to looking after Boud, who, although she recovered from the bullet wound, had become strange and childish. This much I knew from my sisters' letters; Nancy had written saying that Boud herself half realized her condition. "Once she asked me do you think I'm mad? I said yes of course darling Bonehead but then you always were." I did not seek to find out more from Muv. When she left, she asked if I had any messages for Boud; I merely replied that I should like to send my love.

MY FONDNESS for Muv, and my appreciation of her remarkable qualities, dated from this visit to Oakland. Years later, in 1971, Nancy and I exchanged some letters in which we discussed and sought to analyze our respective relationships with "that enigmatical, generous, great-minded matriarchal figure . . . with the philosophical detachment of a mariner," as Jim Lees-Milne had described her. Unaccustomed though both Nancy and I were to shared introspection, I think we each tried to be as candid and explicit as we knew how.

"All very well for Jim," I wrote to Nancy, "but who wants to be brought up by a mariner? And, at that, a fairly ancient mariner by the time I came along. I think one trouble is that people sometimes get militantly nasty in middle age (oh dear, my age now) which was the time of her life when I was growing up," and I cited my unsuccessful attempt to get Muv to let me attend the grammar school science courses when I was twelve. "Naturally I didn't tell *you* about it, Susan,"* I wrote, "because whenever one told you one's deepest ambitions it was only to be TEASED UNMERCIFULLY and laughed off the face of the earth, do admit.

"But then after re-getting to know Muv in 1948, I became immensely fond of her, really rather adored her. Therefore in my memory she turns into two people; although I'm sure she didn't really change much, because people don't except for a certain mellowing with the onset of old age. More likely we did. Or the balance of power changed once one had flown the coop, so one met on totally different terms."

Nancy, who was contemplating writing her own memoirs (she never did, alas, for she was already suffering from the illness that killed her two years later), wrote back: "It is probably we who changed & not her there's nothing so awful as teen aged girls. Didn't know abt. scientific interests—yours—one thought of them as literary. Susan you might have invented the Bomb what a wild tease—still there's always the Mitford to help suffering humanity.

"I shall say what an unsatisfactory relationship I had with Muv. I had the greatest possible respect for her; I liked her company; but I never loved her, for the evident reason that she never loved me. I was never hugged and kissed by her as a small child—indeed I saw very little of her.

"Certainly Debo always loved her & Diana did in old age but not when we first grew up. She was very cold & surly with me. I don't reproach her for it people have a perfect right to

* To the confusion of acquaintances, Nancy and I called each other Susan.

dislike their children but it is a fact I think I must mention. If you write memoirs at all they must throw some light on the personality of the writer."

During Muv's stay in Oakland, both she and Aranka, in New York, expressed a desire to meet. Though dubious as to the wisdom of bringing two such wildly disparate characters together, I was nonetheless intrigued by the situation-comedy possibilities their meeting might offer. I was put in mind of one of Dink's skip-rope chants: "My mother, your mother lives across the bay, / Every night they have a fight and this is what they say: / Ickabacker soda cracker, Ickabacker boo. / Ickabacker soda cracker out goes *y-o-u*." I yielded to their insistence and arranged for Muv to spend a day with Aranka during a stopover in New York on her return journey. If this worked out well, I said to Bob, I would make our fortune by opening a West Coast–East Coast Mother-in-law Coordinating Bureau, charging steep fees for arranging transcontinental encounters between unlikely in-laws.

The meeting was a huge success. We got rave reviews from both participants. Aranka wrote in her idiosyncratic spelling, "Your mother is a wonderfull person, a real laddy, so greatfull for everything, I loved her." And Muv: "Mme. Aranka was *too* kind, she gave me the most beautiful hat it will be my summer joy."

A few years later an even stranger bond was formed between Aranka and Nancy. Each year Aranka went to Paris for the fashion shows, where she bought hats and studied styles for Madame Aranka's Exclusive Clientele. She always went to see Nancy on these occasions, and would report to us on her next visit to Oakland. "I went to tea with Nancy. She is so beautiful, so chic, so elegant—she is dressed by Dior"—wrinkling her nose critically in my direction. "Well, Aranka, next time you see her, tell her I'm dressed by J. C. Penney."

Nancy in turn reported on her encounters with Aranka—who was not always quite recognizable, to me, from the letters. Thus shortly after their first meeting, in 1954: "Aranka. Well I absolutely love her, she is a *dear*. Also she's the only person who gives me news of you, so I eat her up whenever she comes. She simply thinks the world of you, she says you're so wonderful that I thought you *must have altered considerably*."

More typical was her letter just after the Mexican earthquake of 1957. Dinky, aged sixteen, had gone to stay with a Mexican family for the summer. Early one Sunday morning a friend telephoned to say she had just heard on the radio that Mexico City had been razed by an earthquake. Some very nasty moments followed for us—we had no way of reaching Dinky—until the telephone rang and the operator announced a call from Mexico City, person-to-person for Alice Oakie. Frugal Dinky! It was, of course, her way of informing us without paying for the call that "All is O.K." We breathed again.

Aranka was on her annual buying trip to Paris, and I got a letter from Nancy: "I saw my publisher yesterday, Mr. Cass Canfield. I said is Cass short for Cassowary but no, Cass is his name. Really, Americans!

"As for Aranka, she might be called *Cass*andra, I never knew such an old gloom-pot. She began about how Dinky was certain to have been killed in the earth quake so I said people like us are *never killed in earth quakes* & furthermore only 29 people were, all non-U. I envy her the fun of it. Next day I got a letter from Muv saying she'd slept through it (hard cheese) so I reassured Cassandra on that point. Then there was talk about Russia & I said 'You must realize that to us in Europe Russia & America seem exactly the same: two enormous countries where you can't get servants & where everything in the shops is machine-made.' She said I'd got it all wrong & her customers have gracious lives like anything."

After Muv's visit we had but one other envoy from my family: Debo, who to my surprise and joy came over for a Honnish reunion in 1950. We relived the ploys of childhood— all that we really now had in common. We were back in the Hons' Cupboard, our secret meeting place at Swinbrook, talking our secret language. Nancy, we both agreed, had completely falsified the origins of the Society of Hons in her novel *The Pursuit of Love,* in which she said Hons derived from us being Honourables; in fact, it was Honnish for Hen, the sweet chickens we used to keep. As a child, Debo had spent hours in the chicken house learning to copy the exact expression on a hen's face while laying an egg (one of earnest, pained concentration), and she did this for Bob and the children. "Hen, do show Bob your deformed thumb," I urged and she did; since she had sucked until the age of nine, one thumb is half an inch shorter than the other. We sang the Deformed Thumb song to Bob, to the tune of "You're Going to Lose Your Girl," a popular song of the thirties: "You're going to lose your thumb / You're going to lose your thumb / And when it's gone / It won't come back, / They never do come back. / You can't have your thumb and eat it / You're going to lose your thumb."

It is said that all the world loves a lord; what I had not realized is that this goes double for duchesses, even the world of Oakland Communists. The comrades craved to meet Debo, and they did; a great dinner was given in her honor—that is, great by our standards—to which at least twenty flocked. We introduced them CP fashion, in which one indicates the area of a person's political work: "This is Andy Johnson, he's active in the Youth Movement. Phyllis Mander, active in the Peace Committee. Dr. Pierson, active in the CRC," and so on. It was rather a rum party; the locals seemed oddly constrained, overawed by and deferential to the guest of honor. There was one lively moment when Bob, trying to get a bit of conversation going, said, "Debo, when you arrive in New York you'll probably be besieged by reporters asking what you think of American men. What are you going to say?" "Tell 'em we're iron-hearted!" shouted a Negro comrade, thumping a surgical cast he was wearing on his chest, which produced a tremendous clang and caused Debo to jump violently.

That Christmas she sent us a card with an official-looking photograph of herself and Andrew, dressed in their ducal robes as for a coronation, garlanded with orders, chains, jewels, staring stonily ahead. Under the photo she had written: "Andrew & me being active."

CHAPTER 8

Mississippi

BY EARLY 1951, each mail was bringing an extraordinary assortment of mimeographed directives, all sent airmail, many special delivery, all marked "Rush!" from the CRC national office in New York, for Clarence Rossman was now working there as organizational director. Sometimes, if I happened to be in a rush myself, I would stuff his letters into the wastepaper basket unopened, say quietly to myself, "Rush!" and rush.

One day things were slow at the office and I was desultorily opening the familiar envelopes and glancing through the contents: *"Absolutely essential* you get full page ads in all local papers calling for letters to Mississippi Governor Fielding Wright demanding reprieve for Willie McGee. . . . *Even more essential* you send your quota of $10,000 [dashed in by hand] to the National office to cover expenses of legal defense and mass mailings." I skipped on through *"Vitally important* you get your local city council on record against this legal lynching . . . resolutions from Young Democrats and Young Republicans condemning this flagrant frame-up." Somewhere buried away were the words: *"Imperative* you send your full quota of 4 [written in] women on the White Women's Delegation to Mississippi." Followed the time and place where the delegation would forgather—March 10 at an address in St. Louis, Missouri.

Madman Rossman had scored again. He knew very well that we could not afford the full-page ads; that no local city council was going to put this case on its agenda; that no Young Democrats or, *a fortiori* (as Clarence himself might have said), Young Republicans would bestir themselves over this issue; he also knew that no ten thousand dollars for the national office would be forthcoming. But a White Women's Delegation sounded to me like a marvelous idea. If four were expected from Oakland, there would be scores or hundreds from such Party strongholds as New York, Chicago, Los Angeles, and our accomplishments could be great. I was determined to be part of this great conclave.

Willie McGee, a thirty-six-year-old black truckdriver in Laurel, Mississippi, had been convicted of raping a white woman despite persuasive evidence that his accuser had long been his mistress. He had been in prison, under sentence of death, for more than five years. The court transcript and eye-witness accounts of the three trials, together with stories from the local Mississippi press, made sickening reading; at the first trial, which lasted less than a day, the jury had taken two and a half minutes to reach a verdict. It was obvious that a ritual race murder was in the offing. At the heart of the case was the fact that no white had ever been condemned to death for rape in the Deep South, while in the past four decades fifty-one blacks had been executed for this offense.

The CRC had entered the case at the appellate level, after the first trial. Thanks to the skillful work of Bella Abzug of New York and John Coe of Florida, members of the CRC legal panel, there had been two reversals of the guilty verdict and new trials granted. After McGee was found guilty in the third trial, all legal remedies had been exhausted, the only remaining hope being executive clemency. Under the direction of the Party and the CRC, the campaign to save McGee's life had reached worldwide proportions. *Political Affairs,* theoretical journal of the Party, reported "protests of millions in the Soviet Union, the People's Republic of China, the Peoples' Democracies and the people's movements in the capitalist and colonial countries . . . resolutions from the 600,000 strong London Trades Council and the Caribbean Labor Congress." Alas, as was so often the case, the response from London to Peking outshone our home-grown efforts; yet considering the inclement political climate, these were considerable.

The McGee case had been designated a "national concentration" by the Party, which meant that Party clubs everywhere, in trade unions, neighborhoods, professions, would swing behind it in a style of work dating from the days of Sacco and Vanzetti and the Scottsboro case. Tirelessly we labored, in keeping with United Front strategy, to "broaden" the campaign, to enlist support of trade unions, liberals, churches, the community at large. The *Peoples World* meticulously recorded every action, its job as Party newspaper to inform, encourage, exhort, stimulate. It reported daily on endeavors and developments, some on a minuscule scale: "200 protest postcards signed . . ." "$8 collected for telegrams . . ." "35 signatures gathered outside Sears . . ." "24 graduate students and junior faculty members at U.C. send a telegram to Governor Wright . . ." And some of more substantial dimensions: "Marine Cooks & Sewards distribute 10,000 leaflets . . ." "day of prayer set by Interdenominational Ministerial Alliance . . ." "strong protest from African Methodist Episcopal Bishops' Council . . ." "Los Angeles CIO urges stepped-up campaign . . ." "National CIO appeals to Governor Fielding Wright . . ." "six state legislators agree to wire Truman . . ." "Albert Einstein, Josephine Baker, pledge support . . ."

I did my part—writing leaflets and resolutions—fairly mechanically, believing in the justice of the cause yet finding it impossible to think myself into the actual situation of blacks in Mississippi; the daily horror of their lives was too far removed from any experience of my own to permit of taking it all in, except in an abstract fashion. The realities of Mississippi began to come alive for me when Willie McGee's wife, Rosalee, arrived in Oakland on a national speaking tour that had been organized by the CRC. She was accompanied by CRC national director William L. Patterson's wife, Louise Patterson, herself an important figure in the Party's black leadership and veteran organizer in the International Labor Defense. I went to meet them at the airport with Mrs. Lofton, powerful church sister of the Mount Zion Baptist Church, deep in the Oakland ghetto. A member of the CRC executive board, Mrs. Lofton ran her church, its huge congregation of over two thousand, its board of deacons, and its minister with an iron hand, and had swung them behind many a CRC fight. Much later, Louise giggled affectionately at her recollection of this, our first meeting: "There you were, looking so English and proper in your tweed skirt, and Mrs. Lofton in her pink satin toque and matching high-heeled shoes. I thought to myself: What an odd pair they are!"

Rosalee McGee, a diminutive twenty-eight-year-old woman who looked much older, had never before been out of Mississippi. On the first lap of her plane journey, from Jackson to New York, many hours in those pre-jet days, she had forgotten to bring the lunch that neighbors had packed for her, and arrived famished. Stewardesses had solicitously offered meals, which she refused, having no idea they were free.

From her account of life in Laurel, and the genesis of the rape charge against her husband, one began to see the macabre contours of oppression in the Deep South. If McGee was executed, she said, he would be the third man in her family to die violently at the hands of white Mississippi. "I saw my nephew lynched by six white hoodlums, and my first cousin was put to death in the electric chair."

Mrs. Hawkins, the white accuser, had pursued McGee relentlessly for years, said Mrs. McGee. "People who don't know the South don't know what would have happened to Willie if he told her no. Down South, you tell a woman like that no, and she'll cry rape anyway. So what else could Willie do? That's why I never got angry at Willie." Eventually, after years of acquiescence to Mrs. Hawkins, McGee did decide to break off the affair. It was at this point that she pressed the rape charge. According to her testimony at the trial, McGee had come into her bedroom in the middle of the night; she did not cry out, she said, for fear of waking her husband and baby, who were sleeping in the next room.

All court appeals had been exhausted. The year before, Clarence himself had gone to Jackson with a delegation in an effort to persuade the governor to grant executive clemency. Alone in his hotel room, he was ambushed and severely beaten by five men, who had gained access by calling out, "Western Union." A friend of ours in San Francisco had telephoned that evening, sobbing bitterly as she spoke: "Clarence is dying in Jackson." He was in the hospital with a fractured skull, and in terrible danger of lynch mobs gathering outside, she said; we should try to reach the governor to demand his safe conduct out of the state.

Frantically I started telephoning, and to my astonishment soon heard the voice of Governor Wright at the other end. "We don't know nothin' about it, ma'am," he drawled. "But our folks down here sure don't 'preciate outsiders meddlin' in our affairs." Actually, Clarence had escaped without serious injury; he returned radiating his usual bouncing self-confidence: "I pulled over the chair like *this,* grabbed the lamp like *this,* and really whammed them. They were cops, though, make no mistake about it. Probably sent by the governor." In the myth-bound mind of the South, the sanctity of white womanhood, nothing less, was at stake in Jackson. Any man, black or white, who dared to intercede for the life of Willie McGee would be fair game for the local Klansmen. Some of that sanctity, the CRC reasoned, might rub off on us, white women from the North, perhaps protect us from physical assault. "Although, Dec, don't be too surprised if them Ku Kluxers give you a whupping," Buddy Green sympathetically suggested. And I still have Virginia Durr's letter, in which she wrote in her nonstop, unpunctuated style: "Now honey you be careful they'll likely tar and feather you and run you out of town on a rail." This unpleasant fate, she said, had almost overtaken a librarian friend of hers in a small Southern town who had permitted blacks to use the library facilities.

These warnings only whetted my desire to go, to escape from the routine of mass mailings, leaflet distributions, and protest meetings, into the very stronghold of the enemy. Perhaps people generally act from a mixture of motives, and it is hard to sort out mine at this distance in time. For one thing, I did feel Clarence had hit on the only scheme that might have some remote chance of saving McGee's life: to take the case directly to the people of the state that sought to execute him. But I should admit I also hoped it would be a thrilling adventure (a thought it would have been injudicious to communicate to the comrades, as the Party was squarely opposed to "adventurism" as a manifestation of "left-wing infantilism"), let alone a welcome breather from diapers and housework. Bob, of course, understood immediately, for like me he got positive pleasure out of crossing swords with the Class Enemy. He readily agreed that I should take our car, and he would assume the onerous job of lone coper with house and children for the duration of the expedition.

It was not hard to recruit three others to make up our quota of four. They were Evie Frieden, a rollicking, jolly warehouse worker; an absolutely silent young woman of nonexistent personality known as the Youth Comrade; and Rita Baxter, dour top-rank Party leadership cadre. They volunteered, despite a certain amount of grumbling from their husbands, at an Oakland McGee protest meeting. In fact, it was the husbands who saw themselves as the real sacrificers. Their complaints, at first suitably muted, grew louder as the journey progressed. A mere report on mechanical difficulties with the car—"We are in Needles, California, having our valves ground" was the simple postcard I had dispatched—brought anguished phone calls from our Menfolk at home. Rita was a great one for the Menfolk at home. On the first night out she whimpered more than once about her darling Geordie and the boys, only to be brought sharply to book by me. We were all in the same boat, I pointed out, had left our husbands and small children, but we had come of our own accord, so what was the use of complaining?

Evie and I chatted about all sorts of trivia as we drove. It was, after all, in those days a tiresome five-day journey to our first destination, St. Louis, where we were to meet the rest of the Women's Delegation. "Clarence will probably be there in a wig and dirndl," I suggested hopefully. "Knowing him, he wouldn't miss this for anything." Rita glared disapprovingly into the rear-view mirror. The Youth Comrade said not a word.

None of us knew each other especially well. I had run across the others from time to time at meetings. Evie occasionally volunteered to come down to the CRC office to help on emergency mailings or leaflet distributions. She had always seemed to me to be an interesting one, with her enthusiastic and dashing way of doing things, her distinctive laugh somewhere between a giggle and a guffaw. I was somewhat leery of Rita. As county ed. director she sometimes toured the clubs to give an Educational on some topic of current interest. She would go on interminably, in a creaking monotone. As the goal of Educationals was to link theory with practice, her customary peroration was: "So, Comrades, we must soberly estimate the contradictions flowing from the situation, mobilize our forces, and mount a campaign, however limited." I hated "however limited"; however vast was more to my liking. The Youth Comrade seemed a cipher. First impressions turned out, as they often do, to be pretty accurate.

"I hear Bert and his wife have broken up," Evie said as she settled comfortably down into her seat. "Do tell. Is there another man?"

"Comrades, I don't think we should gossip about *other* comrades on this trip," came the Voice of Doom from the back seat. Not that of the Youth Comrade, who was possibly suffering from *mal d'auto*.

Evie and I groaned the groan of the well-advised, and I tried another tack. "There's a frightfully nice Russian comrade in our branch," I started telling Evie. "Oh, he is sweet. He might even be a Comintern agent, because his reasons for leaving Russia are obscure, to say the least."

Great sniffs were emanating from the back seat. I recklessly continued: "He really is a brave and devoted one. During the election campaign one of the comrades complained that every time she advocated the Progressive Party in her precinct, people looked at her as though she was a 'Russian with a beard.' Naturally, all eyes turned to blissful George Bratoff. He had a lovely beard, looked just like Lenin. But the dear thing! Next meeting, he showed up completely shaved, a different person, just so he could do better precinct work."

The sniffs turned into verbal complaints. "I regard this whole discourse as an attack on our Foreign Born comrades."

"*Attack!* How could you! I'm most terrifically fond of George; in fact, he is my favorite thing. Oh, all right, we'll change the subject."

Evie started telling some dirty stories her husband had heard on his job, but these also were put down as unsuitable topics in view of the high purpose of our delegation.

It was not until the third day out that I blew up. Rita had just reproved me for using the term "cracker," which she considered an unacceptable way of referring to the exploited masses of poor white tenant farmers, sharecroppers, and other victims of the absentee landlords and their Wall Street partners in infamy. She was drawing breath for the purpose, no doubt, of delivering a lecture on the historic task before our Party, that of aiding in the building of a United Front between the poor Southern whites and their natural allies the Negro people; but I had had about enough, and said so loudly. Evie backed me up, the Youth Comrade's eyes popped in a scared way, and the fight was on.

Evie and I felt right was on our side. All of us believed in the political importance of our mission, were anguished over the suffering of Willie McGee and his young wife, had thought long and hard about what we could accomplish in Mississippi, where we knew we might face certain dangers. There was nothing in the nature of a "lark" about the undertaking. Nevertheless, Rita's insistence on an atmosphere of unremitting reverence and gloom did cast a certain unnecessary pall.

No sooner did we forcefully point this out to Rita than she began to see the point, for she was fundamentally a good-hearted creature. She even went so far as to be self-critical for setting herself up as chief censor of our conversation. I in turn apologized for rounding on her when she was nattering on about how much she missed her family, and we made up.

I often speculated on what might have become of Rita had her life taken a different course. She was an extremely intelligent, well-educated woman of great drive, little humor, and modest appearance. She seemed driven by an overriding need to sublimate something, somewhere. At first blush one might have dismissed her as one who could as easily have become a fanatic Catholic, or a hopeless alcoholic, as a Party member; one whose inner compulsions might as well, given the opportunity, have taken any one of a number of erratic paths. For she was in a sense one of those Party caricatures, a worshipper of the Line, starry-eyed idealizer of the leadership, stern frowner upon deviationists. Had the Party forged the mold into which a once flexible, pliant Rita had eventually jelled? Or was it the other way around—was she drawn to the Party, had she become one of its devoted handmaidens, *because* of a streak of Original Rigidity handed down through the ages from Puritan forebears?

To write her off—and many like her—as one with a neurotic need to "believe" in something, to be led, to feel important and superior among her peers, would be too simple, for although there was an element of this in Rita's personality, it was not, of course, the whole of it. If the Party had fed this quality of compulsiveness in her, it had also given her a purpose in life, had opened up the way for her to become an effective person in her own right, had provided her with a philosophy and direction towards progress in which she could feel at one with vast humanity. In other words, had it not been for the Party, Rita might well have been far more impossible than she actually was.

Evie, no less ardent in her devotion to the Party, was in all other ways the complete opposite of Rita. She had grown up in

Chicago, where her Hungarian-Jewish immigrant parents had long been rank-and-filers in the radical movement. She had once thought of becoming a teacher. She had not finished college, but both she and her husband, Mike, who had completed a year of law school, in response to the Party's call willingly abandoned their ambitions for professional careers in favor of factory jobs. As Communists, they were prepared to accept the Party's view that they could better carry out its vanguard role by working in a warehouse or on the assembly line—Basic Industry, we called it. It would never have occurred to them to regard this as a "sacrifice"; it was natural for them to put the Party's needs first in all aspects of their lives.

Evie infused everything she did with her own buoyant *joie de vivre* and a kind of moral toughness that I found most attractive. She hadn't an ounce of sentimentality in her make-up, which was such a mercy (there was all too much mawkishness in some Party members for my liking), but she had boundless compassion for human suffering. While Rita had, one felt, grimly steeled herself to make the dangerous journey to Mississippi as a sort of religious atonement for the myriad sins of whites against blacks, Evie approached it in a joyful spirit of comradeship with all oppressed people, as being a good and useful step to take.

We had only one other slight altercation, which ended rather sadly for Evie and me. Dead tired after a full day's driving, we broached the subject of buying a bottle of whisky to revive us. Rita expressed herself as unalterably opposed to this; it might expose us to the possibility of a police frame-up on charges of drunk driving, it might get us into all sorts of trouble. We argued the point for a good hour. Finally a compromise was reached, and feeling extremely daring, we bought the smallest bottle to be had, a half pint, which we passed around in the car. To our dismay, Rita, perhaps to show she was really a good fellow after all, downed almost all of it at a gulp.

We had no idea what would be expected of us once we were in Mississippi. We assumed that after the meeting in St. Louis we would become foot soldiers in a large army led by seasoned organizers from the higher echelons of the CRC, that our operations in the field would be mapped out for us by comrades knowledgeable in the ways of the South. Meanwhile we decided to try to mobilize support for Willie McGee along the way. Rita thought it unwise for us to proceed thus on our own initiative, unaided by directives from the national office, but she was outvoted by Evie and me, the Youth Comrade abstaining. Early in our trip, we had two hours to spare while the car was being repaired in Needles, a railroad town in the Mojave Desert. After some quick research in the yellow pages, we called on two white ministers, a black minister, the secretary of the local NAACP, the local newspaper editor. We were elated by the response; all were sympathetically interested. The ministers said they would pray for us, which was comforting, and promised to circulate petitions demanding executive clemency. We could never have accomplished as much in the Bay Area, where the noxious miasma of redbaiting that hung over the Willie McGee case would have poisoned such an effort.

I was delegated to write up reports of our doings for the *Peoples World,* which I first submitted to the others for collective criticism. Quoting the white Methodist minister who directed us to Reverend J. M. Cadell, the seventy-six-year-old black pastor of a Baptist church, I wrote: "Reverend Cadell has won the respect, the love, the sympathy of the community." Rita, ever ready to inject what she conceived of as the "correct approach to the Negro question," suggested, "I think you should say that Reverend Cadell is 'a man of tremendous stature.' " Later in our travels I noted that she invariably proposed inserting this phrase when we were reporting on conversations with blacks. I managed to resist these suggestions, fearing that our readers might suppose we had encountered an outbreak of gigantism, a dysfunction of the pituitary gland.

After Needles, we drove night and day to reach St. Louis at the appointed time. We found our way to the hall; it was locked, with a note on the door directing us to somebody's house. Arriving there, we were greeted by the local CRC chairman and a beaming Clarence, who had come down from New York to give us our marching orders. "Where are the others?" I asked. Clarence, not in the least abashed, explained there *were* no others—we four were the whole delegation, the generals and soldiers of this great nationwide call to action. Apparently no one else in this wide land had read down to the final *"Imperative"* in Clarence's directive. Nor was there any blueprint, or plan of campaign. Mississippi was pretty much uncharted territory, said Clarence. We should have to develop our plans on the spot when we arrived in Jackson, and he would do his best to get other women to join us there.

We were unlikely to find any local inhabitants who shared our political outlook. Evie had seen a recent news story giving the FBI's estimated strength of the Communist Party in various parts of the country: New York, 10,000 members; San Francisco, 5,000, and so on. For Mississippi, the report gave the disheartening figure of 1. There were to be times when we longed for that lone Mississippi comrade. Clarence, had he known his or her whereabouts, would have been prohibited from telling us for security reasons, and we never did summon the courage to inquire at FBI headquarters.

When we finally got to Jackson, we drove cautiously downtown and headed for the YWCA, which we hoped would be something of a sanctuary if trouble should threaten. Ordinarily,

I would have resisted the oppressive gentility of a YWCA, but Southern friends had told me they often found the Y to be an oasis of decency in otherwise hostile territory, a gathering place for liberals and racial "moderates." The Y director, a pleasant-faced youngish woman, greeted us with that extra degree of courtesy so often encountered in the South, and gave us two large rooms for one dollar a night apiece. We settled in to plan our next moves.

The CRC national office had conceived of the White Women's Delegation as a group large enough to organize demonstrations, picket lines, and leaflet distributions like those we had up North. But the pathetic size of our group, even if it was augmented by Clarence's promised reserves, was clearly inadequate for all this. We discarded the mass approach in favor of the next best thing: an effort to reach as many white Mississippians as possible on an individual basis with the facts of the case, an appeal to white consciences to act.

We drew up strict rules of conduct: never venture from the Y except in pairs; work from early morning until sunset but never after dark; wear hats, stockings, and white gloves at all times. Readying ourselves to work behind enemy lines, as it were, we felt the appearance of respectability was essential both for our own personal security and for the effectiveness of our work among white Southerners. So each morning we checked each other over for hats-gloves-stockings and straightness of stocking seams (a constant preoccupation in those days) before setting forth two by two on our respective rounds.

We made visits to clergymen, clubwomen, and other persons of local prominence whose names we culled from the city directory and telephone book. We buttonholed delegates to a statewide teachers' convention which by a fortunate coincidence was being held in a Jackson hotel. We did door-to-door canvassing in white neighborhoods, roughly based on tech-

niques I had learned in my old market research days, taking
random samplings of opinion in working-class, middle-class,
and upper-class territories. Each evening we reassembled at the
Y for a quick supper of black-eyed peas, grits, and other Southern delicacies, then met far into the night, comparing notes
and writing up a report of our findings.

Soon Clarence's promised reserves, some of them Southerners, began to arrive. Some stayed only a short time, but at its
height our delegation numbered eleven. The Southerners, from
Tennessee, North Carolina, and Louisiana, were a delightful
and exhilarating addition, their native accents a great asset in
gaining entrée to Jackson households.

As time wore on, some of my preconceived notions about
the white South were dispelled. Far from encountering the im-
penetrable wall of hostility I had anticipated, we found many
people willing to talk with us about the case and not a few who
ventured to express a guarded sympathy. Feelings on both sides
of the issue ran far deeper here than in California, more promising in a way than the frustrating indifference that pervaded
the "liberal" North. When the change did come, one felt, it
would come sharp and fast.

Painstakingly we tabulated the results of our survey of forty-
three white working-class families for the *Peoples World:*

Hostile	12
Listened to us but wouldn't express an opinion	8
Convinced of McGee's guilt but willing to listen	7
At first convinced of guilt but changed mind on basis of discussion	5
Convinced of his innocence but made no commitment to act	7
Pledged action: talk to neighbors, write Truman, Gov. Wright	4

The hostile twelve met us with invective, threats, and variations on the theme "They should have hanged him the day it happened." Among the four who "pledged action" we encountered some surprisingly emotional responses. One woman said, in shaken tones, "The way the Negroes have been treated is a blot upon the South. We'll all suffer for it one day." These four—slightly less than 10 percent of our meager sample—seemed to represent some hope for the future.

As to our middle-class survey, in the privacy of their homes many of the ministers, teachers, and clubwomen declared their belief in McGee's innocence; others, unwilling to go that far, nevertheless deplored a double standard of justice under which scores of black men had been executed for rape while no white had ever received the death penalty for this offense. A few even showered us with embarrassing praise for coming. More prayers than I care to remember were offered for our safety and success.

Yet there was an almost universal reluctance to take any sort of public stand, to sign a petition or write a letter to the governor. "I have to think of my husband's job"; "It would wreck my son's career"—all the familiar reasons for inaction were given, plus that hoary rationalization: "I've worked for years for Nigra rights in my own way. If I speak out on this case, it will ruin my long-range effectiveness." Or: "I'm already labeled; my position on these questions is known in the community. I would do the case more harm than good by speaking out." There were some who proclaimed their "love" for "our Nigras." One of these, a clergyman's wife, deplored the new-fangled Northern habit of addressing blacks as Mr. and Mrs. "We call them Auntie this or Uncle that—it's so much friendlier," she said. "Then how does it feel to be murdering one of your first cousins?" Evie shot back acidly.

Our sojourn at the YWCA was short-lived. Soon after we arrived the director approached me and asked if we had come

to Mississippi about the Willie McGee case. I replied that we
had. She said, "Well, you don't have to be so secretive about it."
I was somewhat taken aback, and assured her we were not
trying to be secretive; on the contrary, our whole purpose in
coming to Jackson was to talk about the case to anybody who
would listen, and that I would like to discuss it with her, too. To
my surprise, she was quite willing to chat. As a member of a
local church fellowship she worked with groups in Jackson and
elsewhere, she told me, trying to improve race relations by issuing Christian tracts about the brotherhood of man and the need
for "treatin' the Nigras more human." She often went to Laurel,
ninety miles away, to meet with colleagues in this endeavor.
Friends there told her it was pretty common knowledge that
McGee had been falsely accused; they said his relationship with
Mrs. Hawkins had been the talk of the town for years.

That afternoon Evie and I had an appointment with a Mrs.
Stevens, a civic leader who had been recommended to us as one
who had worked for many years to abolish lynching. She turned
out to be just another of those self-styled "friends of the Negro
people" who abound in the South. She informed us that she had
"put an end to lynching in Mississippi by educational means,"
thus circumventing any need for an anti-lynch law; that she
held classes in her home for "Nigra" girls, "to teach them how
to live"; that groups such as ours were doing more harm than
good by undermining the people's reliance on the courts for
justice. But in this case, Evie insisted urgently, the courts may
well be perpetrating a terrible injustice; what if McGee was
convicted on a trumped-up charge? I told Mrs. Stevens of my
conversation with the Y director, and repeated what she had
said about the McGee-Hawkins affair being common knowledge in Laurel.

Ten minutes later we were back at the Y, and the director

peremptorily summoned me into her office, apoplectic, all her Southern civility evaporated.

"I don't want you using my name any more in connection with this case!" she shouted in near frenzy. I observed that I did not even know her name.

"Well, Mrs. Stevens just called, and it seems you told her I said the case is a frame-up."

"But didn't you say that?"

"I may have, but you shouldn't have told Mrs. Stevens. She is a member of the YWCA board, and I'm likely to lose my job."

I reminded her that Willie McGee would surely lose his life if knowledgeable people like her and her Laurel friends refused to speak out, that she had already surrendered her right of free speech by allowing herself to be terrorized into silence by the hysteria surrounding the case. She kept backing away from me, repeating, "I don't want to have anything more to do with you people!" It came as no surprise when, later that day, she ordered us to move out immediately, as our rooms were "already engaged." We packed our belongings and drove around looking for a place to stay. A hotel, we decided, would be both too expensive and—in view of Clarence's experience—too dangerous. Eventually we found a ROOM FOR RENT sign on a dilapidated little house on the outskirts of Jackson. This time we decided to tell the owner in advance why we were there; apparently in this poverty-stricken part of the town the lure of five dollars a night for the room, in which we slept two to a bed, outweighed other considerations, and she took us in.

I often wondered what became of Mrs. Stevens and the Y director, what shape their lives took in later years. For despite their infuriating attitude to the McGee case and their timidity, they probably did typify a somewhat more decent than average breed of white Southerner. Ten years later, when I visited the Deep South in the wake of the Montgomery bus boycott and the sit-in movement, I found women like them who had been propelled forward by the force of black resistance and were giving positive encouragement to the student militants. But in 1951 Jackson was a veritable concentration camp of the mind in which people like Mrs. Stevens and the Y director were themselves prisoners, confined by tradition and their keepers within strict boundaries to their Christian tracts and classes for "Nigra" girls, their tiny, tentative efforts to do right as they saw it.

Mississippi's largest and most influential newspaper, the Jackson *Daily News,* furnished some insight into the source of this intimidation. We scanned the editorials, written in the folksy, down-home style of the region, for glimpses of received Klan doctrine as preached by the *News* and practiced by the Mississippi authorities:

The Negro race, unfortunately, has not thus far produced any worthwhile literature and mighty little in the way of high-class music. Their melody consists mostly of spirituals. . . .

Ruby Keeler,* announcing herself as "regional coordinator" for the NAACP, proclaims from Birmingham that she will file court proceedings in Mississippi and Alabama to compel the admission of Negroes in all graduate and professional schools. In other words, she wants to fling open the doors for the admission of Negro students. . . . The intelligent and influential Negroes of Mississippi should tell Ruby Keeler, whoever the hell she is, to stay away from our state and not try to meddle in racial relations. Mississippi is still Mississippi. . . .

---

* A black NAACP leader, not to be confused with the white entertainer of that name.

Congress may be about to decide that the Armed Forces are not the proper place for institution of proposals by starry eyed citizens designed to bring on the millennium by requiring mixed intermingling of the races.

The McGee case was featured almost daily. There were insistent editorial demands for his execution:

In a petition for the pardon or commutation in behalf of Willie McGee, condemned rapist, Communist-paid lawyers perpetrate the same old poppycock and time-consuming palaver with which they have afflicted the courts of Mississippi for more than five years. The time for this shystering and nonsensical nagging should now be brought to a close. . . . Willie McGee should be given a new date with death, to be met at the earliest moment.

And direct incitement to lynch him:

Paul Robeson, Negro singer and notorious Communist, who declares he prefers Russia to the United States, blew off his loud bazoo to the effect that the next step should be to get Willie McGee out of jail. It could happen—but not in the way Robeson is thinking about.

Came the inevitable day, shortly after we had moved out of the Y, when the Jackson *Daily News* learned of our presence in town. The banner headline announcing it streamed across the front page: 150 WOMEN CANVASS HOUSEWIVES HERE ASKING AID FOR MCGEE. The story went on: "Two barelegged Chicago women chugged down East Fortification Street in a battered old car. One of the 'civil rights' crusaders was described as dark-haired, about 23, and looked Italian." Obviously Evie, who was bitter about being described as bare-legged; she loathed wearing stockings, but dutifully put them on each morning in compliance with our collective decision. "I suppose they've never seen sheer nylons down here before," she said crossly.

We were enchanted to find that the *News* had magically succeeded, where Clarence had failed, in multiplying our number more than tenfold, and gratified to see that our modest effort had indeed resulted in a breakthrough; for the first time, a Mississippi newspaper had published the full details, hitherto completely suppressed in that state, of the CRC's frame-up allegations. The next day's *News* reported that the mayor of Jackson had hastily convened an emergency meeting of top law-enforcement officials to deal with the crisis—the city prosecuting attorney, the city attorney, the chief of police. He had emerged with the pronouncement: "If strangers come to their door, homeowners should ask them away. If they persist in staying, the Jackson police will cooperate."

Huddled in our sad lodgings, we pondered what to do. Rita thought we should telephone to the national office for instructions, a move I opposed since we had already been "instructed" by Clarence to make our own decisions on the spot; what guidance could the national office, hundreds of miles away in New York, possibly offer us? We decided to press forward and continue the door-to-door canvassing as though nothing had happened. As we emerged from the lodging house, we saw a message scrawled in thick black ink on an adjoining wall: "Behold, a people shall come from the North, and a great nation and many kings shall be raised up from the coasts of the earth. Jeremiah, 50:41." We stared at it in fascination, and decided it was not the random work of some Bible Belt fanatic, but one of the few ways people in this fear-ridden town had of expressing their feelings.

Despite the publicity, few people did call the police. To our relief none of us was arrested; the police just "asked us away." Perhaps the thought of tackling all 150 of us was too much for them? Or more likely the order not to arrest us had come from on high, possibly from the governor. We took this as a sign that CRC's slogan, "The Eyes of the World Are on Mississippi," might after all have been prophetic, that those eyes may have influenced the decision of Mississippi authorities to allow us to proceed unmolested.

We had already overstayed our time in Mississippi. The four weeks allotted for the trip stretched into five, as we did not wish it to appear we had been chased out by the Jackson *Daily News*. But we decided we could not leave the state without attempting to see Mississippi's most—indeed its only—illustrious resident, William Faulkner. The reserves having drifted back to their respective homes, it was the original four of us who drove down to Oxford. We asked a gangling, snaggle-toothed white boy for directions to Faulkner's house. "Down the road a piece, past the weepin' willa tree," was his response, which I took as augury of our arrival in authentic Faulkner country. We turned through a cast-iron gate into a long avenue of desiccated trees leading to a large, run-down plantation-style house, its antebellum pillars covered with grayish moss. Through the window we saw Faulkner, a small man in a brown velvet smoking jacket, pacing up and down, apparently dictating to a secretary.

We gingerly approached and rang the front doorbell. Faulkner himself came to the door, and when we explained the reason for our visit, greeted us most cordially, invited us in, and held forth on the McGee case for a good two hours. (Later we learned that the Soviet writer Ilya Ehrenburg, on his much-publicized tour of America, had telephoned to Faulkner from Memphis, seeking audience with the great man. When Faulkner told him he could only spare twenty minutes, Ehrenburg had declined the honor.)

Faulkner spoke much as he wrote, in convoluted paragraphs with a sort of murky eloquence. I was desperately trying to take down everything he said in my notebook, and frequently got lost as he expatiated on his favorite themes: sex, race, and violence. The Willie McGee case, compounded of all three, was a subject he seemed to savor with much relish; it could have been the central episode in one of his short stories.

Later it was my job to edit down his rambling monologue as a brief press release to be issued by our national office: "He said the McGee case was an outrage and it was good we had come. He cautioned us that many people down here don't pay much attention to law and justice, don't go by the facts. He said in this case they are giving obeisance to a fetish of long standing. He expressed fear for McGee's safety in jail. When we left he wished us good luck. . . ."

William Patterson was jubilant when I telephoned to tell him of our interview with Faulkner. It was a major breakthrough, he said. The release would certainly be picked up by the wire services and flashed around the world! But he insisted we show it to Faulkner and ask him to initial it, for fear that pressure from his Mississippi compatriots might later induce him to repudiate it.

This time I drove alone past the weepin' willa tree to find Faulkner in dungarees and hip boots, up to his knees in dank manure, working alongside one of his black farmhands. I showed him the release and explained why I had come: "Mr. Patterson thought I should ask you to sign this, for fear you might later repudiate it." He read it through, initialed it, and as he handed it back murmured softly, as though speaking to himself, "I think McGee and the woman should *both* be destroyed." "Oh *don't* let's put that in," said I, and clutching the precious document made a dash for my car.

One can only conclude that Faulkner gave expression, in his own distinctive voice, to the deep-seated schizophrenia then endemic among white liberals and racial moderates of the region.

After the Faulkner visit we made for California at top speed like horses returning to their stable. (Mississippi had its mean little revenge after all. Soon after we got back the car conked out altogether, never to go again. The mechanic said its engine was hopelessly gummed up by a large amount of molasses that had been poured into the gas tank.) The bliss of arriving home was enhanced by the rousing, emotional welcome given us in the black community. Mrs. Lofton had chivvied her church into opening its doors to a mass meeting of more than two thousand, at which we reported on our expedition. She herself had just returned from Washington, sent there by CRC as part of a nationwide delegation that sought appointments with government officials to present the case for clemency. Relating her experiences there, she told the meeting, "That Senator Nixon, he said it was none of our business what happens in Mississippi, and President Truman, he skipped out on me." Introducing our delegation, she said, "Since going to Washington, I've been called a Communist. I don't know what a Communist is, but if that's what it is, I'm rarin' to go! Show me any other type of white women that would go out and fight for our men—I would die for them."

Three weeks before the scheduled execution date, in the secure anonymity of a crowded downtown cafeteria, Buddy Green unfolded to Bob and me his incredibly daring plan to enlist hundreds of black Southerners in a last-minute effort to save McGee. Not a word of this would ever be breathed in our homes, offices, or even cars, which we assumed (correctly, as we now know) were bugged.

It was Buddy's prescient view that while the White Women's Delegation had broken new ground by journeying to the Deep South, eventually only a movement spearheaded by the organized power of blacks would bring fundamental change there. He was determined to be a catalyst of this change. He proposed to go to Memphis, his childhood home, where he had many friends and relatives, establish headquarters there, and travel through Tennessee, Alabama, Louisiana, Mississippi, mobilizing black ministers, civic clubs, trade unionists for a demonstration to be held at the state capitol in Jackson.

It was a sensational idea, but how to get the go-ahead from the Party leadership, who were bound to spend endless days pondering its "correctness in view of the present relationship of forces" and so on? We decided to broach it first to William Patterson, who was immediately enthusiastic and told Buddy to proceed without delay. Armed with this directive, we had no trouble getting approval from the local East Bay leadership, who furnished Buddy with a "security clearance" for a leave from his job at the *Peoples World,* meaning no questions were to be asked by his co-workers as to the reason for his absence.

Buddy estimated that he would need five hundred dollars for travel and living expenses—a large sum in those days—as he anticipated having to finance the trips to Jackson of blacks from all parts of the South. We hit on a marvelously simple and effective way of raising the money. He and I drew up a list of five people whom we knew to be both solvent and reliable. We visited them one by one, and told each that we were about to impart a tremendously important plan: "Because of its deeply secret nature, we have been instructed to tell no more than five people, of whom you are one." Having exacted a promise from our interlocutor to reveal the secret to no one, we proceeded to divulge it. Came the punch line: "We need five hundred dollars to finance the project. Since we can only tell five people, and we've just told you, your share is a contribution of one hundred dollars." So successful was this approach that we couldn't resist trying it on a few more, to raise our quota of McGee's legal defense costs.

The days after Buddy's departure dragged with nightmare slowness. We expected, and got, no word of his progress. I was assailed by awful fears: if something went wrong, and his purpose was discovered by the authorities, he might be quietly done to death in some remote Southern hamlet and we should never hear of it for weeks, perhaps months. . . . When he did return, to tell a tale laced with spine-chilling episodes, he seemed imperturbable and matter-of-fact as ever, as though to him it had all been in the day's work.

From Memphis, where he was staying with his aunt, Buddy had darted around the South from Atlanta to the Mississippi Delta, creating a network of support for the demonstration like a latter-day Paul Revere. His method was to concentrate on organizational leaders—the president of a ministerial alliance, the Grand Master of a Negro Masonic society, the shop steward of a union. From these his message spread like brush fire through their own organizations and beyond. Within ten days over four hundred people had pledged to attend the "Sunrise Prayer Meeting" on the capitol lawn, a format for the protest urged by the ministers. Prayers would be offered to the Lord asking His guidance for Governor Wright, that he might do justice to Willie McGee. "We weren't even to say, Free the man!" said Buddy. "I had to settle for that, or there would have been no participation. But I figured just the crowd would be a demonstration that people cared."

Relearning Southern ways gave him a little trouble at first. Boarding a bus in Greenwood, Mississippi, he took a seat halfway back in what he assumed was the Jim Crow section, only to be snarled at by the driver: "Hey, nigger, you get up, you get on all the way back there!" He had almost forgotten that a black man was supposed to give way to whites on the sidewalk, to flatten himself against a building or if necessary to cross the street to avoid impeding their progress. He bought a cap for the purpose of tipping it to any white person, such as a bus driver or store clerk, with whom he might have occasion to speak, much as we had adopted the hats-gloves-stockings routine in hopes of merging unobtrusively into the white Southern populace.

Using the alias "Jimmy Brown," Buddy was in daily contact with Patterson at a secret telephone number. "As things began to shape up, and I was sure of at least a hundred people, Pat ran into pressure from the Party Central Committee," said Buddy. "They told him to have me call it off; they were afraid it would end in a massacre. Pat refused, so they sent a white committee member to Memphis. He showed up at my auntie's, and I thought, Oh God, the FBI!" Having convinced Buddy of his identity, the committee member instructed him on Party orders to cancel the prayer meeting. "I said, 'Sorry, I won't do it. There's too much at stake; I can't walk out on them now.' I decided on the spot I'd have to go over his head. It was very shaking."

The night before the prayer meeting hundreds of black men and women, some with children, began streaming into Jackson by car, chartered bus, Greyhound, train, to take shelter in designated black homes near the capitol, ready to converge on the lawn at the appointed moment. Shortly before dawn, it became clear that something had gone wrong. A platoon of fifteen city patrol cars, together with numerous police and plainclothesmen on foot, began slowly circling the four square blocks around the capitol. Buddy, patrolling the patrollers, nipping swiftly, ducking in and out of dark side streets to observe this operation, concluded that a stool pigeon must have given the plan away.

As lookout man for the demonstration, he quickly alerted

some of the more influential ministers who, with their flocks, were quartered in nearby homes. After agonizing deliberation, it was decided to send five volunteers, three men and two women armed with Bibles and prayer books, as "weather vanes" to breach the designated praying ground. As they crossed over to the lawn, police moved in and arrested them. Within minutes, some two hundred city and highway patrol cars were swarming over the area. "The cops put out the word from the moment of the first arrests that if the prayer meeting took place they would 'kill every black s.o.b. in town,' " said Buddy. Sweeping through the side streets, guns drawn, they arrested every black in sight, shouting, "What's your damn business on this street, nigger?" "Put your hands over your head, nigger!" and "Are you in sympathy with nigger McGee?"

Thanks to the high quality of organization and the discipline of the demonstrators, only thirty-one blacks were arrested that morning, of whom Buddy was one. At the city jail, the booking sergeant asked the patrolman who had Buddy in tow, "What's this nigger in for?" "He's in sympathy with nigger McGee like the rest of 'em." The sergeant, scratching his head, turned to the chief of police, who was on hand to supervise the arrests. "How do you spell 'sympathy,' Chief?" "Oh, just abbreviate it. Write s-i-m-p," was the reply.

There was a nasty moment for those charged with the crime of Simp when they were put in a cell with local black prisoners, in for such offenses as shoplifting and drunkenness, to whom police handed billy clubs with the injunction to "show these niggers some of our Mississippi hospitality." "But when the local prisoners found out why we were there, they immediately offered to help; they took up a collection and pinched together ninety-six cents so we could send a wire to an attorney," said Buddy.

From his conversations with Patterson, Buddy knew that

the CRC national office was bending all efforts to get a new delegation of white women to take part in the Sunrise Prayer Meeting. When, several hours after their arrest, he and the other black prisoners were taken down to the courtroom, he was overjoyed to see a large group of white women, also in custody. He immediately recognized two of them: Dobby Walker and Jean Vandever, from the East Bay CRC. "I never thought I'd be *glad* to see friends under arrest," said Buddy. "But I'll be dog, what a relief! All those white people in there with us—it seemed like our only, chance of getting out alive." Dobby, one of the chosen five from whom Buddy and I had solicited their "share" of a hundred dollars, was privy to his presence in Mississippi. Resolutely disciplined as ever, she never told Jean he was there. "On the drive out from California, she must have cautioned me at least a dozen times that if I should see any Negro in Jackson whom I knew, I mustn't give any sign of recognition," said Jean later. "I wondered what it was all about, until suddenly I saw Buddy. So I looked right past him, and he didn't even flick an eye. I thought: Aha, that's why Dobby kept nagging all across the country!"

In all, twenty-four white women had come from New York, Chicago, California, Virginia to assemble that morning at the Y. In groups of three or four they walked the three blocks to the capitol. As they approached their goal, they were hustled into waiting police cars and driven to the jail.

By fortunate coincidence, McGee's lawyers, Bella Abzug and John Coe, were in Jackson that day to make a last-minute clemency appeal to the governor. When they learned of the arrests they rushed down to court—where two hundred armed city police and highway patrolmen filled the spectator benches —and worked out a deal with the authorities: charges would be dropped provided those arrested left town immediately.

The getaway was fraught with terror. There was an awful

moment when the lawyers seemed about to assent to the district attorney's proposal that the white group should leave first, the blacks later. "Dobby immediately knew this was a trap," said Buddy. "She stood up in court and insisted we should all leave together. The other white women agreed; they said they would not leave without us. As we filed out, police muttered, 'We'll meet you niggers down the road.' Highway patrolmen made a quick dash for their cars to make good the threat. Negroes who had come by car were trapped if they tried driving out, and trapped if they stayed in town. So some of the white women volunteered to drive the Negroes' cars to their homes in Memphis or Atlanta or wherever, which meant going hundreds of miles out of their way."

The whites quickly took up a collection of $190 to meet the unforeseen expense of train fares for the blacks, then accompanied them on the fourteen-block walk to the station, with a dozen police cars slowly cruising alongside. "We couldn't walk down the street together; it's absolutely forbidden in Mississippi for a Negro man to walk within arm's length of a white woman. If you are caught doing so, they don't ask you any questions, you are just clubbed and kicked right on the street by police officers 'enforcing the law,'" Buddy explained. "So there was no way of communicating. At the station, we found seven of the same cops who were in the courtroom waiting for us in the 'colored' section. They stood around taunting us, calling us every name under the sun. Hours went by waiting for the train.

"One of the white women tossed us a note. She had overheard a cop telephoning headquarters; apparently he had learned that one of our group had bought a ticket to New Orleans and would be traveling alone. The cop told his colleagues to watch for the train when it stopped at Brookhaven, less than a hundred miles south of Jackson, at nine fifty-five that evening. So we quickly changed the ticket for one to Memphis, where the rest of us were headed. When we boarded the train, northbound, all of the Negroes shook hands and made a pledge—that if any attempt was made down the road to pull one of us from the train, we would all go. And nobody would be taken off that train alive. For we well knew that for the next 210 miles, we would still be traveling in the state of Mississippi."

"My dear Buddy, I must say you are a man of tremendous stature," I observed when he had finished his hair-raising account.

ON THE EIGHTH OF MAY, Willie McGee was executed. That the execution was indeed a surrogate lynching, for the Laurel mob next best to the real thing, can be inferred from the Jackson *Daily News,* which devoted eight pages of news stories, photographs, and feature articles to the event. To ensure that local would-be lynchers would not be cheated of this long-awaited moment, the electric chair had been transported to the Laurel courthouse from Parchman Penitentiary, 150 miles away.

A crowd of a thousand, or one out of every twenty Laurel residents, gathered outside the courthouse. For those unable to attend, the *News* re-created the festive atmosphere, compounded of blood lust and jollity, what James Baldwin described in his short story about a lynching as "a very peculiar, particular joy":

. . . teenage boys did some laughing and there were a few girls and women in the throng. A patrolman shouted, "Let's everyone be nice. We want no demonstrations. You've been patient a long time." Everybody shouted as he said Willie was going to die. . . . A 70-year-old plumber perched atop a 30 foot cedar tree overlooking the courtroom where the execution took place. The nimble old man

excitedly related the events to the eager crowd below as they took place. . . . When the execution was finally completed, witnesses were rushed by hundreds of people asking such questions as "Is he dead?" "How did he look?" and "What did he say?"
A big cheer arose as the body was driven away.

Two separate eyewitness stories furnished minute-by-minute accounts of the execution, replete with detailed descriptions of McGee's clothing, the barber who shaved his head, the black pastor who administered last rites, the executioner and his aides, and the final moments:

WILLIE MCGEE BRAVE IN LIFE
BUT HE SHED A TEAR AS ELECTRICITY TOOK A TOLL

Willie McGee still had a cocky air about him as he took his seat in the electric chair. But he died with a tear in his eye. Almost bravely, almost defiantly he walked to that chair. . . . His face was enclosed in a weird black mask.

SHACKLED WILLIE MCGEE LOOKED SMALL, BLACK,
WITH DEATH STARE IN HIS EYES, SINGING HYMN

By 12.03 a.m. he was strapped to his chair. By 12.04 belts and black fittings about his face were adjusted again. . . . Watson moved the dial. He set 2200 volts for 45 seconds. . . . Willie's mask was removed. His eyes were shut, his mouth was wide open. . . . His body was rigid, his fingers curled. Then a tear trickled across the right side of his black, still face.

A few days after McGee's death, the *News* had this editorial comment:

The recent Willie McGee case was a striking illustration of the desperate tactics Communists use to gain ground for their cause. They spent at least $100,000 in defense of Willie McGee, a proven rapist, not because they cared anything whatever about the defendant, but they were boldly and impudently seeking to create dis-respect for law and order among Negroes throughout the nation, and especially in Southern states. . . . The Communists tell the Negro's plight in all the far corners of the earth. It is their greatest weapon against the Marshall Plan and places us in a false light, especially to the yellow and black races.

Time and *Life* picked up the theme, rounding on the CRC and the Communists, denouncing them for "using" the McGee case to further the cause of international Communism and foment racial strife. Thus *Time* of May 14, 1951:

To Communists all over the world, "the case of Willie McGee" had become surefire propaganda, good for whipping up racial tension at home and giving U.S. justice a black eye abroad. Stirred up by the Communist leadership, Communist-liners and manifesto-signers in England, France, China and Russia demanded that Willie be freed. . . . Not only Communists took up the cry. In New York, Albert Einstein signed a newspaper ad protesting a miscarriage of justice. Mrs. McGee, a captive of the Communists, addressed party rallies.

And *Life* a week later:

There was a bare chance that this sentence might never have been carried out on the reasonable ground that he, a Negro, had been condemned to death for a crime no white man has ever been exe-cuted for in Mississippi. But something very unfortunate happened to Willie. His case fitted too well into the strategy of the Communist International. . . . Money was raised to reopen Willie's defense and to prolong his propaganda value. . . . As the Communists moved in, such groups as the NAACP drew back. . . .

Five years and five months later, after numerous appeals, six stays of execution and three Supreme Court refusals to review the case, the Communists had worked Willie McGee for all they could.

The liberal weeklies, ever alert for an opportunity to prove their own political purity and lack of any taint of subversion, followed in Luce's wake to launch their own peculiar kind of flank attack against McGee's defenders. John Cogley wrote in *Commonweal:*

The Communists vigorously espoused McGee's cause, but their support nowadays is rather a kiss of death. . . . The Communists and fellow travelers have been so thoroughly and rightfully discredited that no decent American wants to have any share in their crocodile tears and phony indignation.

Mary Mostert, writing in *The Nation,* also bought the "kiss of death" theory. While deploring "the new and most dangerous element, conviction by association," she proceeds to buttress the element in her own way:

After the Civil Rights Congress, a so-called Communist Front organization, took up the fight, people seemed no longer to care about any evidence presented by either prosecution or defense. . . . Willie McGee was convicted because he was black and supported by Communists, not on any conclusive evidence.

Thus did *The Nation* and *Commonweal* end up in a cozy, safe alliance with the Jackson *Daily News* and the Luce press. Neither magazine had printed one word about the case when it was being fought through the courts, when there might still have been time to mobilize liberal opinion for a nationwide effort to halt the execution. Gripped by the prevailing hysteria, they joined the chorus: Communism, not racism or injustice, is the issue. There is not a word of criticism of a Supreme Court that tacitly gave its blessing to institutionalized racism, and upheld the double standard of justice by three times refusing to review the case. Nor is there a word of recognition for the inconvenient truth: that had it not been for CRC and the Communists, the McGee case and the issues it raised would have gone unnoticed outside Mississippi, his execution just another local bloodletting in the violent history of black repression.

Evidently Willie McGee perceived his case as part of the continuum of that history. The day before his death, he wrote to his wife:

Tell the people the real reason they are going to take my life is to keep the Negro down in the South. They can't do this if you and the children keep on fighting. Never forget to tell them why they killed their daddy.

I know you won't fail me. Tell the people to keep on fighting.

Your truly husband, Willie McGee

CHAPTER 9

HUAC

A GRAPH OF THE POTENCY of the House Committee on Un-American Activities as an instrument of terror from its inception in 1938 to its demise thirty years later would, I think, have the shape of a parabola. Fathered by Congressman Martin Dies of Texas at the height of the New Deal, it was by and large received at its birth with a certain light-hearted contempt. Was it Tom Glazer or Alan Lomax who used to go around Washington singing, to the tune of "Deep in the Heart of Texas," "I wish the flies / Were eating Dies / Deep in the solar plexus"? In its early days the Committee pulled some delightful boners. One of its first actions was to name Shirley Temple, then aged nine, as an unwitting dupe of the Communists. Gales of hilarity! Another rib-tickler of the period was the indisputably accurate designation of Christopher Marlowe as Un-American.

The jokes stopped after the war. In *Inquisition in Eden*, Alvah Bessie, himself a victim of the Committee, attributes some dozen suicides and numerous premature deaths from heart attack to persecution by the witch-hunting committees in the postwar years, not to speak of "permanent ostracism, divorce and voluntary exile—a list that numbers many hundreds if not thousands." Only much later, in a very different political climate, did the Committee find itself once more the object of derision, when it was virtually laughed to death by the Merrie Men of the New Left who were called to testify in the sixties.*

It has become fashionable of late in some left-wing circles to point scorn at the Communists for clamming up when asked: Are you now or have you ever been? For example, in *Thirty Years of Treason,* Eric Bentley quotes the Communist Manifesto: "The Communists disdain to conceal their views and aims. They openly declare that their ends can be attained by the forcible overthrow of all existing social conditions." He then proceeds to castigate the Hollywood Ten, who "alas, did not disdain to conceal their views. They lacked candor, and if that, humanly speaking, is quite a common lack, it is an impossible lack for real radicals. . . . It is love of candor that makes men radical thinkers . . . a yearning for realities, an appetite for true consciousness."

Yet a rereading of the transcripts of Committee hearings would seem to demonstrate that courage in this kind of inquisition lay not in "candor" but in defiance. Here is the response of Ring Lardner, Jr., one of the Ten, all of whom eventually served time in the federal penitentiary for "concealing their views," and those of their Hollywood colleagues from the Committee. The chairman has just asked what he jauntily refers to as "the sixty-four-dollar question" (happy, preinflation days!):

CHAIRMAN: It is a very simple question. Anybody would be proud to answer it—any real American. Are you or have you ever been a member of the Communist Party?

LARDNER: It depends on the circumstances. I could answer it, but if I did, I would hate myself in the morning.

---

* For example, on one occasion Jerry Rubin appeared in response to his subpoena dressed as a soldier of the Revolutionary War; another time he came before the Committee wearing a Santa Claus costume. This was good theater, hugely enjoyed by the press. In thus mocking the Committee, the radicals of the sixties doubtless helped to hasten its eventual downfall in 1968.

Some years—and one prison term—later, in 1961, Ring Lardner, Jr., explained his refusal to answer in a *Saturday Evening Post* article entitled "My Life on the Blacklist." It struck me at the time as the first words of sanity on the subject to appear in a mass-circulation magazine:

The impulse to resist such assaults on freedom of thought has motivated witnesses who could have answered "no" to the Communist question as well as many, like myself, whose factual response would have been "yes." I was at that time a member of the Communist Party, in whose ranks I had found some of the most thoughtful, witty and generally stimulating men and women of Hollywood. I also encountered a number of bores and unstable characters, which seemed to bear out Bernard Shaw's observation that revolutionary movements tend to attract the best and worst elements in a given society. With both these extremes the relationship had been a confidential one, and an added reason for taking the chance of a contempt citation was the fact that I had no legal defense at all if I first admitted my own membership and then declined to implicate other people.

My own first encounter with the legislative witch hunt came in 1951, when I was subpoenaed by the California State Committee on Un-American Activities. This was, to be sure, not the Big Time; that was to come later. HUAC (as the House Committee on Un-American Activities was euphoniously though erroneously called for short) at that time held the center of the stage, but their subversive hunt was such a proven headline-catcher that politicians below the national level were scrambling to get into the act. California and several other states had established mini-inquisitorial groups modeled on HUAC ("little HUACs," they were called), and not to be outdone, some city governments had adopted "little Smith Acts," making it a municipal as well as a federal crime to "advocate the overthrow of the government by force and violence."

The California Committee swooped down on eleven of us, a mixed bag including the recording secretary of the Committee for Arts, Sciences and Professions (ASP), a young dancing instructor from the California Labor School, housewives bent on abolition of the A-bomb.

Stepping out of our house one morning, I was annoyed to discern the indistinct figure of a process server lurking behind a hedge. Muttering something official-sounding, he handed me a paper, which proved to be a subpoena of the *duce tecum* variety, meaning that I was ordered to bring documents to the hearing: the membership list and financial records, showing names of contributors, of the Civil Rights Congress.

Lengthy strategy meetings with lawyers and Party leaders ensued to discuss the best course to take. The Hollywood Ten had gone off to prison only the year before, the Supreme Court having rejected their contention that First Amendment rights of freedom of speech and association justified their refusal to testify. This left the Fifth Amendment, refusal on the ground that our testimony might tend to incriminate us. While legally safe—for the Fifth had been tested in the courts and judged sound for the purpose—it seemed at first blush a distasteful posture. Did it not imply criminal culpability for political dissent?

Witnesses who took the Fifth before the various investigating committees had been denounced by McCarthy as "Fifth Amendment Communists" and by other critics as unprincipled opportunists. The same sort of criticisms persisted when, long after we had left the Communist Party, Bob and I (and many others in our position) continued to "take the Fifth" as a matter of principle in more informal situations, as, for example, when undertakers demanded that we reveal if we were now or ever had been Communists.

Laurent Frantz, a CRC consultant and expert in Constitutional law, worked through these knotty questions with us. There is nothing, he explained, in the Fifth Amendment that implies an admission of guilt. In fact, the privilege against self-incrimination had its origins some centuries ago in a situation strikingly similar to ours: that of English religious dissenters who refused to reveal their beliefs or inform on their co-religionists to church inquisitors. As Judge Jerome Frank had put it: "they considered it no disgrace to commit the crime of heresy; they were proud of their heresy; if, without fear of punishment, they could have confessed to what the law denounced as heretical acts, they would have been glad to do so."

The experience of scores of witnesses before us showed that only when the Fifth Amendment was used had the Committee been successfully defied, said Laurent; if a witness decided to fight the Committee at all, the weapon was not a matter of choice. Under these circumstances the privilege had become an indispensable shield for the protection of freedom of speech and association under the First Amendment. Without it the power of Congress to investigate and penalize political heresy would have no effective limit.

What if one elected to testify about oneself, but refused to answer questions about others? No good, said Laurent, and he went on to explain the murky doctrine of "waiver": If you answer a single question, the Committee will say you waived the privilege and insist that you answer as to "related facts," meaning the names of your colleagues and other details of your activities. (The following year, Lillian Hellman had just this experience. In response to a HUAC subpoena, she wrote to the Committee declaring her willingness to tell all about herself if she was not compelled to inform on others. This stance, which was never successfully invoked, came to be known as the

"Diminished Fifth." When the Committee refused to make any such bargain with Miss Hellman, she was forced to assert the privilege as to all questions.)

Thus, Laurent explained, the only course for a witness who wants to avoid jail for contempt is to claim the privilege as early and as often as possible. Only in this way could one be fairly sure one would not be trapped into unintentionally waiving the privilege.

While the Fifth Amendment was adequate shelter for the others, whose subpoenas did not compel the production of documents, the lawyers warned that my predicament was somewhat different, since the Supreme Court had recently ruled that the privilege could not be invoked to prevent the *records* of an organization from being subpoenaed. As I obviously had no intention of complying, a contempt citation, followed by a stretch in prison, loomed as a very real possibility. In the end I was spared this inconvenience by a quirky little incident that nobody, least of all the Committee, could have foreseen.

There was the usual front-page newspaper treatment of the hearings (a headline in the *Examiner:* STATE TO OPEN PROBE OF BAY AREA RED FRONT; and the *Chronicle:* LEGION DEMANDS REDS BE PUT IN DETENTION CAMP), replete with our photographs and Committee statements about our subversive connections. Dinky, aged ten, reported a certain amount of teasing by children at her school about the news stories. I decided to see the school principal about this, also to ask that Dinky be released from school on the day of the hearing so she could accompany me; should I end up behind bars as a consequence of refusing to testify, she would at least have witnessed my crime with her own eyes. Quaking slightly (for school principals are, to me, considerably more fearsome creatures than investigating committees), I sought out Mrs. Hill in her office.

Being a delinquent and inactive PTA member, I had not

met Mrs. Hill before. She was a white-haired lady of forbid-
dingly upright posture, like a portrait by Grant Wood. I wondered if she would denounce me and threaten to call the truant
officer if Dinky was absent on the hearing day.

To my astonishment, she expressed hot indignation about
the pending hearing, said it was a disgraceful infringement of
political freedom, and offered to call in Dinky's teachers so that
I could explain the issues involved. They are nice young people,
she said, but wouldn't have the background to understand the
dangers of these witch-hunting committees. The teachers arrived; we had a long and useful discussion in which Mrs. Hill
announced that Dinky would be going with me to the hearing.
Today this might not seem out of the ordinary; but in 1951,
when public employees by the hundreds were being hounded
from their jobs for opposition to the witch hunt, Mrs. Hill's
response struck me as immensely courageous and heartening.

The hearing room was packed with supporters of the Unfriendly Witnesses, and Dink took her seat with these while I
conferred with my lawyer, Frank McTernan. He drilled me
once more in the ritual words: "I refuse to answer on the
ground that my answer might tend to incriminate me." First on
the stand was the dancing instructor, a radiant young blonde
who to the evident chagrin of the Committee persisted in baring
her breast to nurse her eight-month infant. Next came the
secretary of ASP, who had declared in advance that she dis-
dained to invoke the Fifth Amendment, as she had "nothing to
hide." The rest of us thought this rather tiresome of her, since
the implication was that *we* did. Her testimony was illustrative
of the consequences of "candor" in these hearings. For once
having answered the sixty-four-dollar question (in her case, the
answer was no), and thus waived her right to remain silent, she
was soon chivvied by the Committee into naming members of
the ASP executive board and confessing her knowledge of their

other subversive associations: a veteran of the Abraham Lincoln Brigade, a club chairman of the Civil Rights Congress, a teacher at the California Labor School.

The ASP secretary was followed by Edith Jenkins, a leader in the San Francisco Peace Committee, whose performance on the stand was dazzling. For the occasion, she was dressed in unrelieved red from head to foot—matching scarlet hat, dress, gloves, shoes, handbag. Confronted by this Red Front incarnate, the Committee counsel seemed slightly off his stride as he put the question: "Are you a member of the San Francisco Peace Committee?" Edith, eyes blazing, retorted, "It seems peace is a subversive word!" To the delight of the audience she lambasted the Committee and all its works. She spoke earnestly, eloquently about the Committee's assault on Constitutional freedoms, its hounding of thousands because of their political beliefs, its cruelty to children: "My children were intimidated and harassed on the street by San Francisco police serving the subpoena." The audience roared applause; the chairman snarled back at them and ordered the hearing room cleared for the remainder of the morning session.

I was called to the witness stand after the noon recess. The Committee counsel droned out his questions: Are you a member of the Communist Party? Have you ever heard of or read the *Peoples World?* Have you been director of the East Bay Civil Rights Congress since May 1950? Do you maintain a bank account for the Civil Rights Congress in the Wells Fargo Bank? Is your husband, Robert Treuhaft, legal counsel for the Civil Rights Congress? And to each I responded with the memorized incantation: "I refuse to answer on the ground that my answer might tend to incriminate me."

I was beginning to find it most irksome, and should have loved nothing better than to lash back as Edith Jenkins had done, to start a row, to be a Committee-teaser and audience-pleaser. But I was no Edith Jenkins, I had no talent for oratory, could never hope to match her impassioned fluency, and should have felt deeply uncomfortable proclaiming my devotion to the American Constitution in my still unreconstructed English accent. So I grimly stuck to the course agreed on with McTernan.

"Are you a member of the Berkeley Tenants Club?" the Committee counsel suddenly shot at me. At least, that is what I thought he said. I had never heard of that organization, but the name had a distinctly subversive ring—tenants, no doubt, giving some landlords a run for their money? I was puzzled when my reply, the usual "I refuse to answer on the ground . . ." was greeted with an explosion of laughter from the audience—and only then realized that the counsel, trying his hand at heavy sarcasm, had ironically asked if I was a member of the Berkeley *Tennis* Club, a bastion of posh conservatism. The chairman furiously rapped his gavel for order, shouting, "This witness is totally uncooperative! We won't have any more of her nonsense! She is dismissed from the stand!"

I was pleased with myself; albeit inadvertently, I had done almost as well as Edith in gingering up the hearing. As I stepped down and started for the audience section to find a seat near Dinky, McTernan grabbed my arm and pulled me into the corridor. "That was a wonderful performance!" he said enthusiastically. "You got them so rattled they forgot to ask for the CRC records—now get lost, before they come to their senses. Don't go home—that's too dangerous—or to any house that might be under surveillance." He promised to explain the situation to Dinky and get her a ride home, and I dashed out to my car. (Later I learned that no sooner had I left than the Committee counsel, after some whispered words with the chairman, demanded that I be recalled to the stand. McTernan blandly announced that since I had been excused, I had gone off to keep an appointment and that he would be unable to retrieve me.)

But where to go? Most of my acquaintances were likely subjects of FBI surveillance; I yearned to telephone to Bob, but he was himself in hiding to avoid being served with a subpoena. For a while I drove aimlessly around; then I remembered the name of an insurance agent whose house should be safe enough. I appeared at his door, and he and his wife agreed to give me shelter until the Committee left town. A few days later we read in the papers that the hearings were over, so I telephoned to tell Dinky I was coming home. "Thank goodness for that!" she said. "I've been doing all the cooking and we're *so* sick of scrambled eggs for dinner every night."

One became adept at subpoena-ducking. A few people would be served, and the word would quickly spread throughout the ranks, a signal for others to quietly disappear until the particular danger was over. One day I returned from lunch to the CRC office. The volunteer in charge told me in great alarm that a clean-cut young white man in a business suit, carrying a briefcase, had walked in and asked for Decca Treuhaft. What to do? We had a quick conference, and agreed I had better get away while my co-workers telephoned around to lawyers, trade union offices, Peace Committee headquarters to find out if anybody had been subpoenaed, or knew of any scheduled hearings. Nobody had; but the alert having been sounded, several responded by absenting themselves from home and office. I repaired to the house of the long-suffering insurance agent. When after a few days intensive inquiries by the lawyers established that there were no subpoenas out, no hearing in the offing, I returned—only to learn much later that the young man was a friend of ours, a Party member working his way through law school by selling stationery, and that he had merely dropped by to solicit the CRC's business for his firm.

Our next bout with the inquisitors was in 1953, when Bob and I were subpoenaed by the House Committee for its major production in San Francisco. To make it difficult for people to duck, the subpoenas were served many weeks in advance of the hearing, accompanied by the usual blaze of headline publicity: 100 TOP BAY REDS FACE EXPOSURE IN PROBE, as the San Francisco *Examiner* put it. Most of those caught up in this dragnet were trade unionists—longshoremen, seamen, laborers—together with a scattering of civil servants, teachers, lawyers, and other professionals. While then, as now, the Committee's reputation as superbully rested chiefly on its highly publicized selective victimization of Hollywood glamour figures, it was these local heresy hunts that did the deadliest damage in destroying livelihoods and muzzling political dissent at the grass-roots level. Before its demise in 1968, the Committee had compiled, nationwide, dossiers on one million Americans.*

Shortly before the hearing, we learned from the newspapers that Harry Truman, whose presidency had terminated only months before, had been asked to appear for questioning by HUAC. This was news indeed; the old Cold Warrior himself, perpetrator of the loyalty oath—hence begetter of the Climate of Fear—in the toils of the very monster he had helped create!

One night I found I couldn't sleep for pondering this interesting turn of events, so at 2 a.m. I staggered downstairs and drafted a telegram. Rereading it today, I find it rather pompous, sprinkled as it is with "true patriots," "loyal Americans," and so on; yet it did express the views we held at the time, albeit in the

---

* William Preston, Jr., "The 1940s: The Way We *Really* Were," *The Civil Liberties Review,* Winter 1975.

stilted and admonitory style we had adopted as befitting our vanguard role:

Mr. Harry S. Truman
Waldorf-Astoria Hotel
New York, N.Y.

Have just learned of your subpoena by Velde Un-American Committee. As Executive Secretary of East Bay Civil Rights Congress I too have been subpoenaed for hearings scheduled to begin in San Francisco December 1. Civil Rights Congress has repeatedly warned that the witch-hunting activities of the Velde Committee will not stop with the persecution of Communists. We have warned that, following the pattern of Hitler Germany, the Committee will, if unchecked, go on to destroy organized labor, the church, free universities. Acting as prosecutor, judge and jury the Committee destroys innocent people and through this seeks by fear and intimidation to outlaw political dissent. Now the Democratic Party is one of its intended victims. True patriots must challenge the authority of this Committee. I pledge to do my part by refusing to cooperate with this Committee. You have an opportunity to set an example for loyal Americans by defying this Committee and doing all in your power to expose its real aim—Fascism in America.

Decca Treuhaft

Having sent off this rather governessy message, I thought no more about it—until, on the very eve of the hearing, I received a note in a handwritten scrawl: "Your message in support of the Constitution of the United States and our free institutions is highly appreciated. Many thanks. Sincerely, Harry S. Truman." Amazing! We jubilantly photostated it, planning to flash it to press and Committee members. However, Al Richmond, editor of the *Peoples World,* urged against this course. He pointed out that Truman's letter was a private communication addressed to me alone, and should be respected as such; that in the circumstances to circulate it to the press would be a cheap shot, and might be construed as an unworthy effort to rehabilitate myself in their eyes. Regretfully we acceded to his viewpoint and agreed to keep the letter to ourselves, a souvenir that to this day hangs framed on my wall.

The San Francisco hearing lasted five days, in the course of which thirty Unfriendly and four Friendly Witnesses were called to the stand; the latter served up more than three hundred names for delectation of press and Committee. Most of those named found themselves out of work, and unemployable, by the time the Committee left town. I was among those subpoenaed but not called. However, the Party treasury ended up richer by forty dollars as a consequence of my daily attendance at the hearings. I discovered that witnesses were entitled to per diem plus travel expenses, applied for these, and endorsed the Committee's check straight over to the Party, hoping this would tease *somebody,* if only the Committee bookkeeper.

I found it curiously disconcerting to sit in that large audience and see erstwhile comrades up on the witness stand, testifying as informers about our familiar doings; it was like seeing brief, disconnected vignettes of one's life filtered through a distorting mirror. Of the Friendly Witnesses, two stand out in memory: Dickson Hill, former membership director of the Oakland Party club I belonged to, and Dave Blodgett, East Bay reporter for the *Peoples World,* who had worked closely with me in many a CRC campaign. They typified two extremes of the spectrum of informers: Hill, a small businessman, had volunteered his services to the FBI; Blodgett, a devoted Party member for all his adult life, had somewhere along the way found safe haven in a new religion.

Several of us who knew Dick Hill as a fellow club member had spotted him as a possible FBI informer some time before. He and his nondescript wife had been recruited during a

Peoples World subscription drive by some overzealous comrades, who enrolled them on the basis of a card ("Yes, I would like a trial subscription to the *Peoples World*") that the Hills had mailed in to Party headquarters. There was something extremely fishy about them; Sylvia Hill never said a word, but sat through our meetings endlessly working on a hideous floral tapestry. Dick, who showed little inclination for discussion of Party theory or working in political campaigns, had been elected membership director of my club shortly before I transferred into it from San Francisco. This is usually considered a thankless and dull job, but dull Dick seemed to thrive on it; he was diligent and indefatigable, forever nagging people about their lack of regular attendance at meetings. He would appoint committees to chase down the missing members and report back to the club. "Now, Comrade E., you and Comrade B. were to visit Comrade F. and find out why he's been absent for over three months." "Well, we went over there, and he said he won't be able to come for a while; he's building a wall." "Building a *wall?* What a smashing idea," I said. "D'you suppose he'll let us all hide behind it when the Fascists come after us?" Dick responded dourly to such sallies. Absence from club meetings was a serious matter, not to be trifled with.

Although some of us had growing suspicions about the Hills, we had no proof. So we lay in wait for something that might justify formal charges against them. Eventually Dick made some comment (actually rather innocuous, as I recall) about Jewish businessmen; in short order, we called for a trial on charges of anti-Semitism before the Party Security Commission and expelled them. Thus it came as no surprise to hear Dick testify that he and his wife had been asked by the FBI to work as undercover agents, and tell how they joined the Party: "We sent a postcard to the Alameda County office on Webster Street requesting information on various subjects connected with liberal political activity, and instead of mailing it to us, two people brought the literature and became quite closely acquainted with us."

Oddly, testifying up there before Committee, press, and spectators about the hard lot of a Communist Party membership director, Dick Hill sounded exactly the same aggrieved note about his perennial troubles with absentees that I remembered so well from our club meetings. His unremitting efforts to bring the stray sheep back into the fold! His constant anxiety to produce on the job! Did this, I wondered, say something about the psychological difficulties, a kind of schizophrenia, that an informer is condemned to suffer?

After all, he was a *good* membership director, he really tried his level best to get everybody on the ball, as his responses to Committee questioning revealed:

He had slowed down very definitely on attending meetings of our branch, and I brought up in executive meeting one day that I thought that a committee should go and see them and see why they weren't attending our meetings. . . .

We had a great deal of difficulty getting her to meetings; the only way we could get her to meetings was to send someone over after her and take her back. She was very inactive. . . .

I brought the issue up in an executive committee as to why he wasn't attending and why his wife wasn't attending. . . .

I recommended that a committee be sent to contact him and ask him to become active in our branch. And he was pretty cold toward the whole thing; the committee wasn't well received. He had excuses that he was busy building a wall around his home.

(Muffled giggles and nudges in the section of the audience where I was sitting with some of the club members.)

If Dick Hill's performance could have been anticipated, that of Dave Blodgett came as an electrifying surprise. Yet looking back, there had been a sort of forewarning had we known how to interpret it. The last time Bob and I had seen him was in 1949, during the Jerry Newson trial. The defense had just learned of new ballistics evidence that could demolish the prosecution case, and that evening we were restlessly longing to find somebody to discuss it with, to mull over this extraordinary development and its implications for the defense.

Dave immediately came to mind. We admired his coverage of the trial in the *Peoples World,* he had a good grasp of courtroom techniques and strategies; Bob often consulted him on how to handle a witness, whom to bump off a jury. During the CRC's campaign against police brutality in Oakland, Dave had accompanied me to the hospital bedsides of beaten victims and worked tirelessly to spread the story of these outrages, to help bring the state assembly's investigating committee to Oakland. He was one of those intense, superdisciplined comrades— the Party was his whole life. One was almost abashed by the totality and purity of his dedication to the cause. I regarded him as a far better Party member than I, alas, could ever aspire to be.

We had driven to the Blodgetts' house about 10 p.m. and, seeing their sitting room light was on, rang the doorbell. Minutes went by before Dave came to the door, followed by his wife. They stood there rigid, a look of frozen panic on their faces, like the wedding guest in "The Ancient Mariner" when he learns about the ghostly presences on the ship. When they saw it was only us, they relaxed; we apologized for scaring them, for we had evidently shaken them very badly by popping around unannounced. Dave explained that when they heard the doorbell ring unexpectedly so late in the evening, they thought it could mean only one thing: a visit from the FBI. They left the Bay Area shortly after this, and we never saw Dave again until the day of the hearing. Was it, then, sheer terror that led Dave to turn tail, find God, and seek the enfolding security of the FBI?

As Blodgett made his way to the witness stand—unaccompanied by counsel, a tip-off that he was there not under duress but as a willing informer for the Committee—the audience broke into boos and his sister Jean rushed forward, dashed inside the barrier, and spat full in his face. It was a superdramatic moment. The chairman scolded away about "attacks verging on violence" and threatened to clear the hearing room if the demonstrations persisted.

We had known Jean long before we met Dave, when she was San Francisco organizer for the Federal Workers Union during the war years. The two were strikingly similar in appearance and character: the same drawn, tense face, the same grim, utterly humorless approach to movement work. To these Anglo-Saxon progeny of the Middle West the Movement was merely an extension of the Protestant ethic drilled into them in their childhood. Occasionally Jean, in a conscientious effort to unbend, would laboriously try to tell a joke—only, one felt, because the Cause required her to develop a folksier relationship with the union members. "Of so-called funny stories Jean should have a tiny quota / Because the point got left behind in Northfield, Minnesota," we would chant on these occasions. Brother and sister, spat-on and spitter, what propelled these iron souls in their respective directions? Reflecting on this phenomenon, I surmised that, incapable of bending, Dave simply broke under the strain.

After describing his Minnesota upbringing, Blodgett proceeded to his college days: "At the age of seventeen I wanted to make over the whole world into a more perfect sphere of beauty and goodness and found, at least thought I had found, the answer when I met Communists." He joined the YCL, and by 1943 was issuing manifestoes of the Midwest Student Victory Assembly calling for "national unity against all defeatism," the eighteen-year-old vote, and abolition of the poll tax—evidence, observed the Committee counsel, of "a perfect example of the formation of a Communist-front organization and a most successful one."

Moving on to his employment with the *Peoples World,* "there is the whole story of supposed police brutality in Oakland against Negro people," said Blodgett, "which the Party and the *Peoples World* hug close to their chests. You see, they were supposedly interested in stopping this sort of thing from going on in Oakland. . . . It was so apparent that the Communist Party was interested in what? Recruits for the Communist Party and readers for the *Peoples World.* They were not interested in stopping and preventing further incidents of police brutality."

Having explored this subject at some length (and having fingered in his testimony some thirty-five former associates), Blodgett delivered his peroration, confessing "the commission of the main sin, the feeling that Man can be sufficient unto himself, that he can do without a Supreme Being. . . . I once rejected a God that I did not know, and I rejected a church that I knew nothing about because I had only immature understanding of God and the church. I have corrected this."

To which Congressman Jackson of California responded, "I have never heard finer testimony nor a finer summation of what communism does and the emotional and physical experience of passing through it. . . . Again may I say how deeply we appreciate your splendid cooperation, and we wish you Godspeed." With this benediction Blodgett was dropped forthwith into the shadows.

To me—and, judging by audience reaction, to many others —the high point of the hearing was Bob's testimony, which followed that of Dave Blodgett. It was a lovely little exposition of stiletto-sharp thrust and parry; when it was over, one felt that a lion or two had succumbed to the Christians that day.

Before the hearing, all the other Unfriendly Witnesses had retained counsel and were as usual represented by a handful of left-wing law firms, members of the National Lawyers Guild, officially designated as subversive. Bob decided to try a different tack, to put to the test some Oakland lawyers who had no allegiance to the left but who, in private, expressed disapprobation of HUAC. Would they now come forward publicly to represent a fellow member of the bar before the Committee? He compiled a list of seven lawyers, all supposedly stalwart defenders of Constitutional rights and the right to counsel, and methodically called on them one by one to sound them out about appearing as his counsel at the hearing. I accompanied him on some of these visits. The responses were depressingly reminiscent of some of our encounters with liberal white Mississippians in the Willie McGee case. All seven deplored the forthcoming HUAC extravaganza, some tentatively agreed to represent Bob, only to renege later. By the eve of the hearing all had turned tail in fear of incurring the displeasure of the Committee, leaving Bob the choice of seeking counsel among Lawyers Guild members or representing himself.

He decided on the latter course, determined to reveal through his testimony the full extent to which the Committee had succeeded in terrorizing the bar. As Committee rules prohibited statements by witnesses, his strategy was to attempt to use the routine first question of Committee counsel—"Are you accompanied by counsel?"—as jumping-off point to describe his unsuccessful peregrination through Oakland's leading law firms.

He skillfully circumvented the hurdles erected by Committee counsel to prevent him from doing so.

Q. Are you accompanied by counsel?

A. Mr. Tavenner, I am obliged to appear as a witness before this Committee—

Q. Will you answer the question, please, sir?

A. I am answering the question.

Q. Mr. Treuhaft, will you please answer the question, sir?

A. I am answering the question.

Q. I fail to hear the answer to the question. I heard you begin to explain that you were obliged to appear as a witness, which is quite an obvious fact.

A. I was asked whether I had counsel.

Q. That is correct.

A. I am answering that question.

Q. Do you have counsel? His answer is not responsive.

A. May I be permitted to answer the question?

Q. I wish you would answer the question.

A. I am obliged to appear before this Committee without assistance of counsel, Mr. Tavenner, because of the fact that the repressive activities of this Committee have made it impossible for me to secure the assistance of attorney of my choice.

From then on, it was fairly plain sailing and Bob managed to finish his remarks. To avoid embarrassing the lawyers he had consulted, he named no names but assigned each a number. Lawyer No. 1, he said, holds high office in the Alameda County Bar Association and is known for his civil libertarian views. When first approached, this lawyer agreed to represent him; "the next day, however, he informed me that he felt he could not do so because of the controversial nature and the publicity attendant on these hearings." Lawyer No. 2, a former judge, agreed fully with Bob in principle that he should defy the Committee and rely on the First and Fifth Amendments in refusing to testify. "He told me that he would like to represent me. After conferring with his associate, however, he called me in again and he said that he was very sorry that he could not. . . . He said to me, although he is a well-established lawyer, and older than I am, 'Why don't you find some older lawyer, someone who is in a better financial position, to take this risk?' " Which led to Lawyer No. 3, also a high official of the American Bar Association, with a reputation as a champion of the right of advocacy. "He told me, 'Try to find a younger lawyer. The activities before this committee would be too strenuous and the publicity would be harmful.' "

And so it went. Lawyer No. 4, a distinguished criminal lawyer in the East Bay with whom Bob had been on friendly terms, readily agreed to represent him; when offered a retainer, he said that he would not accept a fee from a fellow lawyer. "Three days ago he called me, and he told me that his partner had just returned from out of town; the partner felt that the attendant publicity would be so harmful to them that he insisted that they could not represent a witness before this Committee." (Actually, the partner had recoiled in terror at the thought. He had told Lawyer No. 4, "If you represent Treuhaft, Internal Revenue will be in here looking at our books—and if that happens, I'm going to jump straight out of that window!") Lawyers 5, 6, and 7, all distinguished members of the bar, feared loss of corporate clients, financial hardship, adverse publicity. . . .

At the end of his recital of these sorry responses, Bob lashed out at the Committee: "I am prepared to fight this evil at every level, and I intend to ask the state bar to look into a situation which I think is truly disgraceful, where lawyers with real courage and standing are afraid to come forward and represent clients before this Committee. . . . Your bible is guilt by association!" The spectators, who had been reprimanded several times for applauding during Bob's testimony, were now unable to contain themselves and broke into a thunderous ovation, upon which the chairman ordered the hearing room cleared.

Although the legal raison d'être for HUAC, as for all congressional committees, was to conduct investigations with a view to proposing legislation, no such proposals ever came out of these hearings. They were conducted purely as exercises in harrying the Left, spreading terror throughout the country, all to the glory of the distinguished congressmen who composed the Committee.

For Bob, there were a couple of minor repercussions. That evening the Oakland *Tribune*'s main headline ran: "OAKLAND LAWYER CAUSES ROW AT HUAC HEARING." The story recorded that "Treuhaft's wife rushed up, hugged and kissed her husband. Outgoing spectators slapped him on the back and shook his hand." Bob was somewhat upset over the headline, thinking that the lawyers he had approached to represent him might assume he had behaved irresponsibly at the hearing. But there was a silver lining: his secretary told me she got dozens of telephone calls, mostly from blacks. "Is this the office of the lawyer who caused the row? He's the one I want to represent my son." And a few days later, Bob's law partner overheard a conversation between two policemen at city hall. "Do you think Treuhaft really wants to overthrow the government?" said one. "Well—no," was the reply, "but I think he wants to get somebody else to do it."

My mother had the last word on Bob's skirmishes with HUAC. In 1959 we had gone to stay with her at Inch Kenneth and Bob produced for her edification a HUAC pamphlet, hot off the press, entitled *Communist Legal Subversion: The Role of the Communist Lawyer,* in which he had been accorded the signal honor of a listing among the thirty-nine most dangerously subversive lawyers in the country. My mother, always on the lookout for additions to her vast family scrapbooks of press clippings, photographs, and other memorabilia, seized it and started reading the charges against Bob: "In 1950, the East Bay Minute Women for Peace were circulating petitions on outlawing the atom bomb. Robert Treuhaft was the lawyer who explained the legal rights of petition circulators to the organization."

"Mi-*nute* women for peace!" exclaimed my mother, pronouncing it to rhyme with Canute. "Oh, the *sweet* little things!" Whereupon she stuck the pamphlet in her scrapbook, between an invitation to George VI's coronation and a card dated 1940 that read: "Authorization for Lady Redesdale to visit Lady Mosley in H. M. Holloway Prison."

CHAPTER 10

Going Home Again

A CURIOUS FEATURE of the Cold War was the prohibition against travel abroad by Americans suspected of Left leanings. From 1952 until 1958, when the Supreme Court took a hand in the matter, passports were arbitrarily withheld or revoked at the whim of two formidable women who ran the Passport Division of the State Department: Mrs. Ruth Shipley, and her replacement, Miss Frances Knight, who took over the job as director in 1955 (and who, at this writing in 1976, is still at the helm, her sails, however, drastically trimmed thanks to the successful Supreme Court challenge of her operation).

The State Department guidelines, adopted in 1952, under which the director could deny a passport were breathtakingly simple: she had but to decide that the applicant's travel was "not in the best interests of the United States." A sampling of the criteria used by Miss Knight in making such a determination is contained in her letter to the artist Rockwell Kent, one of the successful appellants in the Supreme Court case, explaining why he was unfit to travel abroad: "You were a speaker at a dinner in 1954 in honor of Eslanda and Paul Robeson. You are a sponsor of a four page petition addressed to Attorney General Herbert M. Brownell criticizing the use of paid informers . . . signer of a petition sponsored by the Peace Information center urging ban on use of atomic bomb . . . it has been alleged

that you urged clemency for the Rosenbergs . . . urged release on bail of Steve Nelson who was convicted of sedition in
Pennsylvania. . . ."

Thus for almost a decade only the true blue, the politically
and intellectually untainted, were permitted to travel abroad. I
have often wondered if this accounted for the generally low
esteem in which American tourists were held by Europeans.
Ironically, it was not the U.S. State Department but the
Alameda County Committee of the Communist Party that first
denied me and Bob the right to travel abroad. We had obtained
a family passport with no difficulty in 1950, and had made all
plans for Bob, Dinky, and me to go to England. I still have the
passport photo of the three of us, Dinky looking as though she
were about to burst with secret excitement. We had looked
forward to this trip as the absolute treat of all time. While I had
not longed passionately to go to England (for I was too intensely busy to long much for anything), now that the trip was
almost a reality it was the most savorous thought, a dream of
dreams.

But alas! The Party had other plans for us. The long-feared
Mundt-Nixon bill (renamed the McCarran Act) was passed by
Congress a few weeks before we were due to leave. The East
Bay Party chairman, a gloomy fellow who looked as though he
had the weight of the world on his shoulders, sought us out.
Impossible for us to go now, he said. All hands would be
needed to deal with the anticipated wave of arrests, prosecutions,
and general harassment; no lawyers could be given leave of
absence by the Party in this emergency. In my case, as a
naturalized citizen I might never be able to get back into the
country. Sadly, but flattered withal by the Party's recognition of
our indispensability, we conceded the soundness of his position,
and submitted.

By the time our 1950 passport expired a few years later,

the curtain had been rung down on travel for the likes of us. Bob sent it in for renewal with the required fee; after several weeks Mrs. Shipley merely returned his uncashed check in a plain envelope, without comment.

Once more the task of doing battle against a repressive government fell exclusively to the lawyers of the Left. The passport issue would seem to have been made to order for the ACLU, but it responded by sitting bravely on the fence, a posture that had become habitual in the fifties whenever those denied civil liberties happened to be Communists or suspected fellow travelers. I. F. Stone, commenting in 1952 on the ACLU's report on the right to travel, noted its maddeningly flaccid posture:

Paragraph No. 1 climbs arduously up the libertarian hill, asserting the right to travel and recommending that free speech for American citizens should be "as untrammeled abroad as at home." Paragraph No. 2 climbs quickly down again, asserting "it is equally important to recognize that the right of free travel must be subject to limitations —on the basis of a preponderance of the public over the private interest. . . ."

"It will hardly be disputed," it is argued by the ACLU, "that a nation may properly deny the right of free travel when its exercise would endanger the safety of the nation."

This formula is tailor-made for the Passport Division. It is wide enough to cover all the abuses of which the ACLU complains.

The ACLU having capitulated, the legal battle was undertaken by the newly formed Emergency Civil Liberties Committee and its counsel, Leonard Boudin, who filed suit against John Foster Dulles, Secretary of State, on behalf of Paul Robeson, Rockwell Kent, and other prominent radicals whose passports had been denied. (Robeson's passport had been revoked when the Justice Department warned that if he "spoke abroad against colonialism he would be a meddler in matters within the exclusive jurisdiction of the Secretary of State.") The passport cases slowly wended their way through the courts. The scores of lawsuits pending came nowhere near representing the actual number of people who had been denied the right to travel. In the pervasive atmosphere of fear there were those who preferred not to draw attention to themselves by applying for a passport, let alone suing the government to get one, and others who—like us—had simply abandoned indefinitely any hope of leaving these shores.

In 1955 Bob ran into Leonard Boudin at the National Lawyers Guild convention. Leonard suggested that we renew our application for a passport; when we were turned down, he would take our case up to the Supreme Court along with the others. It seemed a great waste of time to have to go through all the motions of applying—getting a passport photo made, assembling all the necessary documents, waiting interminably in line at the San Francisco passport office—when we knew it would all be for naught. But we went through the irksome ritual, spending one of those lost days that occur from time to time in life, very tiresome at the moment but soon forgotten.

Then came the thunderbolt. In a matter of days, there arrived by post, in one of those cheap beige envelopes inscribed "On Official Government Business," the magic document itself —our passport. It was as unbelievable and stunning as winning the Irish Sweepstakes, a golden moment to treasure forever.

We flashed the news around among our friends. It was hailed by all as a sign and portent—possibly the first tiny indication of a major change to come in State Department policy. Was there not a summit meeting to be held soon by heads of state of Russia and America? Could it be that the government's sudden reversal in the matter of our passport was an augury that a general détente of the Cold War might follow?

There was wild optimism in the ranks. Paul Robeson was in town for a concert, and we met him for dinner at the home of Matt Crawford, an old friend who in the thirties had accompanied Paul on an all-black delegation to Russia. Robeson was jubilant. "This means we've *all* won!" he boomed in his incomparable bass voice. Who could doubt, now, that his own victory would follow—why, his own passport might be waiting for him in his New York apartment at that very moment. We parted with a pledge to meet in London in the autumn.

London in the autumn. The human spirit is so constituted that when a goal is clearly and irrevocably beyond the bounds of achievement, we cease to desire it, or at least we put it so far in the back of our minds that it has no more meaning than a lost dream. Now that we were really going, every aspect of the trip was a delicious, tangible object of anticipation: the sea voyage on the *Flandre,* a dear little French passenger ship on which we at once booked passage; seeing those half-hazy creatures my sisters, friends, cousins, and their unknown children; smelling the almost forgotten smells of the Paris metro and the London fog; being in England once more.

Our days were now consumed with preparations for the journey—not only the usual touristic preoccupations with what to take and where to go, but intensive meetings with various comrades who would give us letters of introduction and brief us on useful things to do. This time the Party threw up no roadblocks; far from it. We were, after all, the first of our little lot to make it for a long, long time, so that (while we were confident that others would soon follow) we were in the proud yet ticklish position of informal pioneering ambassadors from the Left to the European Movement. I had a long session with one of the few comrades in the San Francisco area who had international connections. "You must go to Israel and straighten them out," he said. "Straighten out Israel? What a terrifying thought." But he continued, "And don't miss India, whatever you do." (Later I said to my mother, "A friend in America told me not to miss India, whatever I do." "Well, Little D.," she replied, "India is quite big; you could hardly *miss* it.") He gave me letters to Joliot-Curie and other luminaries at the World Peace Center in Vienna, to the Peace Committee in London, to the *Daily Worker* and *L'Humanité*. These letters were to be but a beginning; we decided I should go to New York ten days before the *Flandre* sailed to line up solid introductions to comrades who would smooth the way for a visit behind the Curtain, especially to Hungary, where Bob dearly longed to go.

The Crawfords gave a rousing farewell party for us. In the course of the evening I had a long talk with their daughter, Nebby Lou, who at the discontented age of seventeen was madly jealous of Dinky's good fortune. She would be company for Dinky, I thought, so I talked to her parents about sending Nebby Lou along with us, and somewhat to my surprise this was quickly arranged.

Nebby Lou, Benjy, and I set off for New York by train two weeks before the scheduled sailing. Dinky was already there, staying with friends. Benj was to be deposited at his Aunt Edith's for the duration of our trip abroad. (We had talked him into this arrangement by cannily asking, "Would you rather go to Europe or Disneyland?" Having got the expected answer, we promised to take him to Disneyland as soon as we got home if he would be a good fellow and go to school with his cousins in Queens while we were away.) Bob was to fly to New York to join us there just before sailing.

Insulated during the three-day train journey from all family news, we arrived at Grand Central Station to descry Dinky, grim-faced, flying down the platform to meet us, followed by a weeping Aranka. "Watch out—Aranka's *hysterical*," Dink whispered, and she quickly imparted the shattering news: Bob

224 A FINE OLD CONFLICT

had received a telegram from the State Department. It said the passport had been issued by mistake, must be surrendered immediately, we were not to use it under penalty of the law. This odd message had been followed by the corporeal appearance of State Department officials looking for Bob and the passport. Teams of them had shown up at our house in Oakland, Bob's office, at Aranka's New York apartment, and at her shop. Bob, who had thus far managed to elude his pursuers, had telephoned the day before to say he had changed his plans, Dink said; he was taking a night flight out of San Francisco and would arrive in New York within the hour.

We all piled into a taxi and rushed to the airport to meet him, Aranka moaning piteously the while: "For this I brought him into the world? To be hunted by the State Department? Aiee! You people are crazy, throwing away your life. . . ." There was a good deal of lurking around at the airport while Bob was waiting for his luggage to appear—hiding behind pillars, ducking into the lavatory if an official-looking person should loom into view—in which the children enthusiastically joined.

Our immediate problem was to find shelter both from the rain, which was coming down in torrents, and from the State Department agents; somewhere to touch down temporarily to consider the Present Situation and the Next Tasks. Aranka's apartment was obviously unsuitable, since it had already been staked out by the State Department; other friends in Manhattan might under the circumstances be embarrassed by our presence. Besides, there were rather a lot of us. We settled on Bob's sister's flat in Queens, about an hour's subway journey from Manhattan.

Having deposited the children at Edith's, Bob and I spent the rest of the day rushing from point to point, in and out of subways, conferring with Leonard Boudin, William Patterson,

and other trusted advisers, all against a background of drench-
ing rain. Although I had relinquished all hope that our trip
could now be salvaged, Bob decided on a plan of action. As no
legal papers had been served on us (the telegram, he pointed
out, might very well have been a practical joke—or at least we
could pretend we thought it was) and we still had possession of
the passport, we would try to make our getaway the following
day. It seemed supremely unlikely that we should succeed, for
surely the officials at points of exit would have been alerted to
look out for us. But Leonard assured us that the Passport
Agency's files were in a state of total disarray. "Many of them
have long since been eaten away by rats," he said in his reassuring way; we could lose nothing by trying.

Early the next morning, feeling strangely like prisoners
about to go over the wall, Bob and I set out to reach Cook's by
the time they opened at 9 a.m. The S.S. *Liberté* was sailing that
day at noon; we had three hours in which to perfect our escape
plans. We left Dinky and Nebby Lou in Queens with strict
instructions to be ready to dash into a taxi and meet us with the
luggage should our efforts be successful.

At Cook's, everything seemed to go in slow motion. The
Liberté was fully booked, we were told—or was it? No, there
was one cancellation, space for four in cabin class, said the
Cook's man, languidly thumbing the pages of his reservations
book. But we should have to pay cash in advance; our tourist-
class tickets on the *Flandre* were unrefundable unless bought
later by other travelers. Impasse: we hadn't got the cash. The
relentless clock said ten-thirty. Aranka, who had accompanied
us to Cook's looking and behaving like the chief mourner at a
funeral, suddenly entered into the spirit of the chase: she
sprinted for the bank and joyfully returned with a handful of
bills, the price of our four tickets. Wonderful Aranka! It was
then, I believe, that I felt the first stirrings of appreciation for

her sterling qualities, her valiant support of us despite her implacable disapproval of our way of life.

A maddening wait now ensued for Dinky and Nebby Lou, alerted to get a cab and come at once. Later we learned that the naughty creatures, never dreaming we could pull it off and resigned to forgoing the trip, were lolling about in their nighties making hot chocolate when our frantic telephone call had come.

There was one more hideous, heart-stopping moment. We were the last arrivals on the dock. Bob casually proffered the passport; the official as casually glanced at it—but then he looked again. He stared at Bob and scrutinized the passport. Suddenly Bob understood why: the photograph showed him with a mustache, since shaved off. He covered his upper lip with a finger; the official, smiling, stamped the passport and handed it back. We all emitted the polite, restrained ha-ha-ha's of seasoned travelers accustomed to these funny little misunderstandings and proceeded swiftly up the gangplank.

The unbelievable had happened: the *Liberté* slowly pulled out to sea with us on it. In an excess of caution we forbade the children to go near the cabin until the pilot had been dropped and we were safely out of New York harbor limit. Bob and I sat in the cabin-class bar giggling insanely and drinking to *"Liberté! À nous la Liberté!"*

We whiled away the blissful five-day voyage concocting rather transparent code messages to our friends in California, where, we learned later, all sorts of wild rumors had circulated —one had it that we had been arrested at the New York airport and were languishing on Ellis Island. "As the travel posters say, getting there is half the fun, certainly true in our case," I wrote. "We decided to leave NY in a bit of a hurry as America's getting Dulles dishwater. Will close with love as it's dinner time and soon Knight must fall."

We disembarked before dawn. Dinky, who had been practicing her French on the *Liberté* crew, mumbled a sleepy *"Merci"* to the docker who helped her down the gangplank. "Wot's that outlandish thing she said? You're not in France now, you know," said the docker jovially. Somehow his remark—or rather the familiar cockney accent in which it was delivered—set off in me a wave of nostalgia to which I should never have thought myself subject. The odd feeling of déjà vu but not really déjà observed stayed with me for days and weeks. The brilliant little gardens on the outskirts of Southampton that we passed in the train; the half-remembered English countryside, so green, so rolling, so carefully cultivated, so unlike the bare brown hills of California—I suppose I had never really noticed it all before.

In London, too, I found myself in thrall to the past, hurtling back through time. "Could we possibly go to Lyons Corner House and have some delicious Bovril sandwiches?" These, consisting of beef soup concentrate spread on white bread, did not find favor with the rest of our group; for me their taste evoked a thousand buried memories.

Even the distinctive nastiness of a certain sort of English person seemed almost endearing, so long had it been since I had encountered it. I was in Harrods one day looking through a rack of dresses when I heard behind me the unmistakable tones of a county lady, lilting yet masterful, with an underlying suggestion of bullying, as she addressed the saleswoman—she could have been one of my more unpleasant aunts. "I have an extraordin'ry commission," she said. "My daughter-in-law is going to Inja and she wants me to find something suitable to weah thah." "How old is the lady, Modom?" asked the saleswoman deferentially. "Same age as the Queen," said Modom, causing me to fall headlong into the rack of dresses, whence I had to be rescued by the floor manager.

As for the people I knew, time had altered them in various ways. The most notable change was in those who were roughly my age or a bit older, last seen when they were in their twenties, now approaching middle age. But the old folks—Nanny, now over eighty, aunts and uncles, those who had been in their fifties and sixties when I left—seemed to have changed hardly at all; obviously, I realized, because they had seemed so incredibly old to begin with that a few more wrinkles, a bit more gray, made no essential difference.

The changes were a good bit more than skin deep. I had come back to a different world, and a largely different family, from the one I had left all those years ago. Tom, the beloved Tuddemy of childhood—the only member of the family to be always on speakers with all the others, the only one who made friends with Esmond, frequented our parties in Rotherhithe Street, came to see us off when we left for America—had been killed in Burma towards the end of the war.

The strange and tragic life of Boud was over; she had died in 1948, shortly after Muv's visit to Oakland. In a way I had thought of her as dead to me when political conflicts first parted us, and must have written something of the sort to Muv, for she wrote back: "Yes I suppose Bobo also mourned you in that sense, she knew you would probably never meet again, but her love for you was quite unchanged & she was always going back in her mind to when you were both young & M'Boud was a constant topic of our conversation. She remembered all the Boudledidge songs & used to tell them to the children, they simply roared. When I gave her your love when I came back she knew it was with one part of you, I could see by her face. I think you both understood each other. I remember saying to you, I am so glad you sent a message, after all we shall all be dead soon. But how little did I think she would so soon go away, I thought I would be the first."

Pam was living in Switzerland and Nancy, separated from Peter Rodd since the war, in Paris. The Mosleys lived at some distance from Paris, in a house called Le Temple de la Gloire, with their two sons, imperially named Alexander and Maximilian.

I could not have borne to see Diana again. When I was a small child she, seven years older, was my favorite person in the whole world. She was in all ways marvelous to me: she took me riding every day, taught me to speak French, encouraged me in the forbidden sport of "showing off" in front of grown-up visitors, was my staunch protectress against the barbs of Nancy, my ally in fights with Boud. I could see her in my mind's eye, a radiant beauty of seventeen, shrieking at my jokes, teaching me, helping me through horrid childhood, in general being the best of all possible older sisters. Philip Toynbee once asked me, "But didn't sheer curiosity drive you to want to see her again?" It well might have, I answered, if I hadn't once, long ago, adored her so intensely. To meet her as a historical curiosity on a casual acquaintance level would be incredibly awkward; on a basis of sisterly fondness, unthinkable. Too much bitterness had set in, at least on my part.

This left Debo as a welcoming committee of one when we arrived in London, and what a welcome she had prepared! Her plans had all been predicated on our arrival on the *Flandre* ten days later. I had cabled to tell her about the change, and she had immediately tackled the onerous job of reorganizing our itinerary. "I wasn't a bit surprised; we all *knew* that if you ever came back you wouldn't have proper legal papers," she said.

Our first destination was Inch Kenneth. As Debo explained, it takes slightly longer to get there from London than to Buenos Aires: "Night train to Oban, hang about in Oban until the afternoon, then there are various boats. You get to Inch Kenneth about teatime the next day." We went up with Debo, her

children—Emma, aged twelve, Mornington (named after a
famous English jockey), aged ten—and their nanny. The first
of the various boats is a ferry to the isle of Mull, which rises like
a great unwieldy gray-green whale among the smaller islands
that surround it: "O Sir, a most dolorous country," as Dr.
Johnson remarked to Boswell when they first set foot there.
Muv was on the dock to drive us away from the dolor to the
mysterious island of Inch Kenneth. We all packed into her
beautifully kept-up 1924 Morris, its only function in life the
twelve-mile journey across Mull—a fairly hazardous journey at
that, there being room for only one car on the Mull road. Debo
and I shrieked in simulated terror as a truck came lurching
towards us: "Oh, poor man, I'm afraid you'll have to back up,"
murmured Muv, vigorously honking her horn, and back he did,
for three miles to the next intersection.

I was immensely curious to see Inch Kenneth and to sample
the life there. Claud Cockburn was probably right, I reflected; it
would not have served the purposes of the Communist Party
too well. I could hardly visualize those "pundits of King Street,"
as Philip Toynbee called them, laden with luggage and food
parcels, picking their way over seaweed-covered rocks, wading
through shallow pools to be hauled into the waiting dinghy,
thence transferred into the open motorboat moored nearby—
for such is the final stage of the journey in the last of the various
boats for the half-mile crossing from Mull. Nor would my
mother's assorted retainers—McGillivray, the boatman, and his
wife; Mr. and Mrs. Campbell, gardener and cook; Betty, the
parlormaid—be likely prospects for recruitment to the revolutionary cause.

Inch Kenneth seemed like a child's island, one of those
miniature exhibits set up in natural history museums to display
the natural resources of a region, its flora and fauna and methods of cultivation. In the three miles of its circumference the

shore changes from shell cove to sandy bathing beach to sinister, steep cliffs. There is a tiny hayfield, a potato patch, a walled kitchen garden with little rows of peas, carrots, beans, and cabbages; a Marie Antoinette dairy painted by my mother in white with graceful borders of "Redesdale blue"; a flock of William Blake lambs frisking on the green hill beyond. On a promontory overlooking the sea stand the ruins of a seventh-century chapel surrounded by a graveyard of crusaders' tombs. The house itself resembled a cardboard castle from a child's building set, with fake crenelated battlements put there in the thirties by the former owner. Inside, the décor was incongruously frenchified and elegant, reflecting my mother's taste. "You and Bob will be sleeping in the Tent," Debo said, rather to my consternation; but the Tent proved to be a lovely huge room overlooking the sea, so called because of the elaborate hangings over the four-poster bed.

I found it curiously disconcerting to be once more under my mother's roof, in the time-proofed atmosphere of Inch Kenneth, where every hour seemed like four, where the days drifted slowly by, punctuated by the four-o'clock arrival of Her Majesty's postal service, the six-o'clock BBC news on the wireless. Dr. Johnson, who with Boswell had visited there a century and a half before, had written: "We could easily have been persuaded to a longer stay upon Inch Kenneth, but life will not all be passed in delight." With not even the six-o'clock news for distraction, I felt sure this valediction must have been written tongue in cheek.

Everywhere were reminders of childhood, transplanted from Swinbrook: the high-backed Jacobean chairs from Farve's closing room (so named by me, as a child; since he seldom stirred from it, I thought his old eyes would inevitably close there one day, never to open again); the six drawings of us sisters done by William Acton in 1934, framed in dark pink brocade; the carved round breadboards that my mother bought for 2/6 apiece from a Cotswolds artisan; the bound sheet music of songs we used to sing in the thirties: "Dancing Cheek to Cheek," "Isn't It Romantic?" "Brother, Can You Spare a Dime?;" Boud's gramophone records of Nazi songs: *"Horst Wessel Lied," "Die Wacht am Rhein";* above all, Muv's scrapbooks.

They were great tomes, arranged by subject matter, one consisting entirely of press clippings about the family, one of various weddings, another of family groups from 1904, when Nancy was born, to the mid-thirties, when one by one we went our separate ways. Nancy must have been thinking of these photographs when she wrote, in *The Pursuit of Love:* "There they are, held like flies in the amber of that moment—click goes the camera and on goes life; the minutes, the days, the years, the decades, taking them further and further from that happiness and promise of youth, from the hopes Aunt Sadie must have had for them and from the dreams they dreamed for themselves. I often think there is nothing quite so poignantly sad as old family groups."

Dr. Johnson records that during their visit to Inch Kenneth, "Boswell, who is very pious, went into the chapel at night to perform his devotions, but came back in haste, for fear of spectres." I, too, found the island a haunted place, but my ghosts were all imprisoned in those scrapbooks.

Inch Kenneth housekeeping arrangements had remained unchanged for half a century. The coal boat would call every three years to dump its load of anthracite for the Aga Cooker, a huge, cavernous stove that had to be kept constantly stoked. There was no telephone; if a telegram arrived, the postmistress raised a flag on the opposite shore as a signal to cross over to fetch it. There was no refrigerator. Why not? Bob asked. "Because it would make the food so cold," Muv replied.

Harrods, my mother's favorite shop, a short walk from our house in Rutland Gate but from Inch Kenneth as remote as Buenos Aires, dominated life here as it did in London. The laundry was packed into large wicker hampers for its weekly journey by boats, train, and van to that emporium. One day a bulky envelope arrived from Harrods in the afternoon mail. Noticing that my mother put it aside unopened, Bob asked what it contained. "Just some new pound notes from Harrods bank—so much fresher than the ones you get up here."

In Washington, shortly after we first met, Bob once asked me why I ate as I did, lips withdrawn, clamping down with bared teeth to remove the food from my fork. I explained that it was a habit acquired in childhood to avoid dirtying one's mouth. Muv once worked out the cost of washing and ironing napkins for our family; deeming it excessive, she banished them from the dining room table forever. (To her annoyance, the *Daily Express* had run the story of our napkinless meals under the headline PENNY-PINCHING PEERESS.) "Of course I didn't really believe you," Bob said morosely. "I thought it was just another of your exaggerated stories." As delicious course after course was elegantly served by Betty at lunch and dinner, I would observe poor Bob surreptitiously availing himself of a corner of the tablecloth as substitute for the nonexistent napkin.

From Inch Kenneth we went to stay with Debo at Chatsworth—or rather Edensor, a magnificent lodge on the grounds in which the Devonshires were then living while readying the great house, which had stood empty since before the war, for family occupancy. We had looked up Chatsworth in Bob's 1911 edition of the *Encyclopaedia Britannica:* "one of the most splendid private residences in England . . . great conservatory, unrivalled in Europe . . . fountains said to be surpassed only by those at Versailles," and so on. A few years before, when Andrew Devonshire, then Lord Hartington, had stood for the conservative seat in the district, his mother was asked by a reporter what issues he would stress in his campaign. "Hartington is very keen on housing," she replied. Well, one could see why.

I was fascinated to see what Bob would make of it all—*Qu'allait-il faire dans cette galère?* I wondered. On the voyage over, he had been studying Stephen Potter's *Lifemanship* and *One-Upmanship,* wonderfully funny essays about how to get on in English society chiefly by making others ill at ease. "Listen to this, Dec," he would say, and he'd read out bits as though conning over the rules of an unfamiliar game: " 'Snob and Countersnobship . . . Knights, and how to reassure them of their social position . . . Famous people and when not to recognize them. . . .' " "Oh, poor Bob, I shouldn't even try beating the English at their own game. Remember that if one starts with William the Conqueror, they've had almost ten centuries of practice, how can you hope to compete?"

From Edensor he wrote to Aranka: "If Dec and I had been invited to stay at, say, the White House, at least I'd know what century I'm in and approximately how to behave. But here I'm totally at sea." At first we were very much a nursery party—Debo, her children and nanny, ourselves and the two girls. The children went riding and exploring the vast grounds, Debo showed us the work in progress at Chatsworth, where painters, carpenters, plumbers, were getting all in readiness for the move. (The following year Nancy wrote, "Debo's had 14 bathrooms put in & is wringing her hands wondering what she'll do with 14 guests after they've had their bath.")

Eventually Andrew Devonshire arrived with Lord Antrim, who had come for the weekend. Bob was pleased; now he would get a taste of lordly life as he knew it from literature. The evening got off to a propitious start, the nursery crowd now banished upstairs, a proper air of formality prevailing. When

Debo and I got up to leave the dinner table, Andrew and Lord Antrim also rose and followed us. Bob just sat there looking first expectant then anguished. "Andrew!" he exclaimed, "I *know* this is all wrong, from everything I've read about England. The men are supposed to stay behind for port, cigars, and dirty stories." "Of course, Bob. We will, we will, we were just seeing Debo and Decca to the door." One-down again, said Bob ruefully later.

His crowning moment came when signing the visitors' book at the end of our stay. Looking through it, he saw that some of the previous guests had written their surname only: "Salisbury," "Antrim," "Denham," and so on, standard signature form of titled Englishmen. Deciding this was the model to follow, Bob simply wrote in "Treuhaft," much to the merriment of all.

Actually Bob fared better than I did. For him, my family was a hilarious spectator sport; he was by turn amused and bemused by them, whereas I was in a constant state of ambivalence. What, in fact, was *I* doing in this *galère,* having taken such pains to get away from them, and once away, to "confound their politics, frustrate their knavish tricks"? I had longed to see them, yet found myself constrained in their company, awkwardly separated by the twin gulfs of time and outlook. They were wonderful hosts and I was not a good guest. Years later one of my favorite cousins, Robin Farrer, rather confirmed all this: "You were very *thorny,* darling, when you first came back. *Prickly* is the word, none of us felt we could get near you."

You *can* go home again, I reflected, but only at some risk. I sometimes wondered why I had left the satisfying world I had carved out for myself in Oakland to revive often oddly painful memories and relationships from the vanished past.

As for Dinky and Nebby Lou, it was difficult to fathom

their reactions to the unfamiliar sights, sounds, dramatis personae they encountered in our peregrinations. Perhaps their California public school upbringing had not induced, as mine had, an abiding fascination with the human sort; or perhaps each was too deeply encapsulated in her separate cocoon of self-centered adolescence to notice undercurrents of family relationships. I recently ran across Dinky's trip diary, a prosaic record of our daily doings that contains no hint of introspection or of speculation about her unlikely, newly discovered relations and their way of life.

The girls were good companions, however. In London we packed them off to see the sights while Bob and I sought out the comrades at the *Daily Worker,* the British Peace Committee, the CP headquarters in King Street. So accustomed had we become to the beleaguered semi-outlaw status of Communists in America, and the sense of isolation that had almost imperceptibly crept up on us over the past several years, that we were continually dazzled by the openness and ease with which the Party functioned in the relatively free air of England. At the *Daily Worker* we marveled at the spacious offices and modern presses, so unlike the poor old ramshackle PW. It had what seemed to us a huge circulation, far larger than that of the PW and the New York *Daily Worker* combined—much of it due, we learned, to the wizardry of its racing handicapper, Cayton, whose column, after his sensational selection of Russian Hero as long-shot winner of the Grand National, had become essential reading for track addicts from dukes to dustmen.

In my travels around the United States I had been struck by the instant friendship based on mutual loyalties and shared dangers that one developed with fellow Communists, the total welcome and acceptance by complete strangers once one had established one's comradely credentials. We encountered much the same phenomenon in England, albeit with an English accent: the English Left had been spared the brutal harrying to which American Communists were subjected, and the concomitant provincial hostility to the Left that had seeped into the thinking of all strata of American society.

Unaccustomed to political idleness, I set about stirring up some activity in London on the matter of Paul Robeson's passport. My plan was to secure invitations for him to appear on the great concert stages of Europe, in the hope that if enough were forthcoming from sufficiently august sources Miss Knight would be forced to cave in and restore his passport. The striking aspect, to me, of this mini-campaign was the absence of redbaiting on the part of those whose help I sought. In California, the CRC had made some efforts to organize a protest petition on Robeson's behalf; forever on the prowl for "broad contacts," I had learned to brace myself for the cold and flinty-eyed reception, or the near panic, so often evoked by the very mention of his name. The best one could hope for in this sort of project was to muster the overworked signatures of a tried-and-true handful of hardy small businessmen, black ministers, minor trade union officials.

In London, with the help of our new friends I compiled a list of Members of Parliament and started telephoning. In short order I had a dozen offers of help. I went to see Lord Harewood, the Queen's first cousin and head of Covent Garden, who was shocked to hear that Robeson's passport had been revoked, said he would love to present this great artist at Covent Garden, promised to get impresarios from all over Europe to join in the invitation, suggested writing to the Queen of the Belgians to enlist her support. "How broad can you get?" I exulted in a letter to Paul.

As it turned out, Robeson decided against this strategy. He was no longer interested in the concert stage, he said. He would travel abroad for one purpose only: to speak, as the Justice

Department correctly surmised, against colonialism in Africa and against the genocidal policies of the U.S. government. If my efforts had been for naught, I nonetheless was glad to have had the opportunity to operate in this unfamiliarly decompressed atmosphere in which issues were considered on their merits without regard to labels. The English were perfectly aware that Robeson had been denounced as a "Communist" and "subversive" by his own government, but their attitude seemed to be "So what?"

A MAJOR OBJECTIVE of our trip was to visit Hungary. Aranka had taken Bob there a few times when he was a child, he spoke passable Hungarian, we yearned to see for ourselves a country in which Communism had triumphed and was a reality, and we thought it would be a tremendous experience for Dinky and Nebby Lou. Our "issued by mistake" passport, like all others, was stamped "Not good for" a series of countries, including Hungary. Since our whole trip was illegal, we reasoned, we might as well be hanged for a sheep as a lamb.

Lucky Nancy had been to Russia the year before, one of the very few in those days to visit that country, as a guest of Sir William Hayter, the British ambassador. "Susan aren't you jealous?" she had written. I was indeed, and thought it supremely unfair. Needless to say, her letters to me were one long tease (as my mother once observed, "Nancy's letters usually contain a skillfully hidden dagger pointed straight at one's heart"). "The Russians are very governessy, specially the women. The chaps I feel one could twist round one's little finger, but the women give you a cold blue look out of their little pig eyes which is quite terrifying. One of them asked me if I'd like to see a workman's flat & I said no not a bit, it's the kind of thing I loathe, I want to see old silver & fine morocco bindings. I could see she gave me up for a bad job after that. I asked about meeting some Russian writers & she said they're all away at the Black Sea writing. She said popular novels in Russia sell about 50 million copies goodness the lucky writers. I asked for an example: 'Cement by the author of Glue' was the reply."

Vienna would be our gateway to Hungary. Our letters of introduction to leaders of the World Peace Center, with headquarters in Vienna, would, we hoped, facilitate the granting of necessary travel papers.

Unfortunately all those to whom we had letters were away. At the Peace Center we were ushered into the presence of a tall, dark man of Mediterranean aspect who spoke not a word of English. *"Ce monsieur est responsable pour tout ce qui concerne les États-Unis,"* said our guide. Although we met him many times thereafter, we never did learn his name or even his nationality. I thought I detected a Spanish inflection in his French pronunciation. "Is Le Responsable Spanish?" I asked one of the few English-speaking workers at the Peace Center. "There are many Spaniards working here," she replied enigmatically.

It was all a trifle surrealistic, especially when I began delivering my carefully compiled report on peace activities in California. Le Responsable would interrupt occasionally to inquire which AFL and CIO trade unions were officially affiliated with the California Peace Committee? How many could the Peace Committee assemble for mass meetings? Ten thousand? Twenty thousand? Realizing that the poor chap had no grasp whatsoever of the political realities of his area of responsibility, I soon gave up. However, I continued to frequent the Peace Center, dropping in there daily while Bob laid siege to the Hungarian consulate about the matter of our travel permits. One day Le Responsable told me news had just come over the radio that President Eisenhower had suffered a severe heart attack, was reported to be dying. I fell heavily into a chair. *"Quelle horreur!"* "But, Madame, why does this trouble you?" asked Le Responsable. "Because don't you see, that means Nixon will be President." Carefully and at length Le Responsable explained that in an imperialist country like America, controlled by *les agents de Wall Street,* it made not a whit of difference who was President—"this imperialist tool or that imperialist tool." I crossly countered that in that case he should come over and find out at first hand what it would be like living in a country with Nixon as head of state.

Bob, who made daily visits to the Hungarian consulate, was having no success at all in obtaining our travel papers. The consul did not exactly turn him down; it was always "come back tomorrow." But it was clear that our credentials, consisting of letters from an unknown Californian to various distinguished Communists in Europe, were not quite convincing. We were getting very restive at the waste of precious days. Bob's leave from his office would soon be up; it began to look as though we would have to give up the thought of going to Hungary.

Without much hope, Bob decided to make one more try. He told the consul that our time was running out, that we should love to visit Hungary but if we were not welcome there we would have to make other plans for the rest of our holiday. In vain, he begged him to telephone to Budapest for a prompt yes-or-no answer, and offered to pay for the call. "We do not telephone," he was told. As Bob turned to leave, the consul said, "Let me see those passports again. This one is for your family, yes? And who is this?" He held up Nebby Lou's passport. "Oh, she's Paul Robeson's niece—she's traveling with us," said Bob in an offhand way. ("It was just an idea that popped into my head," he explained later. "After all, she's been calling Robeson 'Uncle Paul' all her life.")

The effect was explosive. The consul stared for a moment, then grabbed a telephone. "Get me Budapest." Bob heard him shouting furiously in Hungarian. "These people are absolutely trustworthy, the delay in granting their papers is outrageous, I demand you cut through the red tape—Paul Robeson's niece wants to visit Hungary!" Within minutes, Bob had the papers securely in hand.

Nebby Lou was exceedingly put out at what she, moralistic seventeen-year-old, perceived as a deception in which she had been used as an unwitting pawn. I calmed her down by pointing out that the fact she was not Robeson's niece was merely an accident of birth and not her fault at all, as she had no control over who her forebears were; that as a putative Marxist she should put no credence in bourgeois notions of the importance of heredity and genetics.

Losing no time, we packed up the car and left for Budapest that day. The morning after our arrival we made straight for the Peace Committee, where once more we were received, as in London, with that extra degree of cordiality that was a hallmark of the fraternity of Communists everywhere. In this case, no doubt the august presence of Paul Robeson's niece in our party was proof positive of our worthiness.

We were assigned an interpreter, an enthusiastic, energetic young woman who was to be our guide. Whom did we want to meet? What did we want to see? We had but to name it. A tour was quickly mapped out that included a drive into the countryside to inspect a collective farm, a workers' rest home, the new steel town of Stalinvaros; meetings in Budapest with lawyers who would brief us on the workings of the Hungarian legal system; visits to high schools where the girls could meet some young people; to the Pioneer Railway, "gift of the Hungarian government to the children of Hungary" (a delightful miniature railway manned by nine- and ten-year-olds); the Hungarian Folk Ballet and other entertainments.

It would be tedious to expand on everything we saw of socialist accomplishment (as a matter of fact when we returned home I wrote a long account of it for the PW; I reread it recently and found it *was* rather tedious). Yet it was for us an exhilarating experience to enjoy the hospitality of a collective farm, to dine sumptuously with the farmers, to learn that the Hungarian peasants, for centuries the poorest in all Europe, now took for granted such former luxuries as sugar, radios, bicycles; to mingle with the workers who crowded the Folk Ballet and Opera; to have tea in Stalinvaros with a Stakhanovite worker and his family (unlike Nancy, I, of course, was longing to see the inside of a workman's flat). Bob, who well remembered the atrocious poverty of workers and peasants in the old Hungary, was particularly struck by the evident prosperity and sense of progress we found everywhere. Nebby Lou, the center of attention wherever we went, lionized and showered with presents for her uncle, was soon happily reconciled to her new identity.

Everywhere we saw the signs and symbols of socialism triumphant. We drove to the Grand Hotel on the Margit Sziget, an island in the middle of the Danube, which Bob remembered from his boyhood visits there with Aranka as the quintessence of prized Gracious Living. The beauty of the island had been preserved, as were the amenities of the luxury hotel, but the change in management was immediately apparent: atop the hotel shone an immense red star. On the magazine stand, in place of *Vogue* and *Harper's Bazaar* or Hungarian equivalents, were displayed *China Today, Soviet Sports Illustrated, L'Hu-*

manité, the London *Daily Worker*—and packets of Five Year Plan cigarettes.

There were two disquieting incidents to dampen our general euphoria over the new regime. One day we were lunching in a Budapest restaurant. A waiter approached us; there was something terribly urgent about his manner. Could we, would we, take a letter to post to his brother in America? But why? we asked. Is there some problem about mailing letters out? He glanced around apprehensively, as though in fear of being overheard, and muttered something we couldn't quite catch. He was evidently in real distress. However, we regretfully decided we could not perform his mission; what if he was a spy, an opponent of the government?

On another occasion we fell into conversation with a young woman sitting near us in the lobby of our hotel. Communication was difficult, as she spoke no English, but Bob was able to puzzzle out most of what she said in a mixture of Hungarian and rudimentary German. She was a schoolteacher, her husband spoke excellent English and was very anxious to meet some Americans, as he would like to visit the States. Would we come to their apartment the next day at six o'clock for a drink? Again there was the disturbing note of urgency in her voice. We said we should be delighted, she gave us detailed directions to her house, we shook hands and parted. The next afternoon there was a terse message for us at the hotel: "Nicht kommen. Magda, Teacher."

We had naturally assumed there was vestigial opposition to the Communist government, yet these two encounters, coming as they did within a few days of each other, would seem to point to a far greater incidence of disaffection than we had supposed existed. We said as much to one of our new-found friends at the Peace Committee. Her response was not particularly reassuring. Service workers, such as waiters, she explained, are notoriously slow to acquire a proletarian outlook and so are members of the professions. Socialism in Hungary was only ten years old; there were bound to be dissidents, hankerers after the illusory delights of capitalist America like Magda, Teacher, and her husband. It would be as well, she added, since we had accepted the hospitality of the Peace Committee, if we refrained in the future from making these chance contacts on our own.

Nevertheless, I thought the incidents of sufficient interest to include them in my otherwise glowing account of Hungary for the PW. But the copy editor cut this portion out of the printed piece for "reasons of space."

In Budapest we spent much time in the company of lawyers, whom Bob had been keen to meet as he was anxious to learn all he could about the Hungarian legal system. It happened that an English-language pamphlet on Hungarian law had just been prepared and was about to be printed for use in England and America. The lawyers gave him a galley proof of this to look over, with the suggestion that if he found faults of English he might correct them. The pamphlet proved to be almost unreadable; the English was deplorable, the explanations of legal concepts hopelessly garbled. Bob offered to rewrite it, and we spent a couple of days holed up in one of the lawyers' offices working it over. Their delight in Bob's production, its clarity and sound organization, was expressed in a typically Hungarian accolade: "We will have your text translated back into Hungarian for our own use here!" In recognition of his services they invited us to an evening gathering, where, as guests of honor, we would be asked to speak on aspects of American law.

To our amazement, the Attorney General, many judges, and the entire Supreme Court turned out for this gala occasion. Proceedings were conducted with extreme formality: there were toasts in Barack Pàlinka, a delicious apricot brandy, to friendship between the American and Hungarian people, to Bob and the new draft pamphlet, to me and Dinky, and the usual standing ovation for Paul Robeson's niece. Bob and I gave our prepared speeches—his on government persecution of left-wing lawyers in the United States, mine on the experiences of CRC in California and the South—which were followed by a period of intensive questioning.

And now, said the chairman, had *we* any questions for our hosts about conditions in Hungary? While Bob and I were putting our heads together, Dinky raised her hand and was recognized by the tolerantly amused chairman; in Hungary, as in other European countries, children are not expected to speak up at adult gatherings. "Do you still have capital punishment in Hungary?" she asked. "Yes," replied the chairman. Her hand was up again. "Is there much of a campaign against it?" There was an uneasy stir at the head table and the chairman responded with a curt: "No, there's no campaign against it." Somewhat to our consternation, once more her hand shot up. "Why not? There is in America," and she launched into an impassioned discourse on the execution of the Rosenbergs two years earlier, the finality and cruelty of the death sentence, the petitions, the meetings, the demonstrations.

There was a prolonged whispered conference among our hosts and this time the Attorney General of Hungary himself rose to respond. He explained that the ultimate goal of a socialist society is the establishment of "socialist legality," which would of course include abolition of capital punishment, but it would be some time before this could be achieved. The immediate task was eradication of the remnants of bourgeois ideology, and to build for a future in which crime would be nonexistent. He assured Dinky that capital punishment was used very sparingly, generally as a last resort against proven enemies of the state.

It was but a few months later that the Khrushchev report burst upon the world, with its ghastly disclosures of rigged trials and summary executions of revolutionary heroes throughout the Communist countries—not the least of which was the execution in Hungary of László Rajk and seven associates for "Titoist tendencies."

As GRAND FINALE of our European tour we were to visit Nancy in Paris. In her letters to me she had been ardent, even passionate, at the prospect of our meeting, abandoning her customary reserve: "Oh darling Susan it will be like a dream to see you again, & my Heiress, oh how I pine for it." (The Heiress was Dinky, to whom Nancy said she was going to leave all her furniture, "the only thing of value I possess"; but some years later she wrote to explain that she had changed her mind about this, as she feared American central heating might cause the furniture to warp.) Whatever our plans, she said, she would fit hers to suit, but we must let her know when we should arrive in Paris.

I was equally longing to set eyes once more on that curious character. But I had not written to tell her our precise day of arrival—we thought it too risky, in view of our already precarious legal position vis-à-vis the passport, to send letters out from Hungary.

We drove from Budapest nonstop for two days, arriving in Paris dead tired after nightfall. As I had idiotically lost Nancy's telephone number, we drove to 7 Rue Monsieur—that familiar address to which I had been writing for years—constantly losing our way in the dark, rainy streets, until finally we arrived and after much pounding on the courtyard door roused the concierge. *"Madame Rodd est partie,"* she said, but her cook, Marie, would know where she was. Marie, an aging, bright-

eyed Bretonne, led us into Nancy's flat. Yes, Madame Rodd
had been expecting us, but not having heard anything, had gone
to England to stay with her sister *la duchesse de Devonshire.*

Much disheartened at this sad news, we flopped down on
various pieces of Dink's legacy, took stock of the beauties of the
flat, pondered what to do next. Why not telephone Nancy, Bob
suggested. I checked with the overseas operator, learned that
one could telephone to England for a surprisingly small sum—
about a dollar—and embarked on the arduous, hour-long task
of putting through a person-to-person call: Crackle-crackle
. . . *"La duchesse de quoi?"* . . . Snap-snap . . . *"Comment? Vous désirez?"* . . . Crash-crash . . . *"De la part de
qui?"* and so on, until finally came the welcome words: *"Ne
quittez pas, voici Madame Rodd à l'appareil."*

"Susan!" I shouted.

"Susan, is that you? Where are you?" The first time I had
heard her voice for sixteen years—an ecstatic moment.

"I'm in your flat, in Paris."

"Telephoning from my flat! You beast! It's *frightfully* expensive." There was a sharp click. She had hung up.

Bob, Dinky, Nebby Lou, and I literally rolled on the floor
helpless and speechless with laughter. Once more Bob, ever
skeptical about my tales of family peculiarities, was forced to
acknowledge the accuracy of my accounts. "Brandy!" he
gasped, and Marie brought a bottle of the best cognac, most of
which we downed.

Half an hour later, as we were about to leave, the telephone
rang. It was Nancy, sounding most relaxed and welcoming—as
Bob pointed out, this time she was "calling on Debo's nickel."

She returned to Paris a few days later in the sunniest of
moods. When Bob and Nebby Lou went home to their respective tasks at law office and high school, Nancy found a cheap
hotel near the Rue Monsieur for me and Dinky. "Mark Ogilvie-

Grant always stays there. He says it's just above the bug level, so it should do nicely."

She pressed upon me a check for fifty pounds. "It's money I owe you," she said offhandedly. "When you left for America I went round to your bed-sitter and got all your books and furniture, and I forgot to pay you for them." I well remembered those books—twelve or fifteen battered Left Book Club volumes that had cost five shillings each new—and that furniture, of which no more than one or two cushions could conceivably have been in usable condition. The fifty pounds, then, was an outright present, proffered in such a way as to give no possible offense and to deflect any implication that she was dispensing charity. Nancy's extraordinarily contradictory attitude to money, her excessive small meannesses alternating with bursts of lavish generosity, never ceased to baffle me.

Dinky and I spent our days at Rue Monsieur, our nights in the supra-bug-level hotel. As always, Nancy was marvelously good company; as always, our conversation skated on the surface. One could only guess at the exceedingly thin time she must have had with Peter Rodd, or indeed at any other aspect of her private life. She was adept at erecting barriers to any such discussion. No wonder she called her collection of essays *The Water Beetle,* and quoted Hilaire Belloc's rhyme of that name as epigraph to the book: ". . . She aggravates the human race/By gliding on the water's face/Assigning each to each its place./But if she ever stopped to think/Of how she did it, she would sink."

I knew only dimly of her long-standing affair with *le Colonel P.* My first inkling of it came when I read *The Pursuit of Love,* published in 1948, in which the heroine becomes the mistress of a Free French leader. I wrote to Nancy at the time, saying that as all her novels were purely autobiographical, and she never wrote from imagination, I supposed she must be having an affair with a Frenchman. She answered briefly confirming this fact. As years went on even Muv seemed to know about it; I asked her what Colonel P. was like—I visualized him as a cross between our uncle Colonel Bailey, a red-faced, hard-riding country squire, and Maurice Chevalier. Muv said that was a very accurate description. I thought so, too, after I met the Colonel, except that unfortunately by then the Maurice Chevalier aspect seemed to have given ground to the Colonel Bailey qualities.

The conversational barrier with Nancy worked both ways. I was not at all inclined to impart confidences about the subjects nearest to my heart—Bob, the children, CRC, and the Party—for fear of inducing that well-known expression, half frown, half wistful smile, that denoted deep boredom. Gossip was not much good, either, as we now knew so few people in common. We resorted to the gambit of "Do you remember?" as with Debo, reliving the days of Boudledidge and the Hons' Cupboard, interspersed with Nancy's idiosyncratic accounts of wartime privations, mostly having to do with her inability to cope with cooking: "I was staying with Farve at the Mews. He'd been awfully ill, but one day he roused himself and said 'I think I should fancy a boiled egg, Koko.' Mabel was doing for us but she had gone out, so I boiled up the water and threw the egg in. Susan, the *most* sinister white stuff started coming out of it, like an octopus, so I threw it away. Then I did another one, and the same thing happened. Then the third one, same thing. Oh dear I was sad, there went our whole week's egg ration, one each for Farve, Mabel, and me."

And once at the height of wartime austerity some friends of Nancy's had been given a goose, prized treat in days when meat or fowl were virtually unobtainable. "They wrung its neck and plucked it, and put it in the fridge meaning to cook it the next day. Susan, in the morning they took it out and *it was still alive,* giving them the *most* baleful look. So they rushed down to the village and used their last clothing coupon to buy some tweed to make it a coat. It stalked round in that coat looking *absolutely livid,* for the whole rest of the war."

I loved Nancy's company and I adored her letters. Yet I suppose I never really knew her very well. In childhood the age difference between us was too great to permit of much companionship; and although I saw a great deal of her in later years, ours was always something of an arm's-length relationship. But then she was not given to confidentiality. I doubt if anybody— even Diana and Debo, her closest companions toward the end of her life—managed to penetrate deeply her lightly worn yet adamantine protective armor of drollery.

Nancy doubtless would have scoffed at the notion that there was a "real Nancy Mitford" to be discovered beneath the glittering veneer, yet perhaps she was groping in the direction of self-discovery when she wrote to Debo in 1971 about the memoirs she was then planning: "If one writes an autobiography one must *unmask* oneself." Harold Acton observes that "Nancy's reticence was too deeply ingrained to enable her to unmask herself." I wonder. Possibly those memoirs, which would have been written at the onset of contemplative old age, might have revealed a great deal not only about herself, but about those of us who had the mixed blessing of coming within the orbit of her potent influence.

FROM TIME TO TIME during our sojourn in Europe we had wondered how we should manage our eventual return home, in view of the dubiousness of our passport. We had presented it at many European borders with nary a cross look from the frontier officials, but had not yet had to face up to the American authorities.

Before Bob left Paris to return home, we were obliged to tackle the knotty matter of applying for separate passports in place of the family one with which we had come over. In some trepidation we had gone round to the American Embassy, where, to our surprise and relief, the application was handled in a completely routine manner. There was one near slip-up: when I went to pick up our new passport photos, the photographer said in alarm, "But, Madame, surely you're not going into the *ambassade americaine* with *that* under your arm?" I looked, and saw that I had inadvertently brought along a copy of *L'Humanité*. I thanked him most profoundly, tucked the masthead inside, and proceeded to accomplish my uneventful errand.

We were puzzled by the ease and speed with which our new passports were issued. Despite what Leonard Boudin had told us, surely Miss Knight's office could not be so disorganized as to wantonly dispense passports to those, like us, whose travel she had determined to be "not in the best interests of the United States." Could she have relented?

Bob's letter describing his arrival in New York quickly disabused me of any such notion: apparently getting back was the other half of the fun. He and Nebby Lou had waited in the long passport line on board ship. Nebby Lou went through without incident. When Bob's turn came, the passport official searched through a list of names on his desk, then shoved Bob's passport into a drawer. "I started making noises like a lawyer," Bob wrote. "The man said he hadn't time to argue, I was holding up the line. He called over a State Dept. official, handed him my passport, and told me to go talk to him." Bob demanded to know on what authority his passport was being taken. The State Department man produced a teletype from Washington instructing him to confiscate it. Bob said a mere teletype carried no authority—anyone might have sent it—and by law he was not permitted to relinquish his passport except on proper authority. "I can only give it up if you show me a signature equal to that of the person who issued it to me. Do you know who signed my passport? Here, I'll show you." The State Department man innocently proffered the document, Bob snatched it, flipped it open. "See? John Foster Dulles signed it, that's who," and he stuck it in his pocket.

Loud protestations ensued. Another official came up to remonstrate with Bob: "That man will lose his job because of this. To lose possession of a confiscated passport is one of the most serious offenses. He has a wife and children to support; don't you have a heart?" Bob said no, he didn't have a heart. "Then you can just stay on board here. We have plenty of time. You won't get a landing card unless you hand over the passport." This was the clincher; Bob saw he couldn't win—and Aranka, waiting on the dock, would be getting frantic when he failed to appear—so he put an end to the cat-and-mouse game and surrendered the passport. But not before he had circumvented yet another State Department ploy: "On my customs declaration there was a note written in pencil: 'Hold for Murphy.' I didn't particularly want Murphy pawing through my luggage so I simply erased the words," he wrote.

This, it turned out, was just as well, for William Patterson, whom Bob met in New York, told him of severe indignities he had suffered a few years earlier at the hands of "Murphy" or counterpart. Patterson had returned from Paris, where he had presented CRC's petition "We Charge Genocide" to the United Nations. On arrival at the New York airport he was held by customs officials for several hours while they rifled his suitcases, photostated the contents of his briefcase, made him strip, and subjected him to a rectal examination. This might well happen to me and Dinky, Bob warned: "Watch out for Murphy."

On our homeward journey Dink and I were encumbered by

a present she had bought for Benjy in Harrods' Christmas cracker department, for which she had saved her entire allotment of pocket money: a giant snowman about four feet high, of immense girth, made of cotton wool with strings protruding which, when pulled (the shopman assured her), would cause the snowman to explode with a bang, revealing wonderful toys at the ends of the strings.

From taxi to boat train, from boat train to ship, Dink had safeguarded and cosseted this monstrosity, clasping it in her arms, refusing all offers of help from taxi drivers, porters, ship stewards. The snowman, which Dink refused to trust to the ship's hold, occupied one of our tourist-class bunks in the *Liberté,* while she and I squeezed into the other one. It was all most annoying.

"Wait until Murphy sees that thing," I said crossly as we prepared to disembark. "He'll tear apart all the cotton wool, looking for secret messages. If it explodes, we'll be charged with sabotage. I do wish you'd bought Benjy something sensible, like books." "Over my dead body will anyone *touch* that snowman," said Dink, eyes blazing. Somehow I knew then that the day was won.

Everything went according to Bob's account. The passport man consulted a list of names, popped our passport in a drawer. "Next, please." I gave him what I hoped was a withering look and stalked off down the gangplank, the heavily laden Dink in my wake. We must have presented a pathetic and unprepossessing appearance: travel worn, our luggage not much improved since the shopping-bag days of our first train journey to San Francisco. Aranka had come to meet us. "You look like steerage-class immigrants!" she exclaimed. "Oh, Decca, when are you going to get some decent suitcases?" However, our bedraggled steerage-class look combined with the sight of the furious Dinky, legs astride, standing guard over the snowman, must have turned the trick, for we went through customs unmolested.

We never heard another word about the passport; the government made no move to prosecute us for using it.

And the snowman never did explode. The day after we got back to Oakland, Benj, in high excitement, invited several school friends to pull the strings and receive the presents. There was no bang, merely a faint ripping sound as the thing tore apart. The toys turned out to be horrid little plastic cars and paper hats. It was all as shoddy, as meaningless, as anticlimactic as the absurd business over the passports.

CHAPTER 11

Leaving the CP

I RETURNED FROM EUROPE in the winter of 1955 to find the CRC in shambles. As we pieced things together from colleagues' reports, it seemed that our organization in the East Bay had become the special target of a massive FBI sweep. Teams of agents, deployed in pairs, had blanketed the area, visiting every member's place of work and presenting their credentials to the personnel manager: "We are checking on subversives in the Naval Supply Depot. Do you have a Roscoe Washington on the payroll here? No, there are no charges; this is just a routine surveillance. We would appreciate being informed if he changes his job." The next day Washington would very likely find himself in the ranks of the unemployed.

As a high percentage of our members worked in government installations, clinging to jobs that had in wartime first been opened to them as blacks, this was a singularly devastating technique; but the FBI did not limit its attentions to government workers. One of our executive board members had a small beauty shop in the West Oakland ghetto. "I was shampooing one lady and had another under the dryer," she told Buddy and me. "These two white men came in, they pulled the lady from the dryer and showed their cards—they were FBIs." Having quizzed the beauty operator about her subversive connections, the agents left, but not before they had thoroughly terrified her customers. A loyal and devoted member of CRC since the Newson defense days, she broke down and wept as she told us she could not afford to lose her business and would have to resign.

I was deeply shaken by these developments. Having worked assiduously to build the organization in the black community, I, safe as houses in my privileged position as wife of a solvent self-employed lawyer, could do nothing but stand by helplessly while the FBI methodically stripped our members of their livelihoods. The sickening fact was that we were impotent. The Party lawyers had filed lawsuits challenging the spurious "security" discharges, and although these were ultimately won in the appellate courts years later, the damage that had been done was irreparable in terms of careers destroyed, lives cruelly disrupted.

From William Patterson we learned that the FBI's concerted drive to crush the CRC was nationwide. In some areas agents had infiltrated the organization to such an extent that it was believed they made up the majority of the membership. In others it had dwindled to the point where the only members were Communists—and who was to say how many of *those* were agents? A telling *New Yorker* cartoon of the period depicts a Communist opening a meeting with: "Comrades and members of the FBI . . ."

In early 1956, the national leadership of the Party, bowing to the realities of a situation in which CRC was becoming more of a liability than an asset, and in which we could provide no effective defense to our beleaguered members, decided to disband the organization.

A concomitant reason for dissolution of CRC was the major policy upheaval that followed the Khrushchev report of March 1956. This report, in which Khrushchev had unfolded in all their grisly details the horrendous crimes of Stalin, sent shock waves through the Party and triggered the most intensive discussion in its history. In *A Long View from the Left,* Al Richmond describes the shattering impact of these revelations on many comrades: "Words for reactions in Communist ranks were used by very political men; 'Shock . . . pain . . . grief . . . bewilderment . . . perturbation . . .' It might appear odd to invoke their descriptions of such intimate feelings and yet I quote them to stress the universality of these responses."

I did not share this anguish to any marked degree, perhaps because I had never been as thoroughly convinced as most comrades of Soviet infallibility. Terrible as the revelations were, it seemed to me that the very fact Khrushchev had seen fit to lay them out for all the world to see signified that the Soviet leadership was set on a course of fundamental change. Surely the report heralded establishment within the Soviet Union of true political and intellectual freedom, and for the CPUSA an overhauling of the entrenched, ossifying leadership with its traditional reliance for direction on the Soviet Union. At least, that was my optimistic reading of the matter at the time—although, as it turned out, I was grievously mistaken.

The Discussions seemed to offer a way out of our irksome isolation. "Comrades, the struggle against Left-Sectarian tendencies must be waged in the factories, the neighborhoods, the fields and farms," as Rita Baxter would say in her Educationals. "We must root out dogmatism"—and she would go on to explain that we must hammer out a new line because the locomotive of history was making a sharp turn. That it was, and a turn, on the whole, much to my liking. The officially launched Discussions were unprecedented in scope, and in the latitude not only permitted but positively encouraged by the shaken leadership.

To record the content of these deeply felt debates would fill volumes. It is the tenor of them that stands out in my memory.

For the first time in my Party experience, one could really express without fear of expulsion any and all criticisms of policy. Massive Discussion Bulletins were issued by the National and State committees, supplemented by county, section, and club memoranda. Long-submerged discontent on the part of the rank and file boiled to the surface; the principal targets were bureaucracy, the "cult of the individual," dependence on foreign Communist parties for the Line. The leadership in our county, sincere folks all, led the field in self-criticism on all these counts.

I found the Discussions all-absorbing, promising as they did a new dawn for an indigenous, American-style revolutionary movement led by the Party, ending our fairly obvious thralldom to the Soviet Union. There was an exciting mood in the air of untrammeled, critical reexamination of old preconceptions. But at the same time many members, their faith shattered by the Khrushchev revelations, flocked out of the Party.

One decision that came out of the Discussions as part of the Struggle Against Left-Sectarianism was to disband the "Left centers," as we called them—the National Negro Congress, Labor Youth League, CRC, Progressive Party, and other organizations that had been largely created and kept going by the CP. "Comrades, we must find our way back into the mainstream of American life" was the slogan, meaning we should work within such established mass organizations as the Democratic Party, NAACP, ACLU, and try to influence their policies. Although I concurred with the dissolution of CRC as inevitable in the circumstances, I mourned its passing. Its short history had been impressive; it had fought valiantly on many fronts against awful odds, had stuck to its principles and held the line when the chicken-hearted liberals of the ACLU stripe had turned a blind eye.

My distress over the demise of CRC was compounded by

the vacuum it left in my own life. Enviously I watched the children leave for school and Bob spring off to the office each morning; I felt useless, at loose ends. I longed to get a job, but doing what? My numerous citations in the HUAC reports would preclude many types of employment; it had been eleven years since I had worked in the OPA, my last non-Party job, years that would have to be accounted for on any application; approaching middle age, I still had no marketable skills. Daily I scanned the HELP WANTED ads, many of which contained the malevolent words "Must be under 35 years of age."

One day I ran across one that sounded ideal: "Would you like to be part of a team in the advertising department of a big metropolitan newspaper?" It was a "challenging job that's out of the ordinary," said the ad, which ended on the encouraging note: "No experience needed. We train you on the job."

There was an intriguing aura of mystery about this job. I rang the number given in the ad to ask what the work consisted of, and was told that no information could be given on the phone, I must come in person to a room in the San Francisco *Chronicle* building. Arriving there, I was received with a few other applicants by the personnel director, who sat us down to fill out application forms. On mine, I deducted a few years from my age and with an inward giggle (thinking of what Bob would say) gave my occupation for the past eleven years as "Homemaker." Again I asked what the job was and how much it paid. The personnel director replied there would be no point in going into that until I had taken the necessary tests to find out if I was qualified.

The tests were staggered over three days. The first was an IQ test, to be completed in fifteen minutes, which looked fairly easy until one came to the last questions, having to do with the circumference, velocity, and rpm's of bicycle wheels. Having failed to finish before the time was up, I told the supervisor that

I had found the test too difficult and started to leave—but no, she assured me after checking it over, I had passed with an exceptionally high score. (Bob said later that had I got all the answers right, I would doubtless have been rejected as "over-qualified.")

Next came a series of personality tests, the most interesting of which was a list of three hundred propositions which the applicant was to mark "Yes" or "No." This must be done rapidly, we were told, as the whole point was to record one's spontaneous reaction to the propositions. However, it was easy to see that they were arranged in sets in which the same person-ality trait would be revealed at intervals of about every fifteen statements in slightly different guise. Thus if one wrote "Yes" next the statement "I would rather be a coal miner than a florist," one should write "No" beside "The sight of dirty finger-nails disgusts me." One of the sets was clearly designed to reveal incipient paranoia: "I sometimes feel I am being fol-lowed"; "I believe my telephone is tapped"; "I think somebody is watching my house." No, no, no, I responded mendaciously to these. Again I passed with flying colors; my personality was unusually consistent, no sign of mental disturbance, said the supervisor.

On the third day came the final hurdle: a telephone voice test in which all one had to do was to chat on the phone for a few minutes with the personnel director. I had passed, she told me, I had done excellently on all the tests, I had got the job, I would start work next Monday in the Oakland office.

Oh, the towering feeling, to be once more part of the work-ing world! But what was the job, exactly? And what were the wages? This was now divulged in a peptalk given by the person-nel director to the successful applicants—who turned out to be all who had applied. We would be working as telephone solici-tors in the *Chronicle*'s classified-ad department, hours eight-thirty to five-thirty, pay fifty dollars a week to start with, regular raises as provided for in the union contract, and tenure after thirteen weeks. We were expected to be prompt and to put in the full eight hours: "Eight-thirty does *not* mean eight thirty-five. Five-thirty does *not* mean five twenty-five," said the personnel director. She was followed by Edna, a classified-ad worker in the San Francisco office and vice-president of the Bay Area Newspaper Guild, who gave a counter-peptalk: "We don't want any eager beavers kowtowing to the bosses. Nobody puts in more than eight hours. Eight-thirty does *not* mean eight twenty-five. Five-thirty does *not* mean five thirty-five. And be sure you take the full twenty-minute coffee break in the mornings and afternoons."

True to the promise in the ad, the job was indeed out of the ordinary; it was also as close to rock bottom as any work I had ever done. Yet I found it most inspiriting to be once more contributing to the family budget after living off the bounty of Bob for all those years, to review for him each evening the strange pursuits in which I had spent my day, to explore at first hand a pocket of industry I had not known existed.

There were eight of us in the Oakland office, working under the supervision of a vibrant, bossy, exhortative young woman named Barbara. Each morning she handed out piles of newsprint—the classified-ad sections of the *Examiner,* the Oakland *Tribune,* the Berkeley *Gazette.* "Now, girls, on the ball! Let's see if we can't top yesterday's production. Jonesy, you had over a hundred lines, excellent. Jessica, forty—that's really good for a beginner."

Boiled down to its essentials, the job consisted of telephoning to advertisers in the rival papers and persuading them to switch to the *Chronicle.* We were each assigned a territory. The plums, handled by the experienced old-timers, were Business Opportunities, Used Cars, Real Estate, which often required dealing knowledgeably with a hard-boiled company representative rather than a "private party." As a neophyte, I was given the easier, predominantly private-party territories of Mobile Homes, Trailers, and Lost & Found.

One was expected to complete a minimum of sixty calls a day—to East Bay numbers only, as there was a crew of more than twice our size working in the *Chronicle*'s San Francisco office. As in certain English houses, where, regardless of their actual names, the butler is always called Perkins and the cook Mrs. Bunts to avoid confusion in case of turnover, so we were assigned a generic name that went with the territory: Jonesy, the real estate whiz, was Miss Miller; I in Lost & Found was Miss Johnson; the person in charge of funeral notices was Miss Black.

Having sorted the ads and marked the numbers to call, we would adjust our headsets and get to work. Barbara, whose extension line in her private office connected to all the telephones, would listen in from time to time to make sure we were on the job and to criticize or commend our approach as called for.

The standard pitch went something like this: "Hello, Mrs. Blomberg? This is Miss Johnson, with the San Francisco *Chronicle*. I noticed your ad in the *Tribune* for a 1950 camping trailer; sounds most attractive." Then would follow a few words about the outstanding success we've had with *Chronicle* ads for camping trailers, possibly because the *Chronicle* has so many more young married readers than the *Tribune*. (Alternatively, if the ad was for a mobile home, one substituted "so many more elderly retired readers.")

If the prospect seemed resistant to switching, one might diplomatically point out shortcomings in the wording of the *Tribune* ad, strongly implying that unlike the *Tribune* employees, we at the *Chronicle* were highly trained in the art of writing brilliant and effective copy: "So many people want chrome finish—of course we can abbreviate that to chr fin—and perhaps we should say 'like new'? Lk nw; it would only count as one extra word."

In my enthusiasm for creative copywriting I made an occasional gaffe. A prospect's *Tribune* ad for a trailer had mentioned "20 ft. bed." Would it not be better to omit those words, I suggested, since despite the alluring implications of that huge bed, buyers might be put off, thinking they would never be able to find sheets and blankets to fit it? Barbara, ever on the *qui vive,* overheard this and set me straight on the basics of trailer terminology: a trailer bed, it turned out, meant the floor of the trailer itself.

Jonesy confided a rather awful ploy that she had used when, as a new employee, she had been assigned to Lost & Found. She demonstrated for me with a *Tribune* ad that read "Lost: Budgie, ans. to Dickie, vic. Shattuck & 61st." Jonesy called the number given. "This is Miss Johnson with the San Francisco *Chronicle*'s classified-ad department. Somebody telephoned here just now to say she'd found a budgerigar that answers to the name of Dickie. . . . Yes, in North Oakland. . . . She wanted to know if anybody had called here to advertise Dickie's loss. . . . No, I'm afraid I didn't get her name. But she's a *Chronicle* reader; I'm sure if you take an ad in our paper she'll see it." I never stooped this low where somebody's beloved budgie, dog, or cat was involved, although I did try it with success in a couple of lost-wallet cases. Day by day I exceeded my rather low quota of lines, and was soon soaring over the hundred-line mark. Barbara was overjoyed with my progress, which no doubt redounded to her credit with the higher-ups in the San Francisco office to whom she was responsible for the performance of her Oakland crew.

Every Friday, just before quitting time, she would call us in for an inspirational chat, and would give out a prize to the one who had exceeded her quota by the greatest percentage. Within a few weeks I had carried off two bottles of domestic champagne and four free tickets to movies. Better yet, I was given an unscheduled raise to fifty-five dollars. "Jessica, you're really on the ball!" Barbara kept saying, and she told me that a girl of my ability really belonged in Used Cars, to which she would soon promote me.

Perhaps my whole life had been a training for this job, I reflected; all those hours on the telephone organizing CRC benefits, wringing money out of Contacts for CRC or CP, striving to reach my PW drive quota, mastering a special shorthand for use in Party meetings: agit. prop., lit., ed., org.—now easily adapted as chr fin, lk nw. . . .

At the end of my twelfth week Barbara asked me to wait behind after the others left. Could it be about the Used Cars? I wondered. She led me into her office and drew a deep breath. "I *like* my job here, Jessica, in fact you might say I *love* it—it's a fun job, and so stimulating," she said earnestly. "But all jobs have their unpleasant moments, and I'm afraid this is going to be one of them." Of course, I knew in a flash what was coming next. "We all like you very much, you know. We think you've really tried hard, and I appreciate that. But all along, I've felt you haven't the personality for this type work. I discussed this over in the city at our staff meeting, and we're really sorry, but we feel we have to let you go. So it won't be necessary for you to come in on Monday."

Now *I* drew a deep breath; this should be more than an unpleasant moment, I decided. Holding her with my glittering eye, I dragged it out to an unpleasant twenty minutes. Methodically I cross-examined her about my work: when had she first noticed my incompatible personality? Before or after the first bottle of champagne? If before, why the first bottle? If after, why the second bottle? What about the free movie tickets? My raise in pay? My consistent performance above quota? Her offer of a promotion to Used Cars?

Poor Barbara got awfully red and flustered. She explained that the quotas don't really mean anything, they're just a gimmick to stimulate competition among the girls, nobody takes them seriously. It's policy to give the prizes to the new girls to encourage them. It's not so much performance as personality that really counts in this job. She said I had a very nice personality but not suited to the special demands of this particular type work. Had I ever thought of being a kindergarten teacher, she suggested, thrashing about desperately. She'd heard there were lots of openings. . . .

"Barbara," said I severely, "I should loathe to be a kindergarten teacher, so let's stick to the point. Now, to go over it all once more . . ." and I did, all the way to the second bottle of champagne. Seeing that she was near tears and that it was getting late, I said, "Well, Barbara, sorry about my personality. I've got to dash home now, but you'll be hearing more about this."

What was behind it all? Obviously, Bob said, the *Chronicle* had found out about my subversive connections—"after all, it's highly classified work." This was my opinion, too. Yet there remained a haunting suspicion that possibly I really was unqualified, in which case what was to become of me? I felt I had reached the lowest possible ebb, unable to hold down even this patently fatuous job.

Bob thought I should appeal to the union. I remembered Edna, who had given that stirring talk on the day I was hired and whom I had seen once or twice since at meetings of the Newspaper Guild. On Monday I telephoned to her at the San Francisco office and unfolded my sad tale. She expressed amazement: *nobody* was ever fired from this job, she said; the

Chronicle had a hard enough time recruiting people for it. The wrong type of personality? She'd never heard of such a thing. We made an appointment to meet.

Edna was a new experience for me: young, bouncy, attractive, an enthusiastic, militant trade unionist, extremely knowledgeable about the union and all its works—but what we would have called "politically naïve," meaning that she had never come anywhere near the orbit of the CP. She became increasingly puzzled as I gave the full details of my brief employment and the final interview with Barbara. Was there anything, any conceivable reason I could think of, why this had happened, she asked.

Her question posed what was to become over the next many years a recurrent dilemma in my dealings with people like Edna, who had no background in our sort of politics. How much should I tell her, how explain my suspicions as to the true reason for my abrupt dismissal? I wanted to enlist her help but feared to lead her unwittingly into the trap of "guilt by association" with me. I should have liked to disclose my Party affiliation, yet feared the consequences; she might well panic at the word Communist, with its connotations in the public mind of traitor, spy, wrecker, and refuse to have anything more to do with me. So I compromised by confiding that I had been secretary of CRC, explained it was on the Attorney General's subversive list, and told about my HUAC subpoenas.

Edna was fascinated by this information; she had heard of HUAC, she said, but had never known anybody who had fallen afoul of it. Far from being shocked, she thought CRC sounded admirable and eagerly questioned me about its work. She was determined to find out whether this connection was behind my firing; if so, the union would surely go to bat for me.

A few days later Edna rang up, exultant. She and some

other union stalwarts had cornered the secretary of the head of Classified. "It was obvious she knew something about your case, but she was terrified; she'd been ordered not to talk. We had to twist her arm a bit, and now we've got the whole story." Sure enough, two FBI agents had come to the office. The secretary had overheard their conversation with the boss, in which they had informed him that I was under surveillance as a suspected Communist. The boss had then summoned Barbara, and together they had concocted her little speech to me, to take place, it was agreed, after the rest of the "girls" had gone home for the weekend so as to forestall any need for explanations; on Monday they could be told I had quit.

Edna was enraged by this underhanded performance; she assured me the union would take my case to arbitration. For a time it looked as though this would happen, but after some weeks the union dropped it. My memory is blank as to the reason they gave me, I suppose because I was so unhappy over it; possibly it had to do with my lack of tenure, since management had cleverly made its move just before my thirteenth week. The truth must have been that the union simply thought my case too hot to handle.

Actually, I was unusually fortunate in having ironclad confirmation that the FBI, rather than my own incompetence, was responsible for my dismissal. In many cases of this kind a special torture was visited upon the worker who lost his job. While he might suspect the FBI was behind it, he would never have proof, and would be condemned to eternal self-doubt: Was he slipping? Losing his touch? Getting too old for the work? I have seen this happen to people in occupations ranging from construction worker to radio commentator. Friends and family would try to reassure them—"Of *course* it was an FBI operation"—but often without much success. Thus one of the crueler consequences of the covert work of the faceless FBI men was that too often the victim, plagued with misgivings as to his competence, became in fact unemployable.

In my case, I felt I had come to a dead end. If the FBI could chase me out of this pathetic job, there was really no point in looking for another. I should have liked to go to college—friends of my age, whose children were growing up, had done so—but this was barred to me for lack of a high school diploma. I sent in for information about a high school correspondence course that I had found advertised on a matchbook cover; the brochure arrived, but the course included algebra and advanced arithmetic—back to the dread circumference and velocity of a bicycle wheel, no doubt. It sounded too arduous, at my time of life.

To fill the empty days I decided to try my hand at writing. *Noblesse Oblige,* a collection of essays by Nancy and others about U and Non-U usage, had just been published. "It is solely by its language that the upper class is clearly marked off from the others," as one contributor observed. An idea flashed into my mind: Was this not also true of the Communist Left? Why not a booklet on L usage, patterned after Nancy's book? The annual PW drive was under way; if I wrote the booklet, charged fifty cents a copy, and managed to sell a hundred of them, I would make my quota for the year.

It was tremendous fun writing it. The title (with a bow to Stephen Potter) immediately suggested itself: *Lifeitselfmanship, or How to Become a Precisely-Because Man.* It was actually a very collective piece of work, although in the end I got all the credit—as, after all, Nancy did for *Noblesse Oblige.* I started out with a few translations. Our friend Betty Bacon happened to drop in while I was hard at it; I showed her what I was doing and she immediately sat down to dash off an L translation of a non-L poem. Bob combed *Political Affairs* for the appendix, "Some authentic examples of recent L-writing," and came up with some gems. Pele de Lappe, then married to Steve Murdock, one of the PW reporters, produced some lovely Thurberesque illustrations. Bob's secretary, herself a staunch Party member, volunteered to cut the stencils. A comrade working in a business office contributed the mimeograph paper, filched at my urging from her boss's supply room (although needless to say, filching was contrary to CP policy).

If ever a book wrote itself, as publishers are fond of saying, this one did; the whole thing* was ready in a couple of days. In fact, by far the most time-consuming aspect of its production was the assembling, collating, and stapling, which we did on our kitchen table. In view of the free paper, we decided to up our first edition to five hundred. I was a trifle apprehensive about its reception. On a couple of occasions in the past I had been brought up on charges for making jokes in Party meetings—which meant a trial before the club executive committee. If the exec. com. thought the charges warranted it, one would then be brought before the dread County Security Commission, which had the power of expulsion; in my case, the exec. had let me off with a warning in consideration of my promise to be less frivolous in future. Hoping to disarm my readers in advance, I added a check list of appropriate criticisms of the author.

Cautiously I sought out a few carefully chosen comrades who I hoped would approve of *Lifeitselfmanship,* to test their reactions: Claire Stark, Al Richmond, Buddy Green, representing top leadership; Evie Frieden, Marge Frantz, Dobby Walker, from the middle echelons—themselves, it goes without saying, L-speakers all. To my absolute delight, they simply shrieked and pronounced it a Contribution to the Struggle Against Left-Sectarianism.

Emboldened by this reception, I set about organizing a sales

* For complete text, see Appendix.

and promotion campaign for *Lifeitselfmanship* that became for a while an absorbing, full-time occupation. I sent samples to Party bookshops around the country and review copies to all the likely publications I could think of: *Monthly Review,* the *National Guardian,* PW and DW, *Political Affairs, Mainstream,* successor to the defunct *Masses & Mainstream.*

The response was nothing short of thrilling. Far from taking a censorious attitude to *Lifeitselfmanship,* as I had feared would be the case, the CP and left-wing press warmly embraced it. Al Richmond gave it a half-page review in the PW, subsequently reprinted in the *Daily Worker;* the *Monthly Review* carried a short but extremely favorable notice; *Mainstream* reprinted the whole booklet, complete with Pele's drawings, as the main feature in one of its issues; Cedric Belfrage, editor of the *National Guardian,* wrote a satirical piece of his own, crediting *Lifeitselfmanship* as his inspiration; Sid Roger, star radio commentator on KPFA, devoted a half-hour to it. Philip Toynbee wrote from England: "I was absolutely delighted by your takeoff of L speech. May we publish a chunk of it in *The Observer,* paying you the usual rates, tributes, etc.?" And he did, to the tune of fifteen pounds. Nancy wrote: "I've been *screaming* over your pamphlet it's too lovely," and Stephen Potter: "If what you sent me is really *scuola di* Potter I feel very honoured and flattered because it amused me *very* much."

Rita Baxter prepared a five-page critique for circulation to all the East Bay Party clubs; perversely, this was my favorite review of all, much as in future years I would cherish denunciations of *The American Way of Death* by Howard C. Raether, executive secretary of the National Funeral Directors Association. She wrote: "The section which is broken down into subheadings contains the terms 'Relationship of forces, dogmatism, tailism' etc. I disagree with the inclusion of this terminology because I believe it to be necessary to our science. Scientific terminology is necessary to the Left because we are *scientists of society*. . . . The scientific terminology of the Left has developed as the theory and activity of the science of society has developed. It is exact in meaning, and in most cases has no proper substitution. . . . I think *Lifeitselfmanship* gives the impression that the solution to our mistakes in Left language is to have no scientific language at all. This doesn't properly open up the question for discussion, in my opinion. Instead of showing us the need for better understanding of the science of society and its activity, it leads us toward a further breakdown of our science."

Orders poured in from bookshops, libraries, and individuals all over the United States, from Canada, England, and Australia. A Japanese student wrote from Tokyo: "I find it is much interesting and feel the Left people has same usage both sides Pacific Ocean." Some comrades in London wrote for permission to reprint the booklet for the use of the Movement over there. A thick envelope arrived from the Four Continent Book Corporation, containing an order from Moscow for one copy, with instructions to fill out the invoice in quadruplicate, allowing best trade discount. (I wrote back: "I'm afraid I don't know how to fill out invoices in quadruplicate nor what is best trade discount so I'm sending this copy as a gift to the Soviet Union." Some months later a letter arrived from Moscow: "Since you neglected to quote our original order number, we are unable to use your gift.")

Steve Murdock wrote a long news story for the PW about the zooming sales and the flood of fan mail: "The postman who serves the 500 block on 61st St. in Oakland has been delivering more letters lately . . ." How I reveled in those fan letters! My days were taken up answering them, my evenings in the endless job of collating and stapling new editions to meet the ever-burgeoning demand. Before it was over we had sold 2,500, enriching the PW's treasury (since there were no expenses) by the undreamed-of sum of $1,250.

The children caught the excitement; they would rush home after school to help staple and fill orders. Dink reported that on a bus ride downtown the adorable Benj, trying to drum up business, had gone around the bus asking each passenger, "Have you read *Lifeitselfmanship* by Decca Treuhaft?" and offering to mail them a copy if they would ante up fifty cents.

I basked in the sudden, unexpected fame I had achieved in our circles, in the ineffable feeling of having produced what amounted to a best seller within the Party, in the delightful mental images I conjured up of the 2,500 buyers and their families sitting around their dinner tables, actually reading something I had written. (I do not know if other writers indulge in these fantasies about their readers; I do, and am kept afloat by them.)

Moreover, I felt I had done something positively useful. *Lifeitselfmanship* seemed to be an idea whose time had come; one could not imagine its smashing reception were it not for the unaccustomed, liberated atmosphere created in the Party by the Discussions. Steve Murdock had written in the PW: "The idea that the American Left can laugh at itself appears to be an engaging one," a thought expressed over and over again in the fan letters. The winds of change are blowing, as we L-speakers would have put it; for an End to Dogmatism! I congratulated myself that *Lifeitselfmanship* might in its small way help to hasten that end.

That autumn, the Party suffered another severe jolt: the Hungarian uprising and its suppression by Soviet tanks. My feelings about this event were very mixed, although one thing was dismally clear: in our visit to Hungary only a year earlier, Bob and I had entirely failed to perceive the widespread discontent that must have seethed below the surface. Of course we now thought back to Magda, Teacher, and the Budapest waiter.

Yet the massive accomplishments we had seen were also real; furthermore, from the news accounts it seemed probable that the legitimate grievances against Stalinist repression were being exploited and manipulated by the CIA from without and counterrevolution from within. Aranka reported that the small handful of her Jewish friends and relations in Budapest who had survived the Nazi holocaust, opponents all of the Communist regime, had welcomed the Soviet intervention, fearing that a White Terror and a return to a Horthy-style regime were in the making. The caliber of "Hungarian Freedom Fighters," many of them grasping neo-Fascist types, who now flocked into the United States under the wing of the State Department lent credence to this assessment.

Apparently the U.S. Party leadership also had trouble sorting out the complexities of these tangled developments; in any event, it stood on the sidelines, neither condemning nor condoning the Soviet occupation of Hungary. One immediate consequence for the CPUSA was an intensification of the exodus that had begun after the Khrushchev revelations. I did not join this exodus. To me, it seemed that whatever the rights and wrongs of the Hungarian situation, it had little relevance to our efforts within the Party to devise our own home-grown program for radical change.

The Discussions were prelude to the CP national convention, first to be held for seven years, to which I was elected as one of four delegates from the East Bay. This was a high honor, and I eagerly welcomed the chance to participate in these momentous deliberations.

I was to stay with some comrades who lived far uptown in Manhattan, near Harlem. Bob and I debated whether I should look up Aranka while in New York. The reason for my presence there would, we supposed, displease her deeply; but if through some one-in-a-million chance she discovered I had been in New York and not gone to see her, she would be even more put out. Better take the plunge, Bob said; just drop in on her without notice.

Arriving the day before the convention started, I made for Park Avenue and walked into Aranka's exquisite little bandbox of a hat shop. She was suitably flabbergasted, and I think genuinely overjoyed, to see me; there was much hugging and kissing. When I confided the purpose of my visit, she actually seemed rather proud that I had been accorded this recognition. "So why didn't they elect Bob, too, after all he's done for them?" Aranka's unpredictability was one of her charms.

Her eye lit on my coat, a beaver mouton that had originally cost twelve pounds, given to me by Debo as a parting present when Esmond and I left for America in 1939. It was my pride and joy at the time, I had lived in it through several bitter New York and Washington winters. But the fashions had changed in the interim, and the passage of eighteen years had not improved the looks of this garment. In fact, I had offered it at several PW rummage sales, with the proviso that if it did not fetch at least $2.50 I should have it back. There had never been any takers.

"Decca," said Aranka reprovingly, "you cannot go to the convention in that awful-looking thing. I will not allow it. What would the other delegates think? That my daughter-in-law is a peasant?" The solution was at hand. One of her customers had gone to Florida for the winter, leaving her mink coat in Aranka's safekeeping. Aranka now pressed this upon me; in truth, it was very luxurious and warm and I thought I looked marvelous in it, so I accepted the loan of it with good grace.

The next morning I set out long before dawn, in the freezing February weather, for the convention hall on Houston Street, at the other end of Manhattan from my friends' dwelling. Jogging along in the subway, I read *The New York Times,* which to my surprise gave front-page coverage to the upcoming CP convention. A horrid thought crossed my mind. If the *Times* story was any indication, the press would be there in force. I could see it now, a news photo flashed round the world, and the caption: "Mink-Coated Delegate Arrives at Red Meet." At the Houston Street subway station I wrapped the mink in the *Times* and dashed through the snowstorm (and past the photographers) in my thin rayon dress to achieve the sheltering warmth of the convention hall.

The convention lasted three days, meeting far into the night. At issue was the future direction of the Party: would it make the "sharp turn" towards inner-Party democracy, towards autonomy in its relationships with foreign Communist parties, towards renovation and the effort to seek an independent road to socialism consistent with the realities of American politics? Or would it remain in the grip of the hidebound, orthodox leadership of past decades?

The sharp-turn advocates, which included our California delegation, led by Oleta, Al, and Claire, were loosely gathered in the camp of John Gates, editor of the *Daily Worker;* the old-liners flocked to the banner of William Z. Foster, veteran CP leader. However, these groupings were not so clear at the time, for there was a third consideration very much on everybody's mind: the necessity of preserving inner-Party unity, of avoiding at all costs another of those splits that had proved so disastrous in the past. As a result there was a certain amount of tiptoeing around issues.

As far as I was able to judge, the prevailing mood of the convention favored the sharp-turners. True, the old-liners had their moments, as when during the debate on the main resolution a comrade rose (perhaps from force of habit) to propose substitution of the word "reject" for the word "oppose," a matter that took a good two hours to resolve; and again, there was a four-hour debate over whether to "interpret" Marxism-Leninism or to "creatively apply" it.

Yet on the whole the entrenched bureaucracy was forced on the defensive. The lines were drawn early on in a heated debate as to whether non-Party observers, a miscellany of pacifists and liberal civil-libertarians, would be admitted to the proceedings. The observers were, in fact, waiting in the wings for the convention's decision. They included A. J. Muste of the Fellowship of Reconciliation, Dorothy Day, editor of the *Catholic Worker,* the writer Stringfellow Barr, Bayard Rustin of the War Resisters League. The motion to admit them was overwhelmingly passed. This in itself seemed to herald a new era; hitherto it would have been unheard of to admit non-Communists to the deliberations of the Party's highest policy-making body, and particularly this group, whom we would formerly have scorned as "revisionist social democrats."

Another surprising development was the unanimous vote for a motion offered by one of the California contingent: that the headquarters of the Party be moved to Chicago, "heartland of industrial America," which relocation, said the maker of the motion, "would place our leadership closer to the areas of basic industry, steel, auto, rubber, packing with their large concentration of Negro workers," and he wound up: "Resolved: that this National Convention instruct the incoming National Committee to move the national headquarters to Chicago within the period of one year."

There was more to this resolution than immediately met the eye. While the New York Party was numerically the biggest in the nation, twice the size of that in California, it was an ingrown organization, largely dominated by European immigrants and their immediate descendants, giving it something of the character of an ideological old folks' home with strong allegiance to the European Communist Parties. The move to

Chicago, I thought, would be an excellent innovation; surely the old-time leaders, reluctant (as anybody would be) to move there from New York, would soon be replaced by younger, more flexible and innovative types.

As the author of *Lifeitselfmanship,* I found myself something of a minor celebrity, and thrilled to the praise of comrades from all around the country, my hitherto unknown readers. However, not everybody appreciated my effort. One night, the convention having adjourned around 2 a.m., I was offered a lift uptown by some comrades who lived in that direction, among them Eugene Dennis, general secretary of the Party. During the long drive he preserved a stony silence, never once glancing in my direction; possibly, I thought with a slight twinge of remorse, because so much of his own work had turned up in my booklet under the heading "Some authentic examples of recent L-writing."

There had, I learned, been much altercation over whether or not *Lifeitselfmanship* should be dignified by a review in *Political Affairs.* Nemmy Sparks, one of the top Party leaders in the country and a frequent contributor to that journal, had written a review when the booklet first appeared. For months it was held up, the subject of acrimonious discussions "at the highest level," Nemmy told me. In the immediate aftermath of the convention, when the spirit of self-criticism was still potent, he was able to sneak it in: "A marvellously funny pamphlet," he wrote. "Most of the 'horrible examples' come from *Political Affairs. . . .* Among the best features of the booklet are the delightful illustrations by Pele." In our accustomed fashion, Pele and I gloated over this review.

AFTER THE CONVENTION the observers said in a joint statement: "We wish to state that the sessions of the convention were democratically conducted with vigorous discussion of all matters brought to the floor. There were many indications that no individual or group was in a position to control the convention." This had also been my impression. However, in the next several months it gradually became apparent that the Discussions and the convention had produced a stillbirth. I was not privy to the high-level infighting that resulted in a recapturing of the Party apparatus and press by the Foster crowd; symbolic of their decisive victory was the fact that despite the unanimous vote of the convention, no move was ever made to transfer the national headquarters to Chicago. Nor was there any explanation of this high-handed disregard of the convention's decision; the subject was never again referred to in the Party press.

Early in 1958 John Gates resigned from the Party, saying it had "ceased to be an effective force for democracy, peace and socialism in the United States," and that he did "not believe it is possible any longer to serve those ideals within the Communist Party." Gates's Party career had been an illustrious one. He had fought in Spain, where he became the highest-ranking officer of the Lincoln Brigade. As one of the first group of Smith Act defendants, he had done time in the Atlanta penitentiary. Under his editorship the *Daily Worker* had been transformed from a house organ for transmission of policy directives by the leadership into a lively forum for debate. His resignation was a heavy blow indeed.

Soon after, several of the California top Party leaders followed suit, including five of the Smith Act defendants, among them some whom Bob and I had long admired and regarded as the most able of the state leaders. Inevitably, they were replaced by lesser lights of the Rita Baxter variety. Membership at the club level began dwindling drastically; while there were few formal resignations, people simply stopped coming to meetings. This meant a doubling up of the exec. com. jobs. I was now both lit. director and PW drive director for our club, which meant carting the lit. back and forth from the Party bookshop, attending the county-wide meetings for both functions, reporting back to an ever-shrinking club. It was dull work, rendered duller by the growing suspicion that the locomotive of history had roared off without us.

Bob and I stayed on for some months after the rash of resignations in early 1958. The East Bay Party, we thought, had managed to preserve much of the spirit of the Discussion period and the convention; there was an openness and flexibility, an allowance for difference of opinion, that on the whole had been snuffed out of existence in most parts of the country. And although many whom we regarded highly had resigned, others, such as Al Richmond, Bill Schneiderman, Hursel Alexander, were sticking it out, determined to fight for their point of view within the Party.

However, from everything one read in the Party press, it seemed unlikely they would prevail. *Political Affairs* was comfortably back on its old track, altered not at all, alas, by *Life-itselfmanship;* the *Daily Worker,* whose columns had been opened to all sorts of diverse opinions under Gates's leadership, had reverted to its familiar role as mouthpiece for the monoliths.

Bob recalls he had felt for some time that only inertia kept him in the organization. For me, the moment of decision came one evening when Mike and Evie Frieden tentatively sounded us out about leaving the Party. They had about decided, very reluctantly, to pack it up, they said; the Party had become a stagnant, ineffective sect, and in view of the direction the national leadership was taking, it was unlikely to revive. Could we not better serve the cause by devoting the time we spent doing Party work to outside movements for radical change (harbingers, as it later turned out, of the sixties) that were springing up in the black community, on campuses, among white liberals? I was swayed by their arguments, and by the fact that Evie, staunchest of comrades, who had spent her whole adult life in the Party, was thinking along these lines.

Rather than steal silently away, as so many comrades were doing, the four of us decided to seek out the East Bay Party chairman and explain the reasons for our resignations. We met with him a few days later at the Friedens' house. While he was predictably not pleased with our decision, there were no recriminations, no bitterness—and certainly no regrets, on our part, that we had devoted all those years to the Party's cause.

CHAPTER 12

Being an Ex

"THE EX'S," as they were called in Party parlance, suddenly freed from years of intense pressure and discipline, ran in a thousand directions, like schoolchildren when the dismissal bell rings. A minority, those tired of the struggle, or bitter and disillusioned, retreated altogether from the political arena to devote themselves to the pursuit of their own happiness. But for the most part the Ex's were endowed with an outsize sense of social responsibility and exceptional organizational skills, legacies from their years in the CP. In search of new outlets for these qualities they fled variously to the Unitarian Church, the Democratic Party, Women for Peace, the Co-op movement. These Ex's had, after all, joined the Party originally because of their vivid desire to improve the world and their conviction that this was possible, and on the whole they continued to be guided by what they had learned in the Party organization. For many of us, I think, the Party experience proved to have been a kind of adult Project Head Start that enabled us to function better than we otherwise might have in the new endeavors we now pursued.

Mike and Evie went back to college, he to become a lawyer, she a teacher. Buddy fulfilled his childhood ambition to become a long-haul truckdriver, an occupation in which he enjoyed enormous success. Claire went into a social-work agency, where she soon became a high-up executive. Bob, together with some members of the Berkeley Coop, devoted all his spare time to organizing the Bay Area Funeral Society. I, unemployable as ever and encouraged by the success of *Lifeitselfmanship,* was slowly getting on with a book I had started writing shortly after the CP convention of 1957.

This book evolved in a curious way. One day when sorting out some papers, I came across a large folder containing all Esmond's letters to me, written in 1941 while he was training for the air force in Canada and later from his air base in England. They were long, fascinating letters written mostly in pencil, indecipherable, I thought, by anybody but me; before long, the writing might fade altogether. To preserve them for Dinky, I spent a week or so making typewritten copies. Pele and Steve happened to come over while I was doing this. I showed them the letters, which they thought gave a wonderfully vivid account of air force life and, as a collection, would make an interesting book. None of us had the faintest idea of how one went about getting a book published; but they did suggest it would be well to write a little foreword which would put the reader in the picture about Esmond and me, how we happened to meet and marry, a few words about our respective childhoods.

I wrote the foreword, nineteen pages long, in one day, hoping they would not think it too discursive; it seemed difficult to condense further. That evening they came over, and together with Bob went over what I had done. "Oh, but you've left out a lot," they all kept saying. "What about the Hons' Cupboard? Your mother and the Good Body? The time you stole five pounds from the Conservative Fête to send to the London *Daily Worker?* You don't at all explain how you and Unity happened to be on such opposite sides. . . ."

The next day I started filling in some of that. And the next, and the next, for almost two years. My production soon dropped to three pages on good days, more often less. By the time the book was finished it had metamorphosed entirely; it ended with Esmond's death and his letters were not in it.

Writing is said to be a lonely task; I did not find it so. Perhaps thanks to my Party training, and to the method I had found so useful in writing *Lifeitselfmanship*, I turned it into a thoroughly collective endeavor, enlisting the help of several friends, who became known as the Book Committee. They were absolutely invaluable, all enthusiasts, each contributing his or her particular skills.

Pele was working in a factory at the time, her hours 7 a.m. to 3:15 p.m. Promptly at 3:30 she would appear at my house (which posed the daily challenge to produce a few pages for her to read), would seize upon the new material, and roar with uncritical laughter. She was, however, infallible at spelling and grammar and would note my lapses in the margin.

This would sustain me until that evening, when Steve had a look; dedicated to the principles of good journalism, in which he had received a rigorous training, he was much harder to please. "No description," he would write in the margin, or: "Date? Place? Time?" He was death on semicolons, which he considered old-fashioned, so I took those out; although being rather partial to them myself, I eventually put a few back in.

Betty Bacon, a librarian and author of the L-translation of "Tell me not in mournful numbers," was by far the toughest member of the Committee. She was a marvelous editor, and would nose out the horrid troubles I had with sequence, organization, antecedents like a truffle pig sniffing for its quarry. "Now look, Dec," she would say patiently, "this is *hopeless*," and her dread yet longed-for red pencil would show me how to get it in better order.

Worst of all was a thing called Transitions, on which Betty

was expert, which means getting elegantly from one subject to another without actually seeming to have done so. "Couldn't I just put: 'And so, gentle reader, we come now to the passage of time with its inevitable . . .' and so on, as Miss Maria Edgeworth used to do?" Absolutely not, said Betty firmly. Gentle readers no longer exist; they quietly passed away at some time in the nineteenth century. Today's readers, hard as nails, might take umbrage at being so addressed.

There were other members of the Committee: Barbara Kahn, a doctor's wife who had once gone to college and hence knew about grammar and would do away with the split infinitives; Dorothy Neville, a tooth-cleaner in a dental office and like Pele a roarer; Marge Frantz, my colleague from CRC days and a student of Marxism, who helped sort out the book's political line.

Bob excelled in all Committee functions: super roarer, super speller, super editor. He cheered when it was going well, sympathized when it was not, egged me on or reined me back, as called for. He also devised what I called the Bob-style Transition, an invaluable writer's aid consisting of a double space between paragraphs. (In fact, gentle reader, you may have noticed not a few of these in the book you are now reading.)

Sometimes the Committee members would find themselves in disagreement. I was writing a chapter about living in Bilbao with Esmond after we had run away to the Spanish war. But what did Bilbao look like? I have a terrible visual memory, and although we were there for a month I could not remember much about the town. So I looked it up in the *Britannica,* and read: "Bilbao is one of the principal seaports of Spain, and the greatest of Basque towns. It occupies a small but fertile and beautiful valley shut in by mountains on every side except towards the sea." I began my chapter with these words. Steve wrote in the margin: "Excellent! At last we have some description." But when Betty saw the manuscript, she wrote in the opposite margin: "This sounds as though it had been copied out of an encyclopedia." Badly caught out, I rewrote that bit: "Life in Bilbao had for me far more the quality of a dream than of a dream come true. . . . It was like living in a protracted vision. . . . I was trying to get in focus this big blur of a grey seaport town. . . ." Steve deplored deletion of the small, fertile, beautiful valley and the mountains on every side, but Betty pronounced the new wording somewhat of an improvement.

The beginning writer is frequently warned to put no stock in the praise heaped on his work by friends and family, who are bound to see it through deeply prejudiced eyes and who have no experience or professional yardstick by which to judge it. I do not agree with this advice; had I not been sustained by Bob and the Committee, I should soon have abandoned my effort, for the professional opinion of my manuscript, when it eventually began to be heard, was almost unanimously adverse.

There were some devastating moments. After the book was half finished, the Committee urged me to get an agent, but how? None of us had entrée into that rarefied world, which seemed to exist only in New York. Finally Dobby's husband, Mason, a PW columnist, gave me an introduction to Barthold Fles, a New York agent who had represented some of the Hollywood Ten and other blacklisted screenwriters. Fles, a Dutch immigrant, had stuck with these throughout the worst years of repression, selling their books to small left-wing firms—Cameron & Kahn, Monthly Review Press, Liberty Book Club—the only outlets in those days for such authors.

I sent him the manuscript and he told me to call him in three weeks, by which time he would have read it and decided whether or not to represent me. The weeks dragged interminably. On the appointed day I rang him up to get his verdict. "Eet ees ex-ecrab-lee typed," were his disheartening first words, but he said he would take it on anyway.

Assiduously Bart sent it on the rounds. Between April 1958 and January 1959 it was turned down by Dial Press; Morrow; Dodd, Mead; Atlantic Monthly Press; Doubleday, and several others. Once or twice it got a good report from some assistant editor, only to founder when it reached the top executives. There was a moment of high hope when Bart wrote to say that Henry Simon of Simon & Schuster had expressed interest; he wanted to read the manuscript and to meet me in San Francisco, where he would be staying for a few days. So relentlessly did I broadcast this exciting news to anybody who would listen that Marge Frantz threatened to have a button made for our friends to wear: "Yes, We Know Decca Has An Appointment With Henry Simon." But two days before the scheduled meeting Bart Fles's letter arrived, its words forever graven on my memory: "I am sorry but Henry doesn't like the book. Hence you are not going to meet him." After this the whole exercise began to seem pointless. The book was still not finished; the hardest part—the ending—was yet to be written. My early confidence seeped away and I put the manuscript aside.

Bob urged me to write an article about the Bay Area Funeral Society. I am sorry to say that I had rather mocked these good folks, an assortment of Unitarians, Quakers, college professors, and other eggheads whose oddly chosen field of endeavor was to fight the high cost of dying by securing inexpensive, simple funerals for the members through contract with an undertaker. I had called them the Necrophilists and teased them about their Layaway Plan. Why pick on the wretched undertakers, I asked Bob. Are we not robbed ten times more by the food industry, the car manufacturers, the landlord? But Bob, whose idea the Funeral Society had been in the first place and who was one of the prime movers in the organization, was absolutely immersed in it.

After I began reading the trade magazines he brought home I could see why. Their very names could hardly fail to invite a closer look: *Casket & Sunnyside, Mortuary Management,* and my favorite of all, *Concept, the Journal of Creative Ideas for Cemeteries.* I was fascinated by the fantasy world revealed in their pages, the world of "Futurama, the casket styled for the future," of burial negligees, street wear, and brunch coats, of Practical Burial Footwear featuring the Fit-a-Fut Oxford, of Natural Expression Formers (an embalmer's aid), and of the True Companion Crypt, "where husband and wife may truly be together forever."

Even more striking were the apoplectic flights of rhetoric in which these magazines denounced the clergy, the funeral societies, and anybody else who favored a return to simpler funerals: "The Menace of the Nosy Clergy"; "Burial beatniks of America"; "Weasels sucking away at the lifeblood of our economy." Drawing on the trade press for inspiration, I wrote the piece, entitled "St. Peter Don't You Call Me," and sent it off to Bart Fles.

Faithful Bart circulated it to numerous magazines and forwarded the rejections that poured in from *Coronet, The Nation, The Reporter, The Atlantic Monthly,* and others. "Eet ees too deestasteful a subject," he told me. But eventually it did find a home, for a fee of forty dollars, in *Frontier,* an obscure liberal Democratic magazine in Los Angeles with a circulation of two thousand. Prodded by Bob, the Bay Area Funeral Society ordered ten thousand reprints; once more I enjoyed pleasant daydreams about those thousands of readers.

As to the book, I hovered uneasily between two views of the rejections. On the face of it, all those editors had found it to be without merit. Yet I clung to the hope that another factor just might be involved: the aversion of publishers in those days to any book that smacked of radicalism or whose author had been tagged with the subversive label.

My Committee loyally adopted the latter view. The publishing industry, they pointed out, no less timorous than the rest of the media, had for the past ten years sedulously avoided books that might incur the displeasure of the various witch-hunting committees. There was every indication that some publishers prudently imposed their own tacit form of censorship, less visible than that of the film industry—which took great pains to proclaim and reiterate publicly its subservience to the witch-hunters—but comparable in its effect.

One last possibility remained. Our passports restored by the Supreme Court ruling, Bob and I were going to England with Benjy, for whom it would be his first visit, in the spring of 1959. I would take the manuscript along, hoping it might have a better reception in that more temperate political clime. If it met with no success there, I would give up the idea of becoming a writer. The book was in any event now in the back of my mind, all thoughts focused on the pleasures of observing Benjy's reactions to England and vice versa.

He and I sailed that April on the *Liberté;* Bob, who could take only a few weeks off from the office, was to follow later. The ever kind and understanding Mrs. Hill, who had let Dinky come with me to the state Un-American Activities Committee hearing, was still principal of the elementary school from which Benj was now about to graduate; she heeded my somewhat specious appeal that the journey would be "educational" for him, and agreed to release him early.

Our friends thought it rather rash to take Benj for such a long holiday; they said I would soon get tired of him tagging along after me—he and I were to stay alone together in Europe until school reopened in September. Bob would be joining us only briefly and Dinky, now away at college, was to spend the summer working. In fact, at the golden age of eleven, Benj proved to be an entrancing companion. On the *Liberté* I saw all too little of him; he was forever away in first class, dining off fine fare with some children he had met there, or on the bridge, helping the captain. "Did you notice that sudden jolt, Dec, when the whole ship shuddered? I was steering, and pulled her around rather too sharply."

On our third day out, a tremendous storm blew up. The captain was shouting over the loudspeaker system, *"Messieurs et Mesdames les passagers! Attention! Nous vous demandons de retourner tout de suite à vos cabines pendant la tempête!"* The solicitous Benj came rushing down from first class to see if I was all right. Safer to sit in the bar, he said; several had been injured getting to their cabins. Having been to the compulsory lifeboat drill (which I had avoided), he knew all the ways to the boats, and at his suggestion we sat out the storm making lists of which of our fellow passengers to save, which to let drown. I was glad to find we were in substantial agreement on both lists.

In London we stayed with Joanie Rodker, whom I had met in 1955 through our English left-wing connections. On our first night there Doris Lessing came to dinner with her twelve-year-old son, Peter, a large friendly bear of a boy, who had set aside his Easter holiday to "show the American boy the sights." For days he and Benj were inseparable. They would sprint off early in the morning with a few shillings for Underground fare, occasionally telephoning for advice: "We're at Greenwich— what should we do here?" "Find out the mean time." Or: "We're in the West End—what should we do now?" "Have cocktails at the Savoy, I should think."

Benjy's other great companion was Marian, daughter of one of the CP solicitors, an appealing, waiflike thirteen-year-old. "Meet you at the Marble Arch in half an hour," I would hear him say on the telephone. "Oh, Benj, the Marble Arch is huge; you'll never find her." But he always did, and together they would set off for the Battersea Pleasure Gardens.

To fulfill the promised educational aspect of the expedition Benj decided to study the English language by racing through all the English children's books we could find: E. Nesbit, *Tom Brown's School Days, Sherlock Holmes.* He applied the lessons learned therein to his everyday speech, with odd results. If we took a cab, he would offer the surprised driver "A sovereign, my good man, if you can get us to Paddington before the night express train leaves." And "I say, Mater, you're a trump!" he would exclaim, or "Crikey! These bangers are topping," to the astonishment of Peter and Marian, unversed as they were in nineteenth-century schoolboy slang.

A few days after we arrived in London, I asked one of the CP lawyers if he knew of an English literary agent who might consider representing me. He suggested James MacGibbon of Curtis Brown, one of the largest and most eminent English literary agencies. I went round to MacGibbon's office, manuscript in hand. We were chatting about this and that when he asked casually, "By the way, Mrs. Treuhaft, are you a member of the Communist Party in California?" I was floored; in America, this could only be a hostile question, coming as it did from a stranger in the course of a business discussion. It seemed too cruel to have it sprung on me in England of all places. I peered closely at his face; disingenuous, friendly eyes gazed back. "Well, I was," I replied, "but I resigned about a year ago because the Party was becoming so inactive and ineffectual." "Oh, *so* was I," said MacGibbon. "I left for about the same reason." What a superbly un-American conversation, I thought.

Developments now unfolded with incredible rapidity, as in a speeded-up movie. James had said he would read the manuscript within the next few weeks. But the day after our meeting he rang up to say he had read it that evening and his enthusiasm was unbounded—not even a reservation about the typing. Which publisher would I prefer, he asked. I explained it wasn't quite like that, and told him about all the rejections. It was settled that he would offer it to Victor Gollancz (whom I had admired from afar since the Left Book Club days before the war) for publication in England, and for the U.S., to Lovell Thompson of Houghton Mifflin, who happened to be in London at the moment. I should expect to wait about six weeks for a decision, James thought.

Three days later, Benj and I, windblown and freezing from hours in an open boat on the Thames (part of his education of me), returned to Joanie's house in the late afternoon. She was outside waiting for us, a bottle in her hand, jumping up and down screaming something we couldn't quite hear. Then we made out the words: "James rang up! Gollancz and Houghton Mifflin have taken your book! You've got to go round tomorrow and sign the contracts! Come in and celebrate—I've bought some whisky!" Benj broke into a crazy jitterbug dance of joy while Joanie and I quaffed the whisky and composed a victory cable to Bob and the Committee members.

The next day Benj came with me to the Curtis Brown office. James handed over the contracts and I was about to sign when Benj, looking at once slightly embarrassed and very determined, stayed my hand. "If you don't mind, Mr. MacGibbon, my father says one should never sign anything without reading the fine print. As he isn't here, I think I'd better do it," and he pored over the numerous clauses while James looked on gravely. "Fine print satisfactory, Benjy?" said James at last. "Very well, then, your mother can sign now."

For weeks thereafter I was consumed with secret excitement about the contracts; I thought it best not to mention the matter to my sisters and cousins until the book was published, for fear of alarming them about its contents, so there were few people to whom I could confide my good news. One day I went to tea in Hampstead with Ella Winter, widow of Lincoln Steffens; her present husband, Donald Ogden Stewart, black-listed screenwriter who in the thirties had written many best-selling books; the novelist James Aldridge and others of the Left literati. I couldn't help announcing to this assemblage, "I've written a book, and it's been accepted by a publisher!" As I wrote to Bob: "The reaction was something like what *you* might expect if you were in the company of several distinguished lawyers, and you suddenly blurted out, 'I'm going to court tomorrow! I'm trying a case before a *real judge!*' "

After Bob's short visit, Benj and I settled into a hotel near Bormes, two miles from the French Riviera, where I was to finish the book. Our life there was idyllic. Benj hitchhiked down to the beach each morning while I worked; at noon I would go down, to find him stretched out on the sand with Lisette, a sloe-eyed French child who had replaced Marian in his affections. One day I chatted with her briefly in French. "What were you saying?" Benj asked anxiously. "Oh, I was just telling her all about you and Marian in London." He was to meet his Aunt Nancy soon, and I thought it would be as well to toughen him up in advance.

I need not have bothered; heredity had evidently done its work, for his revenge was worthy of Nancy herself. On the day the book was finished, I tenderly wrapped it in the stoutest paper to be found and nervously consigned it to the care of the Bormes postmistress, to be sent on its perilous journey over the sea to James. That evening Benj dashed dramatically into the hotel, the very picture of agitated concern. "Are you all right? Oh, I'm so *relieved* to see you're still alive. I was so *terrified* you'd have been hurt in the fire. . . . But hadn't you heard? The Bormes post office burned to the ground this afternoon."

The book was published the following spring, called *Hons and Rebels* in England, *Daughters and Rebels* in America—Lovell Thompson thought *Hons* too obscure for the American public. (Virginia Durr, then living in Montgomery, wrote to say that as a consequence of its title, it was displayed in the Alabama bookshops on the shelves of Civil War books.)

Nancy once told me she never paid any attention to what the critics said about her books. Other writers have said the same. I envy this admirable detachment, which I could never achieve; on the contrary, I lived in dread anticipation until the reviews began to appear. To my enormous relief they were mostly favorable. But for many weeks after the book was published, the opinion I really craved—that of Nancy herself—did not arrive. I had sent her an advance copy and day after day I rushed for the post, looking for her letter. I began to think she had decided not to comment; then, finally, her letter came, postmarked six weeks earlier, having been sent by surface mail. (As she subsequently explained, she thought it non-U to send letters by airmail: "It's very middle-class to be in a hurry.") She wrote: "Many thanks for sending your book which I have read with great attention. I think its *awfully good*—easy to read, very funny in parts. All the reviews have been spiffing, not one adverse note. Clever little thing, you'll make pots." Her usual dagger was contained in the P.S.: "Esmond was the original Teddy Boy, wasn't he."

I heard nothing directly from my other sisters. As Harold Acton writes: "Nancy was not in the least offended by her sister Jessica's remarks in *Hons and Rebels*. On the contrary, she liked the book though her family could not speak of it"—and they never did, to me. But Diana had her say in a letter to the

Times Literary Supplement, whose reviewer had written: "Does Jessica Mitford realize how supremely unpleasant her father and mother appear? If she does, she is too wise and loyal to stress these points."

Diana wrote in rebuttal: "Doubtless the author realizes how 'supremely unpleasant' she makes her family appear. Perhaps the object of the exercise was to demonstrate her good fortune in escaping from them and their way of life. . . . The portraits of my parents are equally grotesque. My sister's book was probably meant to amuse, rather than to be 'wise,' 'loyal,' or truthful." (Incidentally, the *TLS* review was the only one to draw this inference about my parents from what I had written about them. Various other reviewers recorded contrary impressions: ". . . an English couple with some splendid upper-class eccentricities"; ". . . somewhat lovable, if expletive, father"; ". . . charmingly eccentric mother." One reviewer even called my description of our childhood "a joyous account"; another said I regarded my parents "with very little awe and some affection." Who knows? Thinking it all over today, I suppose my book *was* meant to amuse, as Diana said; although I did try to describe the characters therein as faithfully as I knew how.)

Besides Nancy's, the opinion I was most anxiously awaiting was that of the Party, so I was very gratified that the PW review, when it eventually appeared, heaped praise. Actually, I doubt that I should ever have taken up writing had I stayed in the CP, since members were somewhat circumscribed by Party discipline in their choice of occupations. I should have loved to be a reporter on the PW, and once confided this ambition to the county leadership, but they pointed out that I had no experience as a journalist and that my services in the CRC could not be dispensed with. It was not that one was *ordered* to accept certain assignments—at least, not in my experience—but rather that if one showed ability in a given Party job, one soon became pigeonholed in it. The Party leadership, overworked and preoccupied with weighty political and organizational problems, did not take kindly to what they may have seen as whimsical and individualistic suggestions for change of assignment by the members.

But after *Daughters and Rebels* came out, John Pittman, a PW editor who had previously been cool to my ambition to work on the paper, called me in and proposed that I should write a weekly column. I was flattered at this suggestion until he explained that they needed a housewives' column: "How to save money while shopping—that sort of subject." Bob, who does all our grocery shopping and regards me as incompetent at this task because I rush through it without looking at the prices, shuddered at the thought of my column. "How to save *time* while shopping would be more like it."

AN UNFORESEEN BY-PRODUCT of the book was the instant respectability its publication in America seemed to have conferred on me. Suddenly I was in demand for press interviews, radio and television appearances, as speaker at women's clubs and colleges—hardly forums to which I could have aspired formerly. The intention of my hosts was, I suppose, that I should provide fascinating glimpses into the life of the English aristocracy; instead, I used these occasions to blast away at all our old enemies—the FBI, HUAC, the district attorney of Alameda County.

I soon discovered that as a published author one could get away with almost anything. It was a new and curious sensation and one that I found most enjoyable, to be swimming freely in the "mainstream," to find doors heretofore closed to me magically opening on every side.

Furthermore, magazine editors who had in the past contributed their share to my bulging files of rejections now began to ask me to write for their publications. Over the next year or so I pressed this advantage, choosing subjects that I hoped would advance the Fine Old Conflict. I went to the Deep South to write a piece for *Esquire,* entitled "You-All and Non-You-All," on the sit-in movement and Freedom Riders; for *The Nation,* I wrote about the nascent student rebellion at the University of California; best of all, the *Chronicle,* which had fired me only four years before, accepted an article for its book page about the disgraceful cowardice of the American publishing industry during the years of McCarthyism.

The high point of my new-found respectability came when Casper Weinberger, a prominent San Francisco Republican (later appointed by Nixon as head of HEW), invited me to participate in a debate on a half-hour television show, "Profile Bay Area," which he was then producing for the educational channel. The debate was on the subject of the Bay Area Funeral Society. On the affirmative side were a Unitarian minister and me; for the negative, two undertakers who proved to be wildly comic adversaries. Terrence O'Flaherty, television columnist for the San Francisco *Chronicle,* reported that the program had generated more mail to his column than any public event since *The Bad Seed* was shown at a local junior high school, which was highly pleasing news.

Shortly after this I received a telephone call from Roul Tunley, a staff writer on the *Saturday Evening Post,* who was passing through San Francisco. He had heard about the debate from a journalist friend, he said; the subject sounded juicy, and he thought it might make a good piece for the *Post.* I invited Tunley over to have a look at Bob's growing collection of funeral trade magazines, and set up some appointments for him with leaders of the Bay Area Funeral Society. Although I was actually sadly inactive in that organization, Tunley depicted me in his article as "an Oakland housewife who is among those leading the shock troops of the rebellion in one of the most bizarre battles in history—a struggle to undermine the funeral directors, or 'bier barons,' and topple the high cost of dying."

The article, entitled "Can You Afford to Die?", came out in June 1961. The response to it was absolutely astonishing. The *Post* editor reported that more mail had come in about Tunley's piece than about any other in the magazine's history, and observed that it "seemed to have touched a sensitive nerve." The Bay Area Funeral Society issued a frantic appeal for volunteers to help handle the thousands of inquiries that poured in. Bob got a call from the Oakland postmaster: "We have hundreds of letters here addressed simply 'Jessica Treuhaft, Oakland,' giving no street or number." (They were eventually delivered. One envelope bore the stark direction: "Jessica Treuhaft, Cheap Funerals, Oakland.")

Bob was extremely gratified that at last his fledgling organization had taken wing, not only in the Bay Area but nationally, as a result of the *Post* article. Surely this spate of letters showed enough public interest in the subject to warrant consideration of a book about it? I wrote to Roul Tunley, urging him to expand his piece into a book; we would furnish him with any amount of research material, send him all our back copies of *Casket & Sunnyside,* put the files of the Funeral Society at his disposal. He replied that he was too busy with other assignments to take it on. "Why don't *you* write it?" he suggested.

Bob and I discussed this possibility. I said I would consider it only if he would help, and work with me on it full time. We wrote off to James MacGibbon and to Candida Donadio, the young and brilliant literary agent who some months before had agreed to represent me in the U.S., enclosing a brief outline and a copy of "St. Peter Don't You Call Me." Candida replied: "It's a superb idea, so kookie that it is definitely possible." She and

James set about drawing up the contracts with Houghton Mifflin and Victor Gollancz, both of whom seemed moderately enthusiastic. With this encouragement, Bob arranged to take a leave of absence from his law firm and we got down to work.

It was the best of times, it was the worst of times. Bob now spent his days in the San Francisco College of Mortuary Science, where with the help of two professors at that academy named Mr. Sly and Mr. Grimm he penetrated the mysteries of embalming techniques. I visited dozens of funeral establishments, among them Forest Lawn Cemetery in Los Angeles (immortalized by Evelyn Waugh in *The Loved One*), posing as a "pre-need" shopper. Together we sorted out the material, plotted and wrote the chapters.

Since the book was a completely joint effort, in which Bob and I had equally assumed the burdens of research and writing, I had assumed that it would appear cosigned: "By Robert Treuhaft and Jessica Mitford." Agents and publishers alike balked at this; they said that cosigned books never sell as well as those with one author. Bob (all too readily, in my view) fell in with this opinion; as he did not plan to make writing his career, he would defer to the experts.

In his review, Evelyn Waugh said: "It is easy to guess the nature of their collaboration; here is little Decca teasing on the telephone, there is solid Bob at his desk doing his sums." In fact, we each wrote about half the book. It is difficult at this distance of time to sort out exactly which paragraphs were Bob's and which mine. I do know, however, that those portions that appear most frequently in anthologies and college texts on writing were mostly Bob's work.

Our toughest problem was how to write the factual description of the embalming process. Since embalming is the ultimate fate of virtually all Americans, we were determined to describe it in all its revolting details; but how to make this subject palatable to the reader? We thought to solve this by casting the whole passage in mortuary jargon, drawing on the industry's published lists of taboo words and their acceptable synonyms that we had found in *Casket & Sunnyside:* "Mr., Mrs., Miss Blank, not corpse or body; preparation room, not morgue; reposing room, not laying out room . . ." Hoping this would give the subject a touch of macabre humor, we introduced it thus: "The body is first laid out in the undertaker's morgue—or rather, Mr. Jones is reposing in the preparation room—to be readied to bid the world farewell." We were on the whole pleased with Mr. Jones, whose bizarre experiences filled several pages.

By early 1962 we had finished about a hundred pages, which we sent to the agents and publishers for their opinion. James MacGibbon wrote back by return of post: "This is a terribly difficult letter to write because I don't like these chapters, and Victor Gollancz doesn't like them either. The joke, such as it is, surely is going to go on far too long—it already has. I cannot imagine any publisher here wanting it. I find it almost impossible to suggest how you could adapt the book to make it acceptable," and he asked to be relieved as my agent of the obligation to offer it to other publishers.

I was cast into deepest despair by this letter, but Bob said one should not be too depressed about this reaction from England; after all, we were writing about a purely American phenomenon. Houghton Mifflin would no doubt take a very different view of it.

Weeks went by with no word from Houghton Mifflin. Daily I accosted our postman, demanding to look through his bag of mail: "I *know* you've got a letter for me from Boston in there." Finally Lovell Thompson's letter arrived. He said I should "cut out the foolishness," meaning, I assumed, all the jokes, and added, "We think that you make your book harder to sell by going at too much length and in too gooey detail into the process of embalming." In effect, as I said to Bob, Lovell's reaction was the same as James's, only phrased American style, in gentler and less forthright language.

I wrote to Candida, saying we were not going to jettison the embalming passage,* on which the book was now foundering both in England and the U.S.; that we had decided to go ahead, finish the book, mimeograph it, and sell it ourselves, as I had done with *Lifeitselfmanship*. Candida, who had comforted me throughout the crisis caused by James's letter and whose stead-fast faith in the book had remained unshaken, replied by tele-gram: she already had a publisher for it—Bob Gottlieb, an editor at Simon & Schuster, who had offered twice the advance given by Houghton Mifflin.

Years later, Bob Gottlieb told me how this came about. "Candida and I were whining to each other on the phone one night—charter members of the Whiners' Club. Although Candida was already recognized as one of the most successful agents in the business, she was complaining that she was a terrible failure. I was whining back about what a terrible failure I was as an editor. I couldn't think up any good ideas for books, I told her. I'd had only one idea in my whole life: a book about the funeral industry."

Candida said he was too late; such a book was being written by Jessica Mitford and had already been taken by Houghton Mifflin. "I had loved *Daughters and Rebels* and was in despair that another publisher was going to be enjoying this treat. I begged Candida to remember S & S if anything went wrong

---

* In 1965 I was sent a textbook for college students entitled *The Essential Prose*, an anthology, according to the editors, of "prose of the first order from the past and present." There, tucked between Plato and Sir Thomas Browne, in a section captioned "Mortuary Solaces," was our Mr. Jones re-posing in the preparation room! Is there a moral here for the neophyte writer in his dealings with editors?

with HM and said I'd pay twice their advance. Knowing Boston, I thought that would be a safe offer." But neither Bob G. nor Candida really believed anything could or would go wrong. "Months went by," Bob told me, "and one day she called up with the cheery news that Houghton Mifflin didn't like the part about embalming! So it was settled on the spot."

After this, all was plain sailing. In 1962 we went to New York to meet Gottlieb, who at the age of thirty was something of a prodigy of the publishing world. It was love at first sight. He was entranced with the embalming passages and roared at the jokes (although he now complains that for the first year he knew Bob and me, our only topic of conversation was the relative strengths of embalming fluids and the effectiveness of various brands of trocar, a device used by undertakers to pump out the contents of the deceased stomach). He proved to be an uncommonly good editor, at once perceptive, amused, tough, adept at ferreting out one's weak spots, yet sympathetic with one's difficulties—in fact, he was like all the members of my Book Committee rolled into one. (Unbeknownst to him, however, the Committee still functioned. Nothing was sent to S & S until Pele had laughed her head off, Betty had cast her discerning eye, and Marge had monitored the class-struggle aspects of funerals. One disregarded Committee advice at one's peril. Barbara Kahn, who was typing the finished manuscript, came across a passage about the nineteenth-century English cremationists: "They went so far as to cremate each other in defiance of the authorities." Barbara insisted there was something wrong with this sentence; I could not see it, so let it stand. Sure enough, after the book was published, it turned up in *The New Yorker,* captioned "Neatest Trick of the Week.")

Once more, in preparing this book, our CP training, whatever we had been able to absorb and retain of the Marxist method, stood us in good stead. "Dialectical materialism, here we come!" might have been our slogan as we pondered our approach to the funeral industry. We had noted that what little had been published on funeral practices tended to dwell on the misdeeds of the bad apples of the industry. Trade association leaders were not too upset over this kind of exposé because it gave them an escape route, enabling them to utter pious words about their self-policing policies, their ceaseless vigilance and determination to rid the Profession of those who failed to live up to its Code of Ethics.

We decided from the outset to go for the jugular and expose, not the occasional miscreant, but the profiteering and monopolistic practices of the industry as a whole as exemplified by its most respectable and ethical practitioners. We made this political decision clear in the foreword: "This would normally be the place to say (as critics of the American funeral trade invariably do) 'I am not, of course, speaking of the vast majority of ethical undertakers.' But the vast majority of ethical undertakers is precisely the subject of this book. To be 'ethical' merely means to adhere to a prevailing code of morality, in this case one devised over the years by the undertakers themselves for their own purposes." (At one point I wrote to Bob Gottlieb saying, "We have trunkfuls of scandals—bribery of hospital personnel to steer cases, the illegal re-use of coffins, fraudulent double charges in welfare cases—but we've decided not to bother with these." Gottlieb rang up in mock anguish: "You *can't* tell your editor you've got trunkfuls of scandals and won't use them!")

In the course of our happy association with Candida and Gottlieb there was one question that plagued Bob and me—the very same one that I had faced (or ducked, depending on how one looks at it) with Edna of the Newspaper Guild. Here were two brilliant youngsters, undoubtedly on the threshold of distinguished careers. Were we deceiving them by not disclosing our long-time membership in the CP? Suppose it was discovered later by their bosses, and they were fired as a consequence, their future blighted by their association with us? Yet if we sprung the word Communist on them, would they unceremoniously drop us?

Today these worries may seem rather absurd. But in 1962, although the worst years of repression had passed, the Red-hunters were still on the prowl and capable of delivering crippling blows. Again we compromised, dropping many a hint about the dear departed subversive days, but stopping short of mentioning our membership in the Party. Bob Gottlieb since told me, "Of course we were on to you; I spotted you right away as one of those dreary Old Lefts." (I regret to say that Gottlieb, far from assigning noble motives to my long involvement in the Party's struggles, takes the uncharitable view that I joined in the first place and stuck it out for all those years only because I am a "born gutter fighter.")

Months before *The American Way of Death* was published, the funeral industry became aware that the book was in progress, and it was not long before the trade press rounded upon me in full force. A new menace had loomed on their horizon: the Menace of Jessica Mitford. Headlines began to appear in the undertakers' journals: JESSICA MITFORD PLANS ANTI-FUNERAL BOOK! and MITFORD DAY DRAWS CLOSER! When *Mortuary Management* started referring to me as Jessica, I felt I had arrived at that special pinnacle of fame where the first name only is sufficient identification, as with Zsa Zsa, Jackie, or Adlai. Greedily I gobbled up the denunciations: "The notorious Jessica Mitford"; ". . . shocker"; ". . . stormy petrel."

In an article headlined: WHO'S AFRAID OF THE BIG BAD BOOK? the editor of *Mortuary Management* said there was little to fear because books about the Profession never enjoy large sales—he knew this because his dad once wrote a book about funeral service and although he took an ad in the *Saturday Evening Post,* it sold only three hundred copies. "To be sure, Jessica has a captive market, small though vocal, the members of the Nation's memorial societies," he wrote. "But we firmly believe that the public enthusiasm for the book will be of an extremely mild variety and that any storm stirred up will be both non-injurious and of short duration—unless funeral service makes the mistake of dignifying the book with retaliatory endeavors."

Bob and I were inclined to agree with this estimate; we did not anticipate a readership much beyond Unitarians, funeral society members, and other advocates of funeral reform, a relatively tiny group. Not so Bob Gottlieb and his colleagues at Simon & Schuster, who in their skillful fashion managed to create public enthusiasm of an extremely potent variety and to stir up an injurious storm of unusually long duration.

Because of their aggressive merchandising policies, Simon & Schuster had earned the sobriquet "Simon's Shoe Store" in some New York circles. In April, I was summoned to New York to correct the galleys and meet with the publicity department to plot the promotion of the book. How I grew to love Bob Gottlieb's merry crew: Nina Bourne, with her sharp sense of the absurd, in charge of advertising; Tony Schulte, seemingly infallible in his estimate of the potential audience for a book; serious Dan Green, youngest of them all, who worked hard to carry out their directives even if he did not always get the jokes.

I wrote to Bob about this meeting:

It exceeded my fondest hopes, the Shoe Store swinging into action. I'll try to recapitulate the plans. For the annual booksellers convention in Washington they are going to try to get a casket, and are ordering a giant wreath to be made exactly like the jacket design.

Also, getting lots of things from the Forest Lawn Gift Shop such as the Builder's Creed, Forest Lawn ashtrays, Forest Lawn coloring books for kiddies etc. as door prizes for the salesmen.

Discussion turned on how to create national news stories around the book, how to get legislation introduced, how to get somebody to sue us ("Once we're in court, it's bound to be news!"). Goodness you'd have shrieked.

They are making up a brochure of all the attacks in the funeral press, also a special letter to the clergy, possibly a trade union letter, and a letter to the Memorial Societies. All these special letters and special approaches did so remind me of CRC.

They say that 6,000 copies have already been ordered by the bookshops, that their goal is to sell more advance copies than *Daughters and Rebels* sold altogether.

I'm afraid all this is making me fearfully swell-headed, do come to NY and sober me up.

A few months before publication, Bob Gottlieb rang up to say the first edition would be 7,500. Some days later he told us this had been increased to 15,000. Then he telephoned again: the first printing was now set at 20,000. On publication day, the book went out of stock, the first printing having been sold out.

Thanks to Gottlieb, Nina, and the others, what followed was like a rerun of the publication of *Lifeitselfmanship,* only on a larger scale, and without the bother of stapling. *The American Way of Death* zoomed to the top of *The New York Times* Best Seller List, where it stayed for some months. Not only were the reviews almost universally dazzling, the subject became Topic A in the media. CBS made a documentary film based on the book, *The Great American Funeral,* said to have been watched by forty million viewers. Newspapers across the country, including the Miami *Herald,* New York *Herald Tribune,* San Francisco *Chronicle,* Chicago *Tribune,* Cleveland

Plain Dealer, Denver *Post,* published their own in-depth surveys of local funeral costs and practices. One had but to tune in to any radio talk show to catch a clergyman denouncing the pagan ostentation of the modern funeral, or a widow describing how she was fleeced by an undertaker. Walt Kelly and Bill Mauldin mocked the funeral industry in cartoons syndicated in hundreds of newspapers. A *New Yorker* cartoon showed an undertaker in deepest gloom standing outside his establishment and a passer-by calling out to him: "Read any good books lately?"

Benj, now in high school, shamelessly induced a dozen of his classmates to buy copies; they would come trooping in, asking me to autograph their books. One fifteen-year-old girl told me Benj had insisted it would make an ideal thirty-fifth-anniversary gift for her parents; rather to Benj's consternation, I inscribed it for them, "May you be Truly Together Forever."

In October, two months after the book was published, Simon & Schuster sent me on a nationwide book promotion tour, accompanied by Dan Green. (While such tours are now a routine part of book promotion, in those days they were far from common; yet another example of the Shoe Store's innovative and go-ahead merchandising methods.) It was a kaleidoscopic six weeks, enlivened for me by some unforeseen responses of the undertakers and by Dan's earnest efforts to guide me through the treacherous shoals of sudden public figuredom.

I felt deeply for him, for he was, I suppose, in charge of my Image; but every time he got it in focus it would shatter before his very eyes. For example, a review from England (where, thanks to Candida, the book had been published by Hutchinson) began: "Miss Mitford is a minor curiosity of the age." I liked that, and mentioned it during a radio interview. Later

Dan drew me aside urgently: "We want to soft-pedal that aspect. You're *not* a minor curiosity; you're the author of the number-one best seller in the country. You're a major *authority,* whose opinion is sought by legislators and public agencies." I gazed at him down the decades that separated us, trying to see myself as he saw me. To him I'm Grand Old Miss Mitford, I thought, with not a hint of all the odd vicissitudes, contrasts, and surprises my life had afforded.

Sometimes, despite his endeavors to create what he called "name recognition," our hosts proved to be all too dimly aware of what my appearance was all about. The bottom was reached on an early-morning housewives' television show in Cleveland. Arriving in the studio, we watched the act preceding mine, a dozen little tads in leotards doing push-ups while their proud mommies looked fondly on. Then came my turn. The hostess of the show, flashing a bright smile from under her blond beehive hairdo, called me on stage. "And now we are pleased to welcome Mrs. Jessie Medford. Good morning, Mrs. Medford!" She whispered an urgent aside to me: "What did you *do?*" "Wrote a book," I whispered back. "Mrs. Medford has written a lovely novel, and now she'll tell us all about it."

Dan's real troubles began in Denver, where I was to address the Denver *Post*'s annual Book and Author dinner. Bob and I had been somewhat puzzled from the outset at the failure of the funeral industry to play what must surely be their trump card, exposure of our Red background; but in the euphoria of the book's reception by press and public, this question had receded into the back of my mind. It was now brought sharply to the fore.

On the day of the dinner a UPI reporter telephoned. "Miss Mitford? Have you heard about the statement of Congressman James B. Utt of Santa Ana, California, in today's

Congressional Record?" I had not. He said that since it was a rather long statement, he would come over and show it to me. It was a classic of its kind, and I give it here in full:

MR. UTT: Mr. Speaker, I take this time to advise the Members of the House of some rather strange coincidences. At a book-and-author luncheon to be held October 22 at 12:30 in the Waldorf-Astoria Grand Ballroom, and sponsored by the American Booksellers Association and the New York Herald Tribune, there will appear as guest speakers Mr. Allen Dulles, former head of CIA, Hon. Adlai Stevenson, Ambassador to the United Nations, and Jessica Mitford, also known as Jessica Mitford Romilly Treuhaft, author of a recent book entitled "The American Way of Death." Jessica Mitford is the wife of Robert Treuhaft, twice identified as a Communist in the Seventh Report of the Un-American Activities Committee of the California State Senate for 1953, at pages 260, 261, and 262. He took the Fifth Amendment, and so did his wife, Jessica Mitford, to avoid incriminating herself when her associations were documented. Among other things, it was shown that Mrs. Treuhaft—Jessica Mitford—was once the financial director of the Communist-run California Labor School. She was also director of the Civil Rights Congress in the Berkeley, California, area. This organization is cited as a Communist front operation by the U.S. Attorney General. She also was identified as one who attended a closed meeting of the Communist Party on January 28, 1951, at 2002 San Pablo Avenue, El Cerrito, Calif. When questioned on this, she took the Fifth Amendment.

One wonders whether this information is known by Allen Dulles and Ambassador Stevenson, or if they have been made dupes to attract a large audience for Jessica Mitford to plug her new book. While hiding behind the commercial aspects of the mortician and the cemeteries and mausoleums where our dear departed friends and relatives are commemorated, she is really striking another blow at the Christian religion. Her tirade against morticians is simply the vehicle to carry her anti-Christ attack, and I am at a loss to know why Americans such as Allen Dulles and Ambassador Stevenson should create an air of respectability for this pro-Communist anti-American.

Mr. Speaker, I wish to further advise the House that tomorrow night CBS is presenting a 1-hour documentary on the Mitford book and is giving her a national forum from which to spew her anti-Americanism.

You should also know that Dr. Frank Stanton of CBS and Mr. Richard S. Salant, president of CBS News, have been on notice for two weeks regarding Jessica Mitford's Communist-front activities, but they still insist on giving her 1 hour free time to advance the sale of her book, the profits from which, no doubt, will find their way into the coffers of the Communist Party, USA.

It is my belief that this is a pro-Communist documentary and that some patriotic American should demand and receive equal time to expose Jessica Mitford, because you can rest assured that the left-leaning CBS will not put forth one word of identification of Mitford and her Communist-front activities.

The statement ended with the ringing words: "I would rather place my mortal remains, alive or dead, in the hands of any American mortician than to set foot on the soil of any Communist nation."* Had I any comment? asked the UPI man.

This, I decided, called for some high-level deliberations, so I told him I would ring him back later. I telephoned to Bob in California, and together we concocted what we hoped was a statesmanlike comment: I thought Mr. Utt's remarks were beneath contempt, I did not feel called upon either to confirm or deny his charges, loyalty oaths were anyway repugnant to me and particularly when administered by undertakers and their spokesmen in Congress from Cemetery Land, California.

* In 1970 Mr. Utt exercised that option. His obituary in *The New York Times,* with the subhead "Attacked Mitford Book," records that during his ten terms in Congress, "his most newsworthy action came when he called Jessica Mitford a 'pro-Communist anti-American.' "

The UPI man seemed satisfied—"Good for you!" he said— but how would Simon & Schuster react to this development? Poor Dan was distraught when I told him about it, the more so when I proposed to make it the theme of my talk at the Book and Author dinner. "You must issue an immediate denial of any Communist connections, past or present," he urged. I was also distressed, for I could see that Dan's world was rocking dangerously: here he was charged with shepherding me through a dazzling array of public events and interviews, arranged by S & S at enormous trouble and expense, and I kept straying off on my own in unforeseen and possibly disastrous directions.

I told him that since this matter had come up, and would doubtless continue to haunt us for the rest of the tour, I should try to make my position clear to him. I explained that actually Mr. Utt's review of my life was substantially correct; I had indeed been a Party member until just a few years ago. It would, of course, be possible to tell the press that and let them draw their own conclusions as to why I had resigned. For several reasons, I had decided not to do this.

First, Utt's revelation was couched in the form of an accusation, imputing evil to the fact of Party membership. A simple denial would give the appearance of accepting his premise, but I did not see my membership as something evil. Furthermore, there was an important civil liberties principle involved: as long as the government and the courts were still persecuting people because of CP membership or suspected membership, and because the Fifth Amendment was under attack by the witch-hunters on the ground that it was just a shelter for Communists, it would be a form of betrayal of those still in the Party to make public denial of membership.

Second, even if one wanted to prove one's political orthodoxy (which I did not, because I hoped and believed I was as subversive as ever), recent history showed that mere denial of membership was never enough to satisfy the witch-hunters: it must be accompanied by repudiation of the Party and the naming of names. Once you are maneuvered into the position of confessing, Yea, I have sinned, but I sin no more, then you invite the contention that confession is not enough; you must also expiate your sins by denouncing other sinners and naming them.

Third, the whole question was completely irrelevant to the purpose of our tour, a diversion that the undertakers hoped would deflect attention from the book; so why fall into their trap? The best way to deal with it, I said, would be to tease the undertakers by making a joke of it. After all, Khrushchev in his famous statement had declared, "We will bury you!" Obviously Forest Lawn wouldn't like that; they would regard it as muscling in on their territory.

Dan was only partially satisfied with these arguments. We telephoned to Bob Gottlieb, who although concerned (as indeed I was) about Utt's utterance, said firmly that any response to it was up to me; he thought my statement to UPI was fine, if that was how I felt about it.

None of us was prepared to predict the consequences to the book of the Utt revelations, although I braced myself for a cooling, if not a freezing, of its hitherto ardent public reception, accompanied by wholesale cancellations of my scheduled interviews and multitudinous returns of the book by dealers. It was, therefore, a delightful surprise when a few days later *The New York Times* ran an editorial on the fracas, captioned "How Not to Read a Book." The *Times* derided Utt's "McCarthyite attack," noted that the book had "evoked high praise from Catholic, Protestant and Jewish clergymen, as well as from reviewers and other commentators in all parts of the country," and declared that Utt's "credentials as a book and television critic can safely be dismissed as nil." From then on, the tour afforded a unique and fascinating opportunity to observe the paradoxical scene of America on the turn, stirring out of the deep spell cast over it by McCarthyism.

Despite *Mortuary Management*'s wise injunction against "dignifying the book with retaliatory endeavors," the National Funeral Directors Association had hired a Madison Avenue public relations agency to do just that. In all sixteen cities, wherever Dan and I went the agency had preceded us, blanketing the media from the national TV networks in New York to the smallest radio station in the Midwest with their thick kit of information on my subversive background.

In Dallas, the book editor of the *Times Herald* showed me his kit; in Chicago, producers of the "Kup" television show were reading theirs when we arrived; in Tulsa, the host of a local television program flourished his copy before the cameras during our interview: "I don't know where all this garbage came from, but I'm serving notice on the undertakers that I don't want any more of it sent here!"

The packet was in truth a curious mélange, consisting of a reprint of Congressman Utt's remarks; a reveiw in which Howard C. Raether, executive secretary of the National Funeral Directors Association, called my book "a negative diatribe"; a two-page précis of *Daughters and Rebels* ("Jessica Mitford admits she was a shoplifter at the age of 11 . . . hated her parents . . . joined the Reds in the Spanish Civil War . . ."); some copies of *Tocsin,* a Berkeley-based publication subtitled "The West's Leading Anti-Communist Weekly," featuring Bob and me as "identified Communists"; several pages about us from the HUAC transcripts.

Traveling through a dozen states, I encountered a spectrum of responses to this information. The very unpredictability of its effect in any given situation added a certain fillip to the trip; it was like being on a seesaw, never knowing when one would go soaring up or come thudding down, although on the whole the media reacted much as *The New York Times* had done; the undertakers seemed to have misread the mood of the country. A few years before, I reflected, their strategy might have worked very well, they might have succeeded in blasting the book into oblivion. But by 1963, a radical revival was in the making, led by young people and clearly independent of the CP. HUAC had received a well-deserved kicking around by the emergent student movement, and throughout the South blacks were on the march; some of their courage had rubbed off on older folks.

If the Red label had lost much of its magic, the labels Liberal and Conservative also seemed irrelevant in terms of how people reacted to the undertakers' barrage. For example, I learned that my possible political views were a matter of much discussion and concern among the liberals of the Funeral Society movement, some of whom proved to be far more skittish and fearful of being linked with a person accused of being Un-American than many avowed conservatives.

To sketch in some of the more giddying ups and downs of that seesaw ride:

David Lowe of CBS, who was in the midst of producing *The Great American Funeral*, reported that following the Utt blast the network management had instructed him to delete all references to me or my book from his documentary. Lowe angrily refused to do this; eventually a compromise was reached in which the book got full credit, and Utt's statement and my response were incorporated into the film.

On the "Kup" show in Chicago, the host, Mr. Kupcinet, felt impelled to refer to the Utt statement—I had warned him before the show that this would be ill-advised on his part, as I should merely refuse to comment on the charges. When I did so, one of the panel members, the film producer and director Stanley Kramer, who had been silent up to then, suddenly sprang to life: "I must say I think Miss Mitford is perfectly right to refuse to answer! What's that got to do with her book? I'm getting damn tired of the fact that whenever somebody produces a film or writes a book that *says* anything, the opposition immediately brings up the Communist issue."

In Dallas, A. C. Greene, book editor of the *Times Herald,* had written a rave review of *The American Way of Death,* which as ill luck would have it appeared the very week of the National Funeral Directors Association convention there. Mr. Greene described to me a threatened contretemps that developed as a result of this confluence of the stars.

He was called in by the managing editor, a conservative who had on occasion rebuked Greene for taking too radical a position in his reviews. Greene was not reassured when he found Howard C. Raether and a public relations man for the Funeral Directors Association in the editor's office. "As I came in, Raether was saying, '. . . and of course you know that both Mitford and her husband are members of the Communist Party,' " Greene told me. "The editor said nothing, but wrote on a journalist's pad. Raether asked, 'What are you writing down?' The editor replied, ' "Mr. Raether, interviewed today in Dallas, said, 'Of course you know that both Mitford and her husband are members of the Communist Party.' " ' "

"Raether got a bit nervous, he said, 'Well, no, I shouldn't put it like that; I mean we don't really *know* if they are members.' The editor just kept writing. 'What are you putting down now?' asked Raether. 'I'm putting down, "Mr. Raether said today in Dallas, 'We don't really know if she or her husband is a member of the Communist Party.' " ' Raether protested that wasn't right, either. The editor, with great patience, said, 'Then how's this: "Mr. Howard Raether today denied that either Miss

Mitford or her husband is a Communist." ' Exeunt Raether and
PR man, tails between legs!"

Los Angeles was the only city in the country where the
newspapers had printed not a word about *The American Way
of Death:* not a single review, not the slightest comment had
appeared in their pages. The reason for this unkind neglect
became apparent when we saw Forest Lawn's full-page advertisement, which ran day after day for many weeks in the Los
Angeles *Times* and the *Herald Examiner.* The message, in huge
type surrounded by white space, consisted of but eleven words:
"High Cost of Dying? Not at Forest Lawn. Funerals from
$145." Furthermore, Forest Lawn sent a round-robin letter to
all clergymen in the Los Angeles area, stating that "Congressman Utt had exposed Jessica Mitford and the entire controversy
as a Communist plot," and ending with a postscript: "Incidentally, legal counsel for Forest Lawn is preparing libel suits
against the authoress and her publishers." (I *craved* that libel
suit, and should have taken great pleasure in defending against
it, but alas, it never materialized.)

The Pickwick Bookshop, oldest and largest in the city,
gallantly fought back by devoting all its windows to a giant
display of *The American Way of Death,* which, they told us,
was enjoying a vast sale despite Forest Lawn and the newspapers.

Most heartening of all was the Denver experience. Although *Casket & Sunnyside* had joined *Mortuary Management*
in counseling the buttoned lip—as one editorial said: "Stay
silent! That was the watchword passed down when the two-
month siege of Mitford storms started to howl in mid-Septem-
ber"—television producers were occasionally able to flush out
an undertaker for a confrontation on the air. Mr. Van Derber,
owner of Denver's largest mortuary, agreed to a televised de-

bate, which turned into a bit of a comedy act. At one point, defending the notion that mortuaries offer funerals at a range of prices, he declared, "I could put you away for $150," to which I responded, "Sorry, you're too late. Other undertakers have offered to do it for nothing, as long as it's soon."

For several weeks thereafter, Mr. Van Derber ran quarter-page display ads in the Denver *Post* featuring the Utt statement in its verbose entirety. The counterattack was not long in coming, the opening shot a letter to the *Post* protesting the ads, signed by thirty Denver clergymen. Later, when the governor of Colorado sought to appoint Mr. Van Derber to the state morticians' licensing board, a coalition of Republican and Democratic state senators blocked the appointment on the sole issue of the anti-Mitford ads.

ALTHOUGH I relished the support I was getting from unexpected quarters—and the indication it afforded of a new willingness to take a stand against the witch-hunters—there were a couple of uneasy moments when I wondered if I was going too far in my smug acceptance of political respectability.

The *Reader's Digest* notified me that an extract from *The American Way of Death* had been prepared and scheduled for publication in their next issue; the copy they sent me bore the notation "Final." When it was hastily killed without explanation, I was almost relieved; my by-line in the *Digest* might have caused raised eyebrows in our circles, and as Bob said, "In a way you should be glad, because this confirms our view of the world as we've always understood it to be."

And among the stacks of reviews that threatened to inundate our house was one that I quickly hid from my friends: a glowing two-page tribute in William F. Buckley's *National Re-*

view, calling the book "amusing and horrifying . . . a most engagingly macabre survey," and observing: "It is my hope that her book will prove a blockbuster for the whole death industry." I did hope Dinky had not seen it. During her four years at Sarah Lawrence College, Buckley, who was then busy lecturing to college audiences as the young white hope of the far right, had become her personal Enemy No. 1, and on her rare visits home she would regale us with accounts of her occasional bouts with him on the lecture circuit. What would she think of her poor old mother, forever compromised by this accolade in the Buckley press?

Fortunately for my peace of mind, the situation was soon rectified. In the next issue of the *National Review* it became apparent that somebody had slipped up badly in allowing the piece to go through. I was now billed as a "crypt-o Communist" (not a bad pun, I thought), and equal space was given to a denunciation of me on the editorial page. This consisted of a résumé of the undertakers' public relations kit, and ended: "Her record indicates she does deadlier things by far than morticians do."

I cherished that last sentence, which for me summed up the delightful ironies of my situation, a joke within a joke. To have earned this recognition from the very heart of the enemy camp! A chain of absolutely fortuitous encounters—leading from Casper Weinberger to Roul Tunley to Bob Gottlieb—had thrust me for a brief moment into national prominence, enabling me at last to give full rein to my subversive nature in a way that would not have been possible in my CP days, pegging along as a faithful soldier in that army. And here I was reaching people by the millions instead of the dozens with a frontal attack on one of the seamier manifestations of American capitalism! Granted the undertakers were an easy target, hardly a bastion of imperialism, could it be that I had advanced the Fine Old Conflict by one short step in spotlighting their operation as the other side of the coin to the American Way of Life?

SINCE WRITING the above I have received some 350 Xeroxed pages of my FBI file, which I requested under the Freedom of Information Act. In an accompanying letter, Mr. Clarence Kelley, FBI director, explains that he has made some excisions from these documents "in order to protect materials which are exempted from disclosure." That he has, and with odd results. Some pages consist largely of heavy crossings-out: "XXXXXX advised XXXXXXXX XXXXXXXX on XXXXXXX that the Subject was quite active in a union which had been formed among OPA employees in San Francisco. XXXXXX advised XXXXXXXX that he was of the opinion that the union was endeavoring to promote Communism." Other pages have been almost entirely blanked out, leaving merely a tantalizing opener: "Subject was observed entering . . ." The government's charge of ten cents a page for these seems excessive; I am currently appealing the deletions. Nevertheless, what remains legible is a dizzying summary of what I had been doing over the years, much of which I had completely forgotten. Reading it was like seeing one's whole life flash before one's eyes, as is supposed to happen to a drowning person:

"Subject seen at Fair Employment picket line. . . . Subject listed as outstanding worker in Twin Peaks Club of Communist Party. . . . Subject at meeting to protest bombing murders in Florida. . . . Subject present at a Rosenberg clemency rally. . . . Subject chairman of meeting of Committee to Secure Justice for Morton Sobell. . . . Subject signer of Petition to Repeal Internal Security Act . . ." and so on, for day after day, year after year.

One memorandum, from the assistant attorney general, Internal Security Division, to the FBI director, I found of more than passing interest. It is headed EMERGENCY DETENTION PROGRAM, and offers a choice of two boxes to be checked: "It has been determined that Subject's name should be retained on security index" or ". . . removed from security index." In my case, there is a large black "X" in the first box. The date of this memo is October 1, 1962, when Robert Kennedy was Attorney General, a creepy reminder that McCarthyism did not die with McCarthy.

Reading on into the sixties, I learn that Subject was observed at anti-Vietnam War demonstrations, was seen at meetings of the Northern California Committee to Repeal the McCarran Act, was featured speaker at a rally to raise $500,000 to appeal conviction of the University of California Free Speech Movement defendants, was listed as a sponsor of the Spring Mobilization Committee to End the War in Vietnam, was a member of the Jeanette Rankin Brigade for Peace, was trapped by white rioters in a Montgomery, Alabama, church at a meeting for the Freedom Riders, made a speech at a National Lawyers Guild meeting to raise funds for the Student Nonviolent Coordinating Committee, was mistress of ceremonies at a meeting of the Black Panther Defense Committee, was chairman of a meeting to celebrate release of Morton Sobell from federal prison, was believed to be writing a book about the trial of Dr. Spock. The very last entry, for March 1972, reports that "Subject is currently working on a book about prisons and has won a Guggenheim fellowship for a year's study of the United States penal system."

Subject must confess that, as she pored over this telescoped account of her activities through the years, she felt an unbecoming surge of pride, not unmixed with gratitude to the Communist Party for all it taught her, for the avenues it opened up for her to take part in what she perceived as the crucial battles of the day.

True, the CPUSA made some abysmal mistakes, mostly stemming from its unshakable reliance on the Soviet Union for leadership and its resolute blindness to developments in the Communist countries—to the fact that Stalinism did not die with Stalin. Robert Scheer, one of the more perceptive spokesmen of the New Left, writes: "Neither the Old Left nor the New took the building of an indigenous popular radical organization as its main task. And yet without such an organization, no revolution in the world could succeed." This is a telling observation. Preoccupied as we were with the day-to-day tactics of survival, we may well have lost sight of our overall strategic aims. But I do not believe we ever betrayed them. Did we not, in fact, leave something of a heritage—however limited, as Rita Baxter would say—for future radical movements to inherit? That is for new generations to decide.

Appendix

Lifeitselfmanship

or

how to become a

PRECISELY-BECAUSE MAN

« ❖ »

An Investigation Into Current L (or Left-Wing) Usage

by Decca Treuhaft
illustrated by Pele
50¢

CREDITS

The author wishes to extend recognition to the many friends who have encouraged and helped her in the task of preparing this short manual; to her husband, who researched much of the material; and above all, to the editors and contributors of <u>Political Affairs</u>, the <u>Daily Peoples World</u>, <u>Masses and Mainstream</u>, without whose invaluable inspiration this book would never have been written.

The English-speaking world has just been treated to a glimpse into the mysteries of English upper-class usage by the publication of <u>Noblesse Oblige</u> (by Nancy Mitford and others). Because of its immense snob appeal, this book is fair on the way to becoming a best seller. The author points out that "it is solely by its language that the upper class is clearly marked off from the others". Theme of the book is a discussion by the various contributors of what they call"U-usage". U means Upper-class; non-U (obviously) means non-Upper-class. A few examples should suffice:

Non-U	U equivalent
Pleased to meet you	How do you do
Lounge	Hall (or dining room)
Wealthy	Rich
Serviette	Napkin
Dentures	False teeth

Anyway, you get the idea.

Since it's unlikely that many left-wingers will either read the book, or, if they do, find much in it of practical value, we felt that it would be profitable to offer a short course in current L (or left-wing) terminology. A spot-check survey has convinced us that the need for such a course, both for beginners and for more advanced students, has long been felt by many.

This is by no means offered as an exhaustive study of the subject; it is merely a beginning. We sincerely hope and believe that more qualified scholars will take up where this paper leaves off. As a start, we will give a few easy translations:

Non-L	L equivalent
Time will tell whether that plan was O.K.	The correctness of that policy will be tested in life itself. (Alt., in the crucible of struggle.)
At the present time we need to find out what's wrong with some of the most important unions.	In this period there is a need for clarity on the weaknesses of certain key sections of the labor movement.
Suggesting a bum plan.	Projecting an incorrect perspective.

Non-L woman (to husband): I'm having tea with Mrs. Snodgrass this afternoon. Some of the nursery school mothers will be there; we're going to talk about expanding the school.

L-woman (to L-husband): I'm going to spend the afternoon doing mass work. (Alt.: At a meeting of my mass org.) We are projecting some expanded goals on the Woman Question.

An L-man does not speak up at a meeting; he contributes to the discussion.

The following short examination is intended to rate yourself on your own mastery of L-usage. Please use the honor system; cover the answers (on the right) with a piece of paper before attempting to tackle the exam. Do not be discouraged if you make a low grade. There is worse to follow.

Questions	Answers
1. Mo-what-oly what-italism is based on super profits?	1. Nop; cap.
2. He-what-ony of the what-letariat?	2. Gem; pro.
3. List various types of tasks.	3. Historic; immediate; before us; concrete(see Building Trades below); varied, etc. etc.
4. List as many words as you can think of ending in -ize.	4. Mobil; concret; final; political; character; crystal; polemic; etc.
5. List various moods to be avoided. (Hint: moods usually seem to go in pairs).	5. Pessimism and despair; fatalism and complacency; confusionism and obscurantism; recklessness and adventurism; complacency and passivity; etc.
6. What is Wall Street drunk with?	6. Temporary but illusory success (correct answer); Old Grandad (incorrect answer).

moods seem to go in pairs

7. What must we do soberly?

7. Evaluate, estimate, assess, anticipate (correct answers); go down to the nearest bar (incorrect answer).

8. List various kinds of struggle.

8. All out, political, class, cultural, principled, many-sided, one-sided, inner Party.

9. What-illating petit bourgeoisie?

9. Vac.

10. How would you describe labor leaders with whom you are in disagreement?

10. a) The Reuthers, Hutchinsons, Meanys, Wolls, & Co.
b) Mis-leaders of labor
c) The Greens, Hillquits, Thomases, & Co. (obs.)
d) Lackeys of the bourgeoisie.

11. What does one do with cadres?

11. One develops them, trains them and boldly promotes them, poor things.

12. List as many words ending with ism as you can think of. Warning: obvious ones, like fasc, social, imperial, etc., don't count.

12. Chauvin; diversion; narrow-sectional; exceptional; liquidation; adventur; revision; sch (got you there); opportun; confusion; Browder; tail or Khvost (obs.); Keynes.

13. What is happening to the contradictions in the situation?

13. They are sharpening and deepening. Also unfolding. (Sometimes they even gather momentum with locomotive speed.)

14. What must we establish with the toiling masses and their allies?

14. a) closer ties
b) firmer links
c) durable alliances
d) unshakable ideological ties/links/alliances.

15. How do contradictions get started?

15. They either _stem_ _from_ or _flow_ out of situations. Sometimes _roots_ of _problems_ _stem_ from _contradictions_, a botanical anomaly.

16. List various kinds of fronts.

16. Popular; broad; united (if typing, try to avoid a common typographical error, untied front (see Cheesecake Section below); cultural; water.

17. What sort of alliance generally exists between a) the McCarthyites and Dixiecrats, and b) between the police dept. and Oakland Tribune?

17. Unholy.

18. Name some Questions.

18. National, Farm, Woman, Youth; decisive (confronting the American people).

19. List various sizes that farmers come in.

19. Small; middle-sized; family-sized; Associated.

*   *   *

small

middle-sized

family-sized

associated

farmers of various sizes.

Having completed the exam, you are no doubt anxious to dig in further and learn more about the <u>correct approach</u> to L-usage. For the convenience of students, we have <u>attempted to organize</u> this part of the course under self-explanatory section headings:

Retail Selling or Mongering Section:

    War mongers; phrase mongers; hate mongers; fear mongers.

Wholesale Section:

    Doing <u>bidding</u> of monopolists
    <u>Wholesale</u> slashing of living standards
    <u>Wholesale</u> wage freezes
    <u>Wholesale</u> price increases (By the way, this latter always really
       means retail price increases. The authors do not feel equip-
       ped at this time to go into the reason for this.)
    The <u>bulk</u> of the American people

Aquatic, or Water Sports Section:

    In the main
    Mainstream (of American life - we must find our way into it).
    Launching (campaigns, programs of action, etc.)
    Broad current (usually, of political thought)
    Baby and bathwater (not to be thrown out together)
    Fishing (in the muddied waters of popular discontent)
    Herring (red - dragged across path)
    Ships: relation (of forces), unholy partner, etc.
    Liquidationism
    Flowing from

the united front

the line →

in the main

Building Trades Section:

    Architect (of cold war - Dulles & Co.)
    Should start with balanced (or rounded) estimate
    Laying the foundation (for more advanced political thinking)
    Building toward (a firmer foundation)
    Cementing (ties, unity, etc.)
    Forging (links, ties, unity, etc.)
    Welding (ties, unity, etc.)
    Undermining (ties, unity, etc.)
    Levels (of understanding, militancy)
    Concrete (situation, leadership, estimate, appraisal)
        (v.t. concretize)
    Hammering (out the line)

    Locksmithship Sub-Section:

    Key (issue, question, link in chain, concentration)

Canine and Equestrian Section:

    Dead horse (beating a)
    Stable base
    Captains of industry, riding rough shod
    Stalking horse of reaction
    Running dogs of imperialism (must be curbed)
    Mad war dogs of fascism (mustn't be unleashed)
    Galloping to its own destruction (imperialism, or sometimes Wall
    War chariots (of Wall Street, etc.)   Street)
    Dogmatism (for an end to!)
    Tailism (or Khvostism, obs.) (See Exam Question No. 12)

Outdoor (or Camping) Section:

    Areas of agreement
    Camps are too numerous to list. Among them are:
        Camp of peace
        Camp of National independence

Camp of Democracy (usually, enormously strengthened)
Camp of World Imperialism (usually, shaken to its very foundation)

Sub-Section (Scouting):

Tying together key issues confronting broad strata of American
people.

baby going out
with bathwater
and dead horse
(beat)

Electronic Section:

Negative and Positive (approaches, viewpoints, programs, etc.)
Elements (democratic, peace-loving, corrupt, disruptive, vacil-
lating, wavering, honest, rotten, dishonest, petit bourgeois,
etc.) We do not advise being an element as you run the danger
of being isolated from the mainstream (see Water Sports, above).
Charges (things some elements are sometimes brought up on).

Needle Trades Section:

Pinning (down responsibilities)
Hemming (the Labor Movement in with contradictions)
Cloaking (with demagogic phrases, or with left-sounding slogans)
Vested (interests)

Cheesecake Section:

Popular Front
Broad Front
Untied Front (see Exam Question No. 15)

Well Rounded Points (made in discussion)
Broadly Based
Affairs (in non-L usage, means an illicit love relationship; in L usage, fund raising gatherings. This has been known to create moods of confusionism and obscurantism in discussions, e.g. saying to non-L people:"Why don't you have an affair and raise some money?")
Well Developed Cadres
Fresh Approaches

Grammatical Section:

What does Wall Street's Policy spell? (World Disaster)
What does it not spell? (Prosperity for the bulk of the American people. See Wholesale Section, above)
What does complacency spell? (The road to defeat)

Gastro-Intestinal Section:

Assimilate (working-class theory)
Bloated (Capitalists, obs., except in cartoons)
Purging (of disruptive elements. See Electronics Section)
The Movement (also mass movements and narrow movements)
Only through struggle will anything come to pass.

why don't you have an affair and raise some money?

Traffic Control Section:

Crossroads, at the (imperialism, America, etc.)
Approaches (correct, right, left, broad, narrow, fundamental,
It's no accident that   multiple)
Avoid right and/or left errors
We cannot adopt a middle of the road policy
Driver's seat (e.g. "Dulles is temporarily in the")
Roads (to socialism, fascism)
Turns (we must learn to make)
Drives (P.W., etc., known in non-L language as campaigns or
Utilizing all paths   crusades)

Gardening Section:

Rooting (out petit bourgeois influences; oneself in the neighbor-
Growing (political maturity, also various moods)   hood)
Digging (deeper into a host of questions)
Deeply rooted in theory
Flowering (of creativeness, political maturity, etc.)
Fertile fields (for political activity)
Withering (away of the state, obs.)

        Having completed this short course, we believe that the average
L-man will find himself better equipped to go out and start boring -
from within?

Non-L Poem	L Translation
Tell me not in mournful numbers	Do not project to me in moods of pessimism and despair
Life is but an empty dream	The perspective that no positive conclusions can be drawn from the present relationship of forces
And the soul is dead that slumbers	
For things are not what they seem.	For we must focus attention on the key issues.
Let us then be up and doing	Let us therefore mobilize the broad masses
With a heart for any fate	To a realization of their historic task within the political climate
Still achieving, still pursuing	We shall continue to win victories in the crucible of struggle
Learn to labor and to wait.	As we develop correct tactics adapted to the concrete situation.

APPENDIX

Some authentic examples of recent L-writing:

"In striving to liquidate the cold war, the greatest weakness of
the peace forces in the United States is the ultra-reactionary character of the Meany group of mis-leaders now dominating the A. F. of L.
and soon to have their influence spread further, through the current
merger of the A. F. of L. and the C.I.O."
--<u>Political Affairs,</u> Oct. 1955.

* * *

"Our Party must counteract daily and hourly the political, ideological and cultural influences of the war camp, expose and isolate
the reactionary Social-Democratic and labor-reformist ideologists of
Big Business, who strive to demoralize the working class and tie it to
Wall Street's war program."
--<u>Political Affairs</u>, Feb. 1951.

* * *

"Our ideological struggle has to be conducted as a concrete
struggle arising from the unfolding events. It should be carried on
in a language and in forms that the workers can understand and in
terms of their own experience."
--same article, <u>Political Affairs</u>, Feb. 1951.

* * *

"Yet note should be taken of the fact that in the 1954 Program
the previous position of the Party on self-determination in the Black
Belt has been modified--in fact, dropped."
--<u>Political Affairs</u>, June 1956.

* * *

"Therefore one main conclusion that the working class and all
popular forces must draw is that it is necessary at every juncture to
prevent and defeat the stubborn efforts of the economic royalists to
thwart the popular will."
--<u>Political Affairs</u>, June 1956.

* * *

"At this juncture we should particularly stress the next immediate stage of progress for the people of our country--which is insep-
arably bound up with, and requires the crystallization of a broad democratic front coalition, under progressive labor leadership."
--<u>Political Affairs,</u> June 1956.

* * *

"We will likewise focus attention on the main tasks of the movement and the period ahead, especially the forging of a labor-demo-
cratic coalition whose potential for effectively curbing the power of
the trusts will grow ever more mighty."
--<u>Political Affairs</u>, June 1956.

We are quite sure that many readers will now wish to criticize the author. For the convenience of readers, a check-list of appropriate criticisms is given below; however, of course, readers are not limited to the check list.

Anti-leadership ▱   Right-Opportunism ▱

Anti-theoretical ▱   Left-Sectarianism ▱

Rotten Liberalism ▱   Philistinism ▱

Fails to chart a perspective ▱   Petty Bourgeois Cynicism ▱

If you would like to send in suggestions for inclusion in subsequent editions, please use the space provided below (or attach extra pages).